Nationalism in Italian Politics

This book is the first full-length study available in English to trace the extraordinary history of the Italian Northern Leagues during the 1980s and 1990s. At a time when the post-war First Republic entered a crisis amid corruption scandals, the Leagues acted as one of the main protest actors and grew at an unprecedented rate.

Drawing on electoral and survey data, existing research, eyewitness accounts of protest events and interviews with activists and leaders, this book provides the definitive account of the movement. Damian Tambini analyses why the movement was so successful in mobilising support, and focuses on its most novel aspect: its use of nationalism.

This book argues that the League developed a new genre of nationalist protest action, which relied upon spectacular transgressionary tactics. These not only captured the media agenda, but were an effective way of further undermining the legitimacy of the Italian national state. In a period where the nature of the nation has been fundamentally redefined as western Europe integrated, and in which the geopolitical map of central Europe was completely rewritten, the Leagues' secessionist discourse came to dominate Italian politics.

Written for scholars interested in nationalism, ethnicity and citizenship, and for specialists in European studies, Italian and ethnic studies, *Nationalism in Italian Politics* draws on the best Italian and international research to thoroughly analyse the movement, and update classic studies of nationalism in the age of media spectacle.

Damian Tambini is Senior Research Fellow at the Institute for Public Policy Research in London and is also a Research Associate at the London School of Economics. His publications include *Cyberdemocracy* and *Markets, Citizens and States.*

Routledge advances in European politics

1 **Russian Messianism**
Third Rome, revolution, communism and after
Peter J. S. Duncan

2 **European Integration and the Postmodern Condition**
Governance, democracy, identity
Peter van Ham

3 **Nationalism in Italian Politics**
The stories of the Northern League, 1980–2000
Damian Tambini

Nationalism in Italian Politics

The stories of the Northern League, 1980–2000

Damian Tambini

LONDON AND NEW YORK

First published 2001
by Routledge
2 Park Square, Milton Park, Abingdon, Oxfordshire OX14 4RN

Simultaneously published in the USA and Canada
by Routledge
711 Third Avenue, New York, NY 10017

First issued in paperback 2015

Routledge is an imprint of the Taylor and Francis Group, an informa business

Typeset in Baskerville
by Curran Publishing Services Ltd, Norwich

British Library Cataloguing in Publication Data
A catalogue record for this book is available from the British Library

Library of Congress Cataloging in Publication Data
Tambini, Damian
Nationalism in Italian politics : the stories of the Northern League, 1980–2000 / Damian Tambini
p. cm.
Includes bibliographical references and index.
1. Lega nord. 2. Nationalism–Italy. 3. Italy–Politics and government–1976–1994. 4. Italy–Politics and government–1994–. 5. Italy, Northern–Politics and government. 6. Italy, Northern–Politics and government–1996– I. Title.

JN5657.L45 T36 2001
320.54'0945–dc21 00–068999

ISBN 13: 978-1-138-01015-4 (pbk)
ISBN 13: 978-0-415-24698-9 (hbk)

Contents

Figures

Tables

Preface and acknowledgements

This book was recorded live. I was lucky enough to live in Italy during most of the 1990s, and to observe as the Northern League grew at an astonishing rate, galvanising the protest that ended the first Italian Republic. I was present at many of the events I describe in these pages.

Although it can be read as a history of the League, I hope that this book will also contribute to discussion of broader issues beyond Italian politics. The rapid rise of the League had observers all over the globe asking how a movement could mobilise so many thousands so quickly. I seek to answer that question. The League also touched political nerves that in the 1990s were tingling all over Europe and beyond. In the wake of the cold war the National Question was re-emerging, in new and unexpected forms. As a protest movement that based itself so clearly on ideas of nation and ethnicity, the new Italian regionalism posed questions about the very nature of the nation. Those were questions not only for theorists but also for citizens. As the National Question permeated public debate in Italy as it did in other European countries, it threatened to undermine the founding principle of the Italian state: the idea of the Italian nation.

I seek in these pages to inform understanding of the League and of its peculiar version of nationalism through close observation of the movement over time. This book is based on dozens of interviews with the movement's activists and leaders, analysis of existing research, press coverage and the League's own documentation.

The observations and claims offered in these pages, which focus upon the nationalist transgression tactics of the League as a media strategy, are tentative. But I would argue that they are relevant to understanding the National Question outside Italy. Politics everywhere is increasingly concerned with control over the media agenda, and the most successful movements are those that are most effective in generating news. At the same time, processes of globalisation, privatisation and the increasing integration of trans-national trading blocs undermine national citizenship and further sensitise the national nerve in political life. In this context, our understanding of the relationship of ethnic and national identity to collective action needs to be deepened. The account of the role of national identity constructions in social mobilisation that I develop in this book is an attempt to get below the surface of the movement and examine the link between large-scale global processes and political mobilisation.

It has at times been difficult to maintain the analytical distance that is necessary in a study of this type. My natural tendency to reject many of the xenophobic emotions associated with the League had to be balanced with an ambition to stand back and analyse how the movement actually worked. Since the aim was to understand why the movement grew so quickly and how its central dynamic operated, the xenophobic discourses of the League had to be read in terms of their social function, cause and consequences for the movement, rather than merely rejected as a political menace. At the same time, my long conversations with movement members and leaders, many of whom appear to be reasonable people, led to the danger of going native and adopting the movement's perspective. A qualified social constructivism, which is a theoretical position that runs through this book, thus applies also to its author. My claims, like those of the League, need to be read in context, in terms of their function and consequences, and of the factors that explain their emergence.

Luckily for me, my conclusions were developed in the most conducive of social-scientific contexts. This book has its roots in a doctoral research project supervised by Klaus Eder, at the European University Institute in Florence. Klaus taught me a great deal, and many others have had a hand in the work. Steven Lukes was an influence throughout, and an attentive reader. Yasemin Soysal offered welcome encouragement and advice. Adrian Favell, Christian Joppke, Gianfranco Poggi, Oliver Schmidtke, Peggy Somers and many others in Florence made discussing nationalism enjoyable, while Ettore Recchi and Willy Ward helped me decipher Italian political life. Alessandro Pizzorno's and Bernd Giesen's theories of collective identity and comments on this text have been crucial, and Will Kymlicka was an excellent discussant in 1995–6. Isabelle van de Gejuchte was a source of inspiration through much of the project.

The book owes a general debt to the European University Institute, which during the 1990s seemed a magnet to the best minds in the field of nationalism studies. In a genuinely trans-national institution such as the EUI, it is perhaps possible to think thoughts about nationalism that would not be thought elsewhere.

I am grateful to Cath Woollard for patient and efficient editing work, and her incisive comments on the content. I am grateful to Brigitte Schwab of the EUI, and to Eva Breivik, Maureen Leichtener and Marie-Ange Cattotti of the Department of Social and Political Sciences, and

Camilla Salvi for help with translations. The work was completed with the help of a Marie Curie Research Fellowship from the European Union, and additional support from the EUI.

I am grateful to the Northern League for permission to reproduce cartoons and posters.

Damian Tambini

Introduction

On Tuesday 10 May 1994, Umberto Bossi walked through a doorway on Via Uffici dell' Vicario, a narrow street behind the Parliament in Rome. The building he entered housed the parliamentary offices of his Northern League and several other Italian parties. Bossi had just left a meeting of the party leaders of the new Italian government, whose objective had been to appoint the cabinet, dividing the ministries between the recently-elected coalition members. The negotiations over the formation of the government had already taken six weeks, and the League's MPs were waiting for him, eager to know who amongst them would get the ministerial jobs.

Two other party leaders had been at the meeting with Bossi. Gianfranco Fini was hoping to have MPs from his National Alliance at the head of the Ministries of Transport and Agriculture. His party represented the pro-Mussolini minority of post-war Italian politics. Silvio Berlusconi, leader of the coalition and now Prime Minister, was at the head of the newest party of the three. He had rallied the resources of his media empire to create a party in just four months. With more MPs than either of his partners in the right-wing coalition, Berlusconi could call the shots at the meeting. The third party of this trio, Bossi's, was even more eccentric than the other two compared with other ruling parties in Western Europe. Most of the MPs of the Northern League were new to politics, having been elected for the first time after 1992. In ten years their party had grown from a tiny separatist campaign in the region of Lombardy into a united front of Northern regionalists in the Italian Government. Bossi's party had already been promised one of the two Vice-Presidencies, was making a bid for the Ministry of the Interior, and had proposed a candidate for Minister of Justice. In the most complete change of personnel since the end of fascism, the 'traditional parties' of Italy – Christian Democrats, Socialists and Communists, who for years had cooperated with one another in government coalitions – had been swept out of government in a single election.

Bossi's Northern League, a key agent in this revolutionary change, had been ridiculed and snubbed by the Italian establishment during its short history. The party was enjoying its first taste of real power, so the oak-panelled corridors of its parliamentary HQ crackled with anticipation of the outcome of the coalition talks. Bossi took the lift to the second floor. He passed the ground-floor offices, then still occupied by the once all-powerful Christian Democrats, a party now in the wake of electoral humiliation, and soon to split. As Bossi left the lift, MPs, secretaries, and hangers-on rushed into the corridor, dropping whatever was in their hands. A gaggle of journalists followed.

Italian newspapers – which just a few years previously had branded Bossi's League a club for folklore nostalgics, and then a den of racist hooligans – were now queuing to interview the movement's leaders. Most labelled the League as dangerous and extremist. The League had above all become known as the movement that wanted to break apart Italy. Movement spokesmen had demanded increased autonomy from the central state: first of the region of Lombardy, which they insisted was a nation, and later of the entire North of Italy. This had not proved a popular proposition with the existing establishment who had interests vested in the clientalistic Italian political system. When the Lombard League's first local councillors made their inaugural speeches in Varese in 1985, the other councillors left in protest. The first League deputies in the Italian Parliament, elected in 1987, refused to form coalitions with the main parties, opting instead to protest against them from the back benches.

It was only at the end of the 1980s, when the corruption and criminality that had become routine in Italian politics began to come to light, that the League could no longer be ignored. The new movement proposed federalism as a panacea for the clearly malfunctioning Italian state, and since 1987 had begun to win the votes that were to give them this place in the government. In the North as a whole, the League could reasonably claim to be the leading party, winning up to 40 per cent of votes in some constituencies in the period 1992–4, and key offices such as the Mayor of Milan (1992). During the negotiations over the formation of the 1994 government it became obvious that although League MPs were a minority in the ruling coalition, their ideas were high on the political agenda. Even the Christian Democrats and the Democratic Party of the Left, sensing a groundswell of support for state decentralisation, were writing devolution into their party manifestos.

Bossi almost smiled as he invited his colleagues into his office, because he had brought good news. For the League. His good friend, Roberto Maroni, would head the Ministry of the Interior. This was the first time since 1948 that a Christian Democrat would not head the department.

The important Ministry of the Budget also went to the League, plus the post of Vice-President. In all, the party had five of the twenty-five cabinet posts. With the Ministry of Institutional Reform in the hands of Francesco Speroni, they seemed to be in a position to push for the decentralising reforms they had been calling for over the previous decade. It was as though the Scottish Nationalists were suddenly setting the agenda for the British government.

Italy's political class was in shock. While the foreign press focused on worries about the 'post-fascists' (the National Alliance under Gianfranco Fini that had broken away from the Movimento Social Italiano) returning to government, the Northern League raised more alarm within Italy. It seemed impossible that a party calling for the fiscal autonomy of the North of Italy could have control of the ministry responsible for national unity. Within the ranks of the League there was the converse problem: how could the only Italian political movement with 'clean hands', which had called for increased Northern autonomy from 'Roman corruption', now form a coalition in Rome? Weren't they sleeping with the enemy?

The League's coalition partners, however, could also claim to be representatives of The New, untainted by the previous regime. Forza Italia (FI) was even younger than the League. A political vehicle for Milanese media baron Silvio Berlusconi, the party simply transformed the organisational structure, and many of the staff, of Publitalia and other divisions of Berlusconi's huge Fininvest enterprise into a political party and campaigning tool. The constituency of the party was similar to that of the League, and some of the elements of the basic appeal (such as Thatcherite policies to encourage entrepreneurship) were also shared. But the claim to be a 'new' party was tarnished by the fact that Berlusconi's business empire had thrived in the political and economic climate of the First Republic. By 1994 it was widely thought to be impossible to run a business in Italy without engaging in some form of illicit practice, such as the paying of *tangenti*, or bribes, for public contracts. Alleanza Nazionale (AN) also claimed to be something new, after the rump of the old fascist Movimento Sociale Italiano was 'modernised' by its young leader, Gianfranco Fini.

The League had inspired confusion and fear in Italy partly because as a movement it was very difficult to categorise, and partly because its campaign tactics were rough and racist. It was a strange new political animal. In ten years of strategic manoeuvring and publicity-seeking the League at different times had presented itself as an ethno-nationalist movement, an anti-immigration party, a left-wing alternative, a centre party and more recently as part of a right-wing coalition for government. Those desiring a 'mature two-party system' in the Italian Parliament began to hope that the League would opt for a merger with its coalition partners, to form a unified centre-right party. This was not to be.

Cut to two years later. The Northern League organises a three-day ceremony, to mark the declaration of independence of Northern Italy from the Italian state. On a windy Friday in September 1996, Umberto Bossi fills a bottle with water from the source of the River Po. The bottle is then taken, by car and boat, via a series of flag-waving rallies, to the mouth of the Po in Venice. There on the following Sunday, at yet another rally of League supporters, it is poured into the Lagoon, in a ritual to celebrate the Po as the lifeblood of 'Padania', as Northern Italy is thus baptised. Ex-Minister of the Interior, Maroni, is to be seen waving the newly-designed Padanian flag, and most of the League leadership are wearing green shirts, which, since the League brought down the 1994 government, have become the uniform of League militants.

This 'Festa on the Po' was a new ritual: the latest in a series of events and symbols that the Northern League, and its predecessor the Lombard League, had constructed and selected since they began campaigning in 1982. There was the logo of the League, the figure of Alberto da Giussano, hero of the 1187 Battle of Legnano. A picture of this sword-wielding medieval warrior had appeared on League propaganda, and on millions of Italian ballot papers, since 1983. There was Pontida, where the League, in the 1980s, started to hold huge open-air rallies on the site where the Northern cities rallied against Barbarossa in 1167. Even the name 'Padania' was relatively new. Bossi had for some years used the term in his speeches to differentiate the North of Italy from the less developed South, but it was only in 1995, after its brief adventure in government, that the League embraced in earnest the plan to separate North and South, and set up the self-styled 'Parliament of Padania'. By the end of the decade, it appeared that Padania would once again be mothballed as the League attempted to go into an election as part of a broad coalition with government ambitions.

What are we to make of the bizarre changes of direction marked by the new secessionism of 'Padania' and the Po? Had the League leadership really taken the decision that secession was the only way forward for Northern Italy, or was this merely a posture to catch the headlines? Many accused the League of being blatantly instrumental in its use of nationalist themes, and of fabricating this new nation: 'Padania', they insisted, was simply a publicity stunt. There was no such thing as a separate Lombard, or 'Padanian' culture or language, so how could they be nationalists? Why was the propaganda filled with articles about the Celts? Should this movement be read – as it often is – as part of a more general tendency to separatism and regionalism? Is it an agent of the inevitable fragmentation of nation states, sure to occur as their citizens realise national states can no longer deliver on welfare, security, or democracy? Or is it another version of central European post-totalitarian nationalism, as the Italian version of a one-party state under the Christian Democrats breaks up? Is it perhaps a strange new form of communitarianism? Should it be compared to the new forms of identity politics mobilising gender, sexuality and ethnic identities in the wake of universalising projects of nation and class? Or is it 'merely', as many have argued, an instrumental use of identity by a movement that is basically an anti-tax campaign? But if that is the case, there remains to be asked, *why* did they need all the Padanian flags, green shirts and folkloric baggage? Why the 'identity work'?

This book aims to shed light on these issues, through a detailed investigation of the origins and history of the movement. In particular, it aims to understand why this apparently eccentric identity construction of the League was so appealing to the electorate in Northern Italy at this juncture, and how this peculiar new form of movement may be compared to other movements, such as those which we more comfortably label nationalist movements.

There are also basic empirical questions to be addressed: what pushed one of the richest regions in Europe into a revolt against 'exploitation'? How did a tiny regionalist movement grow into a genuine force of government in less than ten years? And why did it then abandon that real government to set up a 'virtual' one: the provisional government of Padania?

In what follows, I tell the story of the League. Chapters Two to Five simply set out the course of events which led to the League going into government, while touching on the deeper questions of the explanations for the emergence of the movement, and for its peculiar use of nationalism. Chapters Six and Seven are more analytical, and return to the questions I just indicated, and Chapter Eight brings the story up to the time of writing, 1999, and outlines some possible future scenarios. Chapter One makes the theoretical framework of this analysis more explicit, and could be skipped by those readers who simply want to understand the movement in its context.

1 Virtual nationalism?

Understanding the League

Writing about an existing movement or political party, one could always be accused of *schieramento*, of taking sides, seeking either to discredit or support the movement. This is a complex problem, particularly when writing about movements that claim to be nationalist: simply by granting them the label 'nationalist' one offers some recognition to their claim that they speak for a 'nation'. So this book will be criticised for the mere fact that it uses the word 'nationalism' alongside the name 'League'. This is a pity, since I have no interest in discrediting or supporting the movement, only in analysing it. The book seeks to use analytical concepts, rather than contested, politicised concepts of practice, to use such concepts to outline the particular tools and strategies used by this movement, and to identify the mechanisms that contributed to its extraordinary success.

A great deal of the initial research on the League was, intentionally or otherwise, *schierata*, in that the concepts used to describe the movement were value-laden, concerned with de-legitimising or, more rarely, with supporting the movement. These same concepts were used as tools to try to grapple with the League analytically: derogatory labels doubled as analytical categories. This was compounded by the fact that the League was so hard to categorise. Should it be seen as another form of populism, as a single-issue protest movement, an anti-immigration movement, a form of regionalism, or a nationalist movement?

A protest movement?

Because of its very centralised, hierarchical structure, the League was able to make very sudden and profound changes of strategy, without detailed elaboration of policies by the party. This led commentators to claim that it was a 'mere' protest movement with no interest in constructive policy-making. It was indeed difficult to pin down the League on policies. Bossi, for example, gave an interview in October 1993 saying that if an election was not called he would withdraw his MPs from Rome, to form a 'Northern' Parliament. The following week he retracted the threat, saying it was made 'to provoke'. When the congress of December 1993 adopted Gianfranco Miglio's constitution for division of Italy into 'three republics' by a near-unanimous show of hands, Bossi gave an interview just a few days later saying, again, that that proposal was merely a provocation.[1] It is clear that much of the propaganda of the League is based on what the League is against, rather than what it is for. Four of every five League posters examined by Todesco (1992) emphasised external enemies, rather than positive proposals for reform (cited in Diani 1996: 15). The League has therefore been compared to the *Uomo Qualunque* (Everyman) movement in 1950s Italy and *Poujadisme* in France, and it was asserted that League voters are merely using the League as a vehicle for anti-regime protest.[2] This argument has found some support in surveys of League voters (Biorcio 1992, Diamanti 1993; see also the discussion in Corbetta 1994). Surveys of League voters do not, however, summarise the position of the entire League, nor do they explain why it is the League, rather than another movement or party, that inspires these people to protest. The label 'protest' is ultimately a rather shallow one: to be against something does not preclude being for something else.

A communitarian movement?

Could the League be described as a reaction of traditional community against the encroachments of the global economic system, or as a rediscovery and defence of local traditions and civic values? This was the assumption of some commentators on the League, particularly abroad. The movement did use a strong rhetoric of defending local traditions (Lombardi 1990), and spoke tirelessly of the history of the Northern Italian communes, which they saw as the basis of the civic spirit of the League. But the entities for which they advocated autonomy (first Lombardy: population 9 million, larger than the Netherlands), and then the North ('Padania'), population around 30 million) cannot be described as communities either in the sense of homogeneous cultural orientations or in the sense of groups forged in face to face interactions and rich in institutions fostering cooperation and trust (Etzioni 1995).

There was certainly an element of communitarian nostalgia in the motivations of League supporters, and in their intermittent enthusiasm for local dialects and history. Many of the areas they come from have developed in two generations from small-scale, peasant communities with distinct identities and dialects, to become a hub of the global economic system. It is clear from surveys, however, that participation of militants in the movement was not principally motivated by such goals (Mannheimer *et al.* 1991: 144).

The League did represent a negative communitarianism in the form of a strong rhetoric of exclusion of outsiders, and often did so by presenting outsiders as carriers of a 'foreign' (dishonest, corrupt) way of life, to be contrasted to what the League saw as the honest, civic values of the North. This applied both to Southern Italian immigration into Northern Italy, and to Third World immigrants. But the League should not be seen as part of a broader, global trend towards communitarian mobilisation. League concern with community occurred in isolation from the rise of communitarian thinking elsewhere (Etzioni 1995; Taylor 1992). Bossi himself, when questioned directly on the topic, was adamant that the League should remain unencumbered by such 'intellectual baggage' (Tambini 1998b), and shows no signs of being aware of such debates. The actions of League mayors in respect to community differed very little from those of their predecessors. The League's rhetoric regarding direct democracy – another communitarian theme – was not developed into concrete proposals for reform, even when the League was, after 1992, in charge of more Northern Italian town halls than any other party.[3] Beyond a vague reference to autonomy, the exact form of preferred political arrangement for the League was in fact never made public, probably in order to retain as broad as possible public appeal.

A racist/anti-immigrant movement?

There were many references to origin and ethnicity in League propaganda, and later I discuss how such ideas helped consolidate the movement identity of the League. But race was not the only concern, and although League members and League propaganda made much of cultural difference, this was explained by reference to the divergent histories in Northern and Southern Italy, rather than biologically reductionist racial theories. The League tended to engage in tactical use of vague ideas of race, when that was convenient for mobilising support. After the League attempted in 1992 to become more accepted in the mainstream of Italian politics, the racial element became more subdued, though it emerged again after 1999 with renewed venom.

The League's rhetoric against South–North migration in Italy dovetailed with its position on immigration from the Third World. The Martelli Law, much discussed in Italy in 1990, was an attempt to control immigration after a large increase during the 1980s. It was devised to bring Italy in line with the other signatories of the European Schengen Agreement. The legislation provided an amnesty for many of the immigrants already on Italian soil, and then the installation of tighter controls on further immigration. The League used the wide public debate surrounding the issue to make its anti-immigration position heard, with the result that the movement was categorised along with the extreme right elsewhere in Europe as an anti-immigrant party.

This was not the first time League propaganda had commented on immigration. The discussion in the early years in League newspaper *Lombardia Autonomista* was phrased in terms of the League's position on modern capitalism. Capital should move, argued the League, but not labour. Just as Southern Italians should have less right to work in Lombardy than Lombard residents, so too should non-European immigrants be 'helped at home' according to the League. The official statements of the leadership and propaganda come from this perspective; racism was generally not open, though there was an occasional speech or remark that was undeniably racist.

Clearly there were many among the League's supporters who were racist in a straightforward, phenotype/reductionist way, but such positions were rarely explicit in League propaganda, and this issue was not the most prominent in League discourse. On the surface, the leadership claims to have made a commitment to stopping the Martelli Law, because it argued that it was too lax in allowing illegal immigrants to stay in Italy. Rather than referring to biological-racial differences, they focused on the illegality of the entry of many immigrants, arguing that they should not be rewarded for this with an amnesty.[4] During the period in which the Martelli Law was being discussed, every issue of the campaign newsletter *Lombardia Autonomista* contained referenda forms in an attempt to collect the 50,000 signatures necessary to repeal the law. The League was unsuccessful in this modest objective, however. Allievi concluded that 'either the League did not have the capacity to do it, or this was not the first strategic objective, but only a tool, a chance to make political polemics' (Allievi 1992: 67).

Bossi himself has always been careful to avoid biologically reductionist racism (he is married to a Southerner), and uses the term 'racist' to describe what he calls the 'colonial regime' in Rome. He is aware that the attitudes of many of his supporters are not so subtle, however, and League propaganda does use very blunt, derogatory terms to describe the enemies of the League: '*terroni*' for southerners, and '*vu' cumpra*' for Africans. Biorcio (1992: 64) found that racist opinions were more likely to be found among the supporters of the League than among the supporters of any other movement bar the post-fascist Alleanza Nazionale.[5]

There are no statistics on physical attacks on Southerners and immigrants in Northern Italy during the 1980s and 1990s. Given the heightened media sensitivity to the issue, it is difficult to say with certainty if they increased. Even if we had figures, it would be difficult to link them to the

League. Daniele Vimercati, however, himself a League sympathiser, was in no doubt that a brawl that occurred in July 1989 in Tramigna, Soave, and resulted in the death of one man from Puglia, in the South of Italy, was triggered by anti-Southern goading, inspired by the League (Vimercati 1990: 66). It is hard to imagine that a political party can somehow use, or exploit prejudice, as the League undeniably does, without feeding and legitimising it.

A federalist movement?

Federalism entered the League vocabulary fairly quickly, and from 1990 until 1995 was the cure-all buzzword of the League. Integral federalism was a particularly central concept. Although ostensibly based on the federalist thought of Brugmans, Proudhon and Hamilton and their conceptions of *federalisme integral*, the idea was little developed by the League. In their hands the term is glossed to represent supposedly non-fragmentary federalism. If *federalismo integrale* is a central plank of League ideology, it is a very flexible one, its meaning changing as is convenient for the League. Leaders such as Rocchetta and Bossi gave vague and contradictory interpretations of the term in 1994.[6] In any case, the federalist stance was dropped at the beginning of 1995 (after it was taken on by the other parties in Italy who announced federal reforms).

A populist movement?

The League has been labelled a form of populism, following the theory of Ionescu and Gellner (1970) (Biorcio 1992). Broadly, populism is described as an ideology that emphasises 'the people' in opposition to an 'enemy'; that emphasises territoriality, nationality and often race; and that articulates the authentic popular will via a strong leader rather than by the formal rationality of democracy (Biorcio 1992: 43). As a broad, catch-all concept this does characterise many aspects of the League, and is good for describing the various stages of the League's mobilisation (Schmidtke 1996: 137; Diani 1996: 11–14). A fraction of foreign opinion sought to define precisely these aspects of League populism as its virtues as a new form of authentic democratic resistance (Piccone 1992).

The analytical value of this term, however, is limited. It is very broad, since it applies to movements as diverse as fascism, communism and various forms of nationalism, and yet does not grasp the particularity of the appeal of the League. Further, it is clear that the League leaders themselves do not consciously frame their own protest in terms of populism. The framework they have deliberately used, I argue in the next section, is that of nationalism.

Beyond essentialism

The League is therefore all these things in part, none of them fully, and more besides. All these labels imply that the League has some essence, or a dominant aim, ideology or voice. This is a misplaced assumption. Statements of the type, 'The League is a federalist party' (Cross 1990) or 'The League wants to break up Italy' or 'The League's main thesis is the "Northern Republic" as a "macro region"' (Poche 1995) imply a conscious collectivity that never existed: the League was in fact unstable, constantly redefining identity, interests and goals. There is no single League that wants or does or thinks. With a trial–error strategist at its head, who constantly tests new formulae with his followers and with the public at large, the League, like most contemporary movements, is certainly not driven by reference to a single unquestionable text, utopia, ideology or article of faith. Analysts attempting to sum up the League in 1990 may have described it as a racist, anti-immigration party as Cross (1990) did; three years previously they may have found it a folkloric, dialect-protecting localist party (see Lombardi 1990). And if it is federalist what does that mean, when there appears to be no stability or agreement even among League leaders regarding what is to be federated?

Many responded to the apparent disorder of the League – its shifts in membership, strategy and goals – by dividing the movement's history into several phases, stressing the discontinuities in the League's electoral strategy, its forms of action, and its support. Ilvo Diamanti, for example, divides the rise of the League into four phases: ethno-regionalism (1983–7); socio-economic regionalism (1987–90); anti-state protest (1990–2); and party of government (1992–).[7] Interestingly, this version of events has also been shared by the leaders of the League themselves, who at certain times found it useful to reject the early 'ethnic' phases as strategic postures.[8] This is a reasonable guide, but by stressing the sudden changes in strategy that the League makes, stage theories may distract our attention from deeper continuities in the politics of the League, and from understanding why changes in political strategy were made. It is necessary to understand the elements of continuity that allow the movement to reproduce itself over time.

Most early research on the League was therefore dogged by essentialism: the desire to reveal the *real* League. This compounded a series of public misconceptions about the League. A sensitivity to the nature of the animal – and its collective identity – was missing. The League, like all social movements, should rather be seen as an unstable configuration moving through time, constantly redefining goals, membership and identity (Melucci 1982, 1985; Touraine 1978).

Researchers would have done well to follow Alain Touraine's advice when he commented on the Occitan movement in 1970s France, a regionalist movement with some similarities to the League:

> Our research rejects the idea that the Occitan movement has a unique or central meaning. It has many. It is part of the broad family of third world nationalisms. It is an action in defence of a pre-industrial economy and society, threatened by advanced industrial society . . . None of these hypotheses could be accepted in its entirety, since they all fall into the same trap, which is to say: here is the essence, here is the true nature of the Occitan movement.
>
> (Touraine 1981: 285–6, my translation)[9]

My analysis of the rise of the League will keep Touraine's advice in mind. We have seen that others tended to treat the movement as a pre-wrapped collective actor: this analysis in contrast will focus on how the League achieved this status as a collective actor. The focus will be on the process through which the League reproduced itself over time, negotiated and renegotiated its goals, and responded to its changing environment.[10] It seems that in all those fields, the nationalist-separatist stance was crucial as the 'organisational form' of the movement. The following are key questions:

> How do the actors construct their action so that we can observe an apparently unified empirical behaviour? What facilitates or impedes the integration of the different orientations in a given collective phenomenon? How does the involvement or defection of the individual occur, if one takes into account this plurality of meanings?
>
> (Melucci 1985: 331)

Nationalism, it will emerge from the next section, should be viewed not as the essence of the League, but rather as one of the main ways the movement answers those questions Melucci describes. Nationalism was the League's dominant political strategy.

Nationalism and the League

> On 28 June 1989 several hundred thousand Serbs gathered on the battlefield site of Gamimestan, outside the Kosovar capital Pristina, to celebrate the six-hundredth anniversary of the Battle of Kosovo. 'After six centuries,' Milosevic told the crowd, 'we are again engaged in battles and quarrels.'
>
> (Malcolm 1994: 213)

In May 1990, the League held its first 'Lombard National Festival' on the site where the Giuramento (Pledge) of Pontida was signed in 1167. 'Nine centuries later,' said Bossi, facing many thousands of League supporters, 'the people of Lombardy are here again, to struggle for the liberty of Lombardy.' The date chosen was the anniversary of the 1186 Battle of Legnano.

What is nationalism, and why does this book insist on analysing the League in terms of nationalism when most dismissed the League's claims to a right to self-determination, and denied that it was a nationalist movement? Was the League in 1989 less nationalist, or less legitimately nationalist than the Serbian movement, and on what grounds can one answer such a question? Here I argue that this set of claims is particularly difficult to understand because it is generally discussed in terms of a concern with issues of legitimacy of movements, and ultimately of states. Nationalism, as Brubaker (1997) pointed out, is a concept of practice, not an analytical concept. Many assessments of the League's nationalism are concerned not with understanding how nationalism works, but with the business of sorting legitimate from illegitimate nationalist claims. The League did not seek to construct itself as a populist movement, as a racist movement, or as a protest movement as such. It did seek to be seen as a nationalist movement. What is analytically interesting about the League is its attempt to be accepted as a legitimate nationalist discourse. In what follows I trace its reasons for so doing.

The League leadership certainly sought to be recognised as nationalist when it was convenient for it to do so. The results of the July 1989 regional elections were celebrated in the League newspaper with the headline: 'A great victory for Lombard nationalism'.[11] League MEP Francesco Speroni wrote the cover article which related the vote (in which the League won 8.1 per cent of preferences in Lombardy) to the Milan insurrection of 1848, and drew parallels with Lithuania, Estonia and Latvia, then about to secede from the USSR. The League leadership sought to demonstrate that their movement was on a par with more conventional 'ethno-nationalisms' such as the Québecois or the Catalan, and thus to increase the legitimacy and visibility of the movement. Speroni was among the first League MEPs who joined the Arc En Ciel group of regionalists in the European Parliament. Through their propaganda organs, the League let it be known that there they were in the company of other more established nationalist parties such as the Flemish Volksunie, the Scottish National Party, and Corsica's Unione di Populu Corsu (Vimercati 1990: 99).

So the League claimed to be nationalist. Clearly, however, if nationalist claims are to convince domestic and international opinion they cannot merely be made unilaterally, but must be recognised by others. It was inevitable that many would question the League's claim to represent a nation. Diamanti (1996b) thus claimed that 'the Northeast is not Catalonia; a homogeneous identity and interest of the Northeast does not exist'. Political scientist Gianfranco Pasquino agreed: 'The League lacks, notwithstanding a few clumsy attempts, the cement constituted by a language and a specific, differentiated culture' (Pasquino 1993: 33).[12] Roberto Biorcio put it as follows: 'There was no autonomous Lombard culture grounded on a specific language and particular traditions' (Biorcio 1992). The argument is that since there is nothing we can identify as a pre-existing Lombard or Padanian culture, the nationalism of the League is an inauthentic posture, rather than a genuine nationalist movement.

Given this conception that separatist claims should be accompanied by some proof that they are made in the name of an existing nation, the Lombard and Venetian Leagues (then the most active among the movements that were to make up the Northern League), did, however, represent areas with several attributes that we would consider national: they had no language but could claim to have a cultural specificity and a unique dialect, and they had long histories as independent states.

There is, of course, no undisputed way to determine legitimate claims to nationality as opposed to illegitimate ones on the basis of objective, national attributes (if there were, and if there were an agent capable of adjudicating such claims, modern history would have been much less eventful). Nationalist claims generally inflate, perform and mythologise cultural difference in their quest for recognition and the League was no exception. As Charles Tilly (1996: 305) put it, 'The prize for a successful "We Are a Nation" performance was control of an independent state'. All nationalisms are performative. It is sheer force of numbers, and the political and structural contexts in which claims are made, that decide whether nationalisms develop into genuine threats to existing sovereignty, or remain in the realm of folklore.[13] It is a question of mobilisation. Nationalist performances are successful when they get people onto the streets and into the polling booths. The 'authenticity' of the nation, or the strength of ethnic consciousness, are one type of resource in such political mobilisation struggles. It is necessary therefore to dispel any lingering notion that the League is somehow different from other forms of nationalism in that it does not represent a 'real' nation. The short answer comes from Gellner: 'Nationalism invents nations, not the other way around' (Gellner 1964). That the League invents and distorts identity and history may be true, but it should be accepted that this is normal in any movement claiming to be nationalist (Rusconi 1993).

The politically charged question 'Is this a nation?' (with all its implications in terms of self-determination rights) is always posed in a historical context: a context in which calculations are made not only about authenticity but about consequences, for example about scale required for independent states. It is generally agreed that nationalist constructions of identity took on a particular political importance only in the modern period.[14] Industrial production makes new demands on central states for a linguistically homogeneous workforce (Gellner 1983) and the new geopolitical conditions require mass volunteer armies backed by bigger industrial infrastructures and territorial units of larger scale. Class conflicts can be abated to a certain extent by national citizenship regimes, and nationalism is a useful symbolic resource to mobilise otherwise conflicting class or sectarian interests in pursuit of common goals.[15] The context in which the League's claims are made is one in which sovereignty and scale are much less clear: new possibilities have been opened up by globalisation and European integration, and others, those of sovereign national economies for instance, have been closed off.

Nationalist attributes are often more flexible than they appear: dialects can be forgotten or taught, cultures can be assimilated or celebrated, and histories rewritten. Whether or not national attributes (such as language or traditions) are retained by a group depends in part on the political consequences of their changing. While the Irish national movement depended on a linguistic argument to support its nationalist claims, the learning of Irish was immensely popular. Soon after independence was won for the South, language learning declined, despite the fact that it was now state-backed. People migrate, intermarry and assimilate. The League exploited the ambivalences that all nationalism brings to light: between willed and God-given identities, between intensively politicised and apparently 'pre-political' communities and attributes.

If pre-existing cultural attributes cannot be relied upon to differentiate real nationalism from pretender nationalism (and thus dismiss the nationalism of the League), what about the goals of nationalist movements? Are certain types of goals defining features of nationalist movements? Gellner (1983) defined as nationalist the desire to match states and (culturally homogeneous) nations: for every nation a state, and for every state a nation. Did the League really have nationalist goals in these terms? It is not clear whether or not the leaders or supporters of the Lombard or later the Northern League genuinely wanted to secede from the Italian nation-state. Some did, some did not, and many were undecided. If we compare the League to other movements that are more widely recognised as nationalist, we find that they too lacked consistent goals, switching from federalism to autonomy, and in some cases supporting integration with other states. This is particularly true in contemporary Europe, where the issue of state sovereignty is ever less clear in a context of European integration. To a certain extent opportunities are structurally determined: nationalism became such an important device for structuring political action in the nineteenth century not because of a trend for new aspirations or goals, but because the process of modernisation undermined existing power structures and revolutionised political opportunities.[16]

All this does not imply that all nations are collectivities consciously designed to solve problems of community belonging thrown up by modernisation, but merely suggests that they are institutions particularly adapted to the resolution of a number of the structural conflicts and functional requirements that are thrown up during the modern era. There is no need to favour one actor or structure in accounting for the modern rise of nations if one accepts that the institution 'the nation' permitted a temporarily stable compromise between various of them. (Class actors, nationalist intellectuals – both liberal and socialist – industrial élites and absolutist states all had their own specific uses for nationalism. While the means – nationalism – was often similar, the ends differed.) Nor is it to claim that nothing of what we consider to be nations existed before they were put to this modern use. Some cultural similarities, awareness of collective identity and forms of patriotism pre-existed the modern era, as Smith (1981, 1991a) and Armstrong (1982) have convincingly shown. But such cultural similarities and collective identities were much less significant in the tasks of distributing risks and resources, political deliberation, and constructing collective actions than were distinctions of clan, village, religion or caste. Nationalism, then, is not defined in terms of a pre-existing 'nation' but is a form of politics based on a posited nation (Brubaker 1997).

It is a central thesis of this book that nationalism remains a useful resource in protest mobilisation even when its other functions are being undermined. Even when state nationalism goes into decline, there remains the problem of constructing social movements and collective actions, and collective identities are crucial resources therein. This explains why political nationalism takes on a particular salience when nation-states go into crisis. The League's nationalism was not concerned with making compromises possible between antagonistic class actors; it was concerned with making a protest movement more compact and united over time.

As Rogers Brubaker (1997) has convincingly argued, the nation should be viewed above all as a contingent event. Under certain conditions, political actors' claims to be nations are recognised as such. If performers had their 'we are a nation' claim recognised, the nation became institutionalised into a citizenship regime and a national public space, thus reflecting that 'nationalist claims are one genre of answers to the question of what constitutes an autonomous political community capable of "self determination"' (Calhoun 1994: 305). It is possible to view the nation-state as a compromise: an institution that serves a slightly different function for each of the actors (such as political parties and movements) that promoted it. It is also possible to focus on one of the functions it serves: the making of movements of social protest.

Thus the dismissal of the League as 'false' nationalism was not an analytical, but a political statement, a calling for non-recognition of the League's nationalist claims rather than understanding of this movement and how it interprets, uses and transforms nationalism. Written from a perspective outside Italian politics, this book is free of such political constraints. In what follows I introduce a schema for understanding the nationalism of the League. For while I dismiss the claim that any element of the League's discourse reveals an essence of the movement, by analysing the League in terms of its nationalism we should better understand not only the League, but nationalism.

Implicit in all critical accounts of nationalism (Hobsbawm 1990; Gellner 1964, 1983) is the idea that nationalism is an effective mobilising tool. When such accounts dismissed nationalism as an instrumental ideology of élites, there remained the questions of how that instrument worked and the degree to which élites in fact knew how to use it. What is missing in such accounts, and what Breuilly (1982) sketched for the last century, was an understanding of just why nationalism is such an effective mobilising framework for political movements: in general terms why it is so good at motivating and organising individuals to act collectively. The fact that nationalism is recognised as a legitimate form of action is only one aspect of that. In the next section I introduce such a model, drawing on theories of collective action and social movements and focusing on the role of identity construction. At the end of the section I update Breuilly's account, asking how nationalism as a form of politics would operate in contemporary Europe.

Nationalism as a tool of political mobilisation: a theoretical framework

Social movements thrive when they motivate many individuals to participate, when supporters have a strong sense of a common purpose, interests and an enemy, and a sense of belonging to a group with a permanent identity. Social movements thrive when they have an efficient organisational structure, are seen as legitimate, and when they face a favourable set of political opportunities. Nationalism is a strategy for providing all those resources but the last.

Nationalist claims are made in a tensely interdependent field of competing actors and structures of legitimisation. Unlike those of unification nationalists a hundred years previously, the claims of the League were made in competition with those of an existing nation-state. Those who opposed the League had to take care not to offer any legitimacy to the movement, and the League themselves had to appeal to any form of authority, discourse or convention that could support their identity constructions. This analysis, I stress again, eschews the role of arbiter of such national claims. I am not interested in whether the League's separatist/autonomist claims are founded or legitimate, earnest or cynical. Rather, I am concerned with explaining how the League works as a movement, and in particular the role of nationalism in its mobilisation.

The key is the relationship between identity and collective action, which, although it has been explored in detail in the theory of social movements, has not been incorporated into understanding of national and ethnic phenomena. The scheme that follows outlines how the sense of permanent and bounded identity that is provided by national constructions serves mobilisation. In short, I will pose the general question of why nationalism is useful to the construction of collective action and offer an answer via a discussion of a specific case of political mobilisation, the Northern League/Lombard League.

The term 'construction' needs some qualification. Some authors take this to mean intentional design. I do not. Collective identities can be socially constructed without their being consciously designed, since all the term means is that such identities do not present themselves as pre-existing, unchangeable structures, but are constituted through the everyday practices of actors in context (Giddens 1991). To identify a social construction is therefore not to identify a conspiracy by intellectuals, populist leaders, states or capitalists to pull the wool of nationalist ideology over the eyes of innocents. It is in myriad everyday decisions about taste and cultural practice that the nationalist boundaries are constructed; decisions which are structured by situations and opportunities, influenced by cultural élites and rewarded or punished by controllers of resources such as states. The power of construction is extremely rarely, if ever, concentrated in the hands of one actor. The resources to which actors have access, and the ways in which they use them, are of course affected by the operations of leaders and by culture industries and education. In explanatory terms the inventions/suggestions/offers of those leaders have then to be constructed by actors within the constraints of their immediate context. Collective identities, such as the national and regional identities with which the League concerned itself, have periods when they are relatively stable, reproduced through actions related to the economic and security functions they serve, and they have periods when political and economic conditions demand their revision. This is similarly done through actions in structured contexts and within the constraints placed by existing resources. Neither mere invention, then, nor pre-existing collective identity, but the social constitution of identity in context is the key to understanding nationalist processes. The context in which the League's nationalist claims were forged was the construction of a political protest movement at a moment when the entire Italian national state went into a crisis due to revelations about corruption.

The constituency of the League was made up of a variety of class and interest groups, with a predominance (see Chapter Six) of owners of small and medium-sized businesses, entrepreneurs and shopkeepers: those benefiting least from the public sector spoils system and most acutely aware that their taxes supported it. The League was not, however, simply an expression of the interests of this sector, since it also received significant support from other groups, such as industrial workers and farmers. The movement faced the problem of coordinating these in a single movement, and it was nationalism that enabled them to do so.

The leadership of the League returned, repeatedly, to the idea of self-determination, and to the justification of self-determination in terms of historical, cultural/linguistic, broadly what we understand as 'ethnic' identity. The League referred to 'ethnic' nationalism not only during one phase of the movement, but repeatedly during its career, and mainly at times of crisis. Did the League do this in order to protect a way of life, a language, a collective identity about to be engulfed, or because its pre-existing cultural habits constrained it to do so? No.[17] The North was not even the central, sacred *Heimat* of the leadership, many members of which advocated abandonment of separatism after 1994. Clearly the nationalism of the League should be analysed as a strategy. This is to treat nationhood not simply as the goal of the movement, or as a set of values, but as a mobilisation tool, assuming that leaders of such movements are most concerned with mobilising collective actions, and keeping support at the highest level possible.

I argue that nationalism served the League in several ways. First, it mobilised individual actors to support the movement, by offering a convincing and simple way of gaining material benefits and recognition. Second, on the organisational level, it provided the sense of identity and a common enemy that are key resources in collective action. Third, the nationalist stance inserted the League in a certain political field of legitimisation: if not as a claim for national self-determination, then as a call for group rights on the basis of cultural specificity.[18]

As such, the identity aspect is crucial to the mobilisation of voters and militants.[19] In fact there is a strong argument to be made that identity is the key resource in any attempt to create a political movement. This, I argue, is the reason that the construction and politicisation of identity accompany protest, and this is the reason that the League dedicates so much time and space to identity work. The League had the problem of making a previously apolitical group self-conscious as political actors, of mobilising them. This is Marx's old problem: a class in itself is not necessarily for itself. As I will show in more detail later, events such as the Festa on the Po, and the folkloric League rallies at Pontida should not be surprising to observers of the League. Rather, such identity work is a key aspect of any attempt to create a political actor. By using the existing identity resources in a way that is most appealing to potential voters, League propaganda constantly reaffirms a 'we', by reference to a cultural identity.

Why is such collective identity so important in political and social movements? An answer to that question would clearly inform the study of nationalism by offering a means to understand both the processes of inclusion and exclusion that nationalism involves, and the processes of cultural creativity and invention that accompany most nationalist movements. I stress, however, that collective identity construction is a general feature of social protest. For example, E. P. Thompson traced the development of working-class identity and culture in England, a process crucial to the emerging forms of class protest (Thompson 1980). There are a variety of approaches that have stressed the importance of identity in action.[20] The League's constituency needed some kind of collective identity construction in order to mobilise.

Definable in terms neither of cultural attributes, nor of goals therefore, nationalism is best seen as a way of doing politics (Breuilly 1982). This approach can be developed regarding the uses of nationalism in social movements. Where Breuilly analyses the functions of nationalism in 'co-ordination, mobilisation and legitimisation' of protest, I develop an analytical schema which separates individual, organisational and legitimisation levels. What, then, are the features of nationalism as a form of politics?

The individual level

The motivations of the individual to contribute to political action vary between activist, leader, voters, and supporters of the movement. I follow Elster (1989b) in assuming that there are basically three forms of individual motivation: the instrumental, the normative and the emotional.

1 Nationalist actions promise material rewards for action through ending perceived exploitation. Nationalist propaganda demonstrates that independence from foreign domination and an independent

state are the means to attain economic prosperity. Such claims assume the existence of a collective identity, which is provided by cultural nationalism. Taxes paid to central, 'foreign' states are calculated, as is the return on those payments in investment and services. Rational actors – or the rational sides or moments of actors – can thus respond to such a calculation, by calling for increased fiscal independence. The League's claim that the 'North that produces' is exploited by the South and Rome is dependent on the claims that the North is naturally more productive, and that the North and South can be understood as separable interests.

2 Successful nationalist actions provide recognition: they offer the release from shame and the key to collective pride, through a process that Greenfeld (1992) dubbed 'the revaluation of all values' and Horowitz analysed as 'group comparison of cultural attributes' (Horowitz 1985: 147–9). Nationalist movements can be interpreted as a collective movement to repair pride by reversing the evaluation of national attributes.[21] Thus German Volk-orientated nationalism emerged, in part, because Prussians and German speakers wished to dispute the very criteria offered by the dominant French culture (Greenfeld 1992). Further, the individual self-respect and confidence thus acquired become crucial resources for the social movement. It is impossible to imagine an effective social movement occurring where self-esteem is lacking. League propaganda absolved the North from involvement in the widespread corruption that was occurring in Italy by representing it as a Southern problem.
3 In addition, various arguments are brought to bear to support the argument that it is morally right to restore a 'natural' state of national 'freedom' with reference to norms of justice and freedom. These are often linked to democratisation and the positing of a natural state of affairs, to which the current injustices can be compared. Thus decisions to support nationalist actions are made in support of these normative goals (Hechter 1995: 55).

This is not to claim that the nationalists are correct or have access to perfect information in making their calculations and decisions to support a movement. As Walker Connor (1978) points out, it is the perception of exploitation, rather than its actual extent, that spurs nationalist actions. Equally, the opposed positions of pride and shame and the normative arguments concerned with the rise of nationalism are performed within the discourse of nationalism. Two important consequences derive from the subjectivity and complexity of individual motivation. First, subjectivity puts a great onus on nationalist propaganda to construct senses of identity in a competitive market for identity construction, and second, decisions to support a movement result from a combination of factors and motivations, rather than a single motivation, as instrumental or rational choice explanation would claim.

The organisational level

As well as the necessity of motivating a number of individuals to vote, to protest or to take to the streets, a social movement has to organise them. I divide the organisational problems into two related groups.

1. The exclusion of free riders and the construction of 'permanent' group identity/boundaries. As I argued earlier, collective action is facilitated by the perception of an apparently permanent collective identity. Nationalist discourse can be read as a means to achieve such permanence, through reference to history, common origin, and tradition. This is why the apparently irrational and folkloric references to distant Lombard, or Northern Italian history and cultural unity, are important: they permit individual actors to imagine that they are contributing to a more general good from which they will in some way benefit in the future.
2. Routine problems of loyalty, recruitment, avoiding contradictions between members, and scripting collective actions.[22] Collective actors require loyalty and tight organisation in order to resist challenges. Concerning recruitment, political research has established the advantages of ecological concentration of support over dispersed support, for example, the value of using existing social networks, and so forth.[23] Separatist nationalism has an advantage in that it guarantees (by making reference to a closed territorial/ethnic unit) a degree of concentration of its potential support, and thus also increases the potential for the use of personal networks as recruitment networks. The nationalist stance freed the imagination of many surrounding the League, and offered militants a script. When the League adopted a national anthem for Lombardy and revived the Lombard flag and when it condemned Roman 'colonialism' and researched the ethnic and cultural particularity of Northern Italians it was using tried and tested nationalist 'action repertoires' (Tilly).[24] The full nationalist armoury of symbolic actions was used by the League: parliamentary boycotts, language protests, cultural festivals, and performance of folklore. National independence was performed symbolically with the minting of League coins, postage stamps, and other paraphernalia. Whereas many political movements have to face problems of coordination and agreement over action repertoires, the League avoided these by simply adopting the script of nationalism.

The external/legitimisation level

In the modern period in Europe, state power has been loosely structured according to principles of national self-determination. If a claim to national self-determination gains recognition in the international system of states, then it will be in a much stronger position also to mobilise domestic support. National identity in Italy is much less stable and self-evident than in other developed countries. The late unification of the country in the 1860s and the high degree of awareness of cultural and linguistic differences, despite the state-sponsored cultural homogenisation programme, leads many Italians to view national identity as an artificial construct to be contrasted with the 'real' entities of town, families and kinship. In such a situation, the invention of new entities such as Padania is less likely to be viewed as a problem per se, and has the further advantage of undermining the state nationalism that tends to favour incumbents. League spokespersons would have defended their position as follows: Italy was invented, so if Italy is not working, then why not invent something else to replace it? According to Gian Enrico Rusconi (1992: 462–3), 'The League operation claims two types of legitimisation. On one side there is a reference to European regionalism and on the other there is the reference to "local ethnies" according to a vague but widespread use in public discourse.'

Symbolic boundaries

Clearly then, nationalist identity work can be a very effective strategy of constructing protest action, and can offer a more profound challenge than the redefinition of sectoral interests within the national polity. Identity is a vague concept, however, and needs to be more clearly defined and operationalised. In this book I see territorial identities such as that mobilised by the League as social constructs constituted through the marking, in public communication, of symbolic boundaries. The idea of symbolic boundaries has a long history in anthropology (both within and outside structuralism) and more recently in sociology. Leading exponents of boundary theory are the anthropologists Frederik Barth, Mary Douglas, and Anthony Cohen. Classical exponents were Durkheim and Levi-Strauss.[25] Barth (1967) applied the idea of symbolic boundaries to identity maintenance in Pathan tribes, Cohen (1985, 1986) to identity maintenance in local British communities, and John Armstrong (1982) has applied it to pre-modern, proto-national identities. The boundaries conception has been applied to the maintenance of ethnic boundaries in multi-ethnic societies (Banton 1983, Wallman 1978) to class identities (Lamont and Fournier 1992) and in the development of national identity (see Giesen and Eisenstadt 1995).

Boundaries theory claims that pre-existing cultural differences alone do not constitute collective identity. Actors select and use criteria of inclusion and exclusion to create/reinforce a 'symbolic' group boundary (a border that exists in the minds of actors, but not necessarily in political or administrative frontiers). Actors thus define their identities by 'heating into significance' cultural differences. How they do this will vary with their goals (struggles for respect, over resources, and so on), and the contexts and opportunities of movement and member.

In this account, the imagined boundary to a collectivity is made by sets of polar oppositions ('criteria of purity') that mark the difference between inside and outside. In the discourse of the Lombard League, for example, Lombards spoke dialects that no Southerners spoke; Lombards were hardworking and Southerners lazy; Lombards were Celts and Southerners Africans; and Lombards were wealthy and Southerners poor. Clearly the process of boundary drawing is involved in the recognition claims that result in the 'comparison of group attributes' (Horowitz 1985: 142). The cultural differences, traditions and practices that are referred to by boundary markers are not stable: the fact of being selected as a symbolic marker of difference generally intensifies a cultural practice, be it a language, a costume or a way of cooking. Even supposedly objective markers such as differences in skin colour can be accentuated or hidden by choice of clothes. These are the key mechanisms at work in processes of politicisation of identity.

The strength of symbolic boundaries (how easy they are to cross, to enter the in-group) depends upon (among other things), first, how recognisable the difference is between members of the in and the out groups, second, how easy it is to gain (or shed) the characteristics specified by the boundary marker, third, how many, and how strongly, people believe in the boundary, and fourth, what sanctions are used in the policing of the boundary, by the in and the out groups. Thus, if proficiency in the Basque language was the agreed definition of Basqueness, the boundary would be as easy to cross as it was to learn Basque. Boundaries based on habits and culture, such as the League's ideas of work ethics, are generally reinforced through constantly reiterating and living by the values that they impose. Ethnic boundaries are usually marked by unstable and shifting combinations of boundaries, which nonetheless can strongly structure interaction and articulate highly consequential processes of inclusion–exclusion. When codified into state citizenship regimes, ideas of ethnic or national belonging are usually simplified into some version of *jus soli* or *jus sanguinis* (Brubaker 1992).

To summarise the use of boundary theory here, 'boundaries' mark off a collective identity by delineating what the group is not. The inside is imbued with positive traits that are the opposite of the negative ones associated with the other. The crucial innovation is that salient differences between groups are not the direct result of differences in the attributes of actors, but are the result of decisions concerning which should be considered as important.[26] In order to legitimise the movement and support collective action, however, boundaries need to be seen as permanent, which creates problems where they are constructed. Boundary construction processes need, therefore, to be 'self-occulating' (Bauman 1995: 19). This is where historiography comes in. Nationalism constructs instant permanence by rummaging in history for precursors to naturalise and concretise the boundary. Hence the medieval staging of League identity.

The nationalist strategy?

Did Bossi and the other League leaders understand the mobilisation functions of nationalist discourse? Probably not, though Bossi certainly had some intuitive grasp of these processes, since he tended to use nationalism most when the movement was fragmenting. Even if we could establish that he did use it strategically, it does not explain why that strategy worked. In the previous section I treated nationalist identity construction as though it were a tool that movements such as the League could use at will, and yet in the first section we undermined the view that the League is a collective actor with the intentions, strategies and rationality necessary to use these tools. Clearly, nationalist identity work is not a tool that can be used to construct in the same way as hammers and shovels can be used to construct. The leaders of the Northern League could shift the stress of the propaganda to a certain extent, but they never had complete control of the ongoing process of identity construction, and they were dependent on the resonances they could create with their followers, which were unpredictable. At times, and this is a danger for all those who seek to use nationalism as a tool, the process of identity construction can take on its own trajectory. Certainly, such processes are not controllable by leaders and therefore not explicable by reference only to the intentions of leaders.[27]

In fact, boundaries to collective identities are rarely stable, especially in mediated, mobile modern societies. They are continually contested and reconstituted through the practices of everyday life, the mobilisation of political movements, and the self-identity construction of members. Individual actors do not have infinite access to the material needed to draw boundaries, but make reference to a limited cultural toolkit (Swidler 1986) of boundary markers to construct identities.[28] This explains the importance of political actors such as the League, whose main political work concerns the reconstitution of identities via the attempt to gain general acceptance for a new definition of group identity in public discourse. In a situation where previous identities are in crisis – and in 1980s Italy the Catholic and communist subcultures were both undermined – it is those able to monopolise the public space with offers of convenient identities that will gain the consensus.

In the preceding sections I have illustrated the variety of ways in which nationalism, that is, the cultural constructions of identity of the type used by the League, is functional for protest mobilisation. It provides emotional, normative and instrumental reasons for individuals to act; it is an excellent resource in the constitution of identity; and it is well equipped to organise the individual actions into collective actions, and legitimise them.

To assert, thus, that nationalism is functional for the making of the protest movement does not, however, explain why nationalism occurs. This would amount to a functionalist, or 'consequence' explanation (Cohen 1981) as it would be the explanation of a phenomenon (nationalism) in terms of its consequences (the benefits for collective action). Most agree with Jon Elster that a functional explanation must be accompanied by a supplementary theory demonstrating the mechanism that links consequences to their causes: a 'feedback loop'.[29]

The feedback loop is in this case provided by the leadership of the League recognising that some aspects of its nationalist identity discourse are more functional for mobilisation than are others. When the leader of the Lombard League announced that the dialect would no longer serve as a principal marker of inclusion, he justified himself on the grounds that the dialect mobilisation had become a liability for the movement. In doing so he claimed that the principal goal of the movement was not to protect the dialect. Further, the functional utility of a boundary may change considerably in a short time. Although in general terms impermeable boundaries serve collective action, recruitment may in a given context be served by more permeable ones.

So the League was using a proven formula: performing a nationalist sense of identity as a means to construct and legitimise political action. But it clearly differed from previous rounds of nation-state nationalism in its methods and goals. How are we to interpret this?

New context: new nationalism?

> Now there is no more crisis of empire, nor the process of decolonisation; nor the crisis of socialism. Now there is only the necessity that productive systems compete and they cannot do that if different parts of the state have entirely different economies.
>
> (Umberto Bossi, quoted in Tambini 1998b)

The structural conditions prevailing in Western Europe during the closing decades of the twentieth century were radically different to those of the nineteenth century, the period when the nationalist mode of 'doing politics' (Breuilly 1982) was perfected. National economies, and the argument that the populations of nations are involved in a common destiny relating to state-regulated economic growth, are undermined by economic globalisation and the emergence of new class inequalities that states seem less able to abate (Crouch, Eder and Tambini 2001). National citizenship is undermined by alternative institutions for assessing rights claims (Soysal 1994), and national culture by migration, relativism and post-modernism (Bauman 1990b). This does not, however, signal the withering away of nationalism per se: while nation-state institutions of citizenship may be failing, nationalism – or something like it – still works very well as a mobilising force for social protest.

In summary, the following are current trends among those that might lead us to expect nationalism, as a repertoire of action, to be transformed in the late twentieth century.

Globalisation

While most analysts accept that nationalist mobilisations tend to appear when empires fail, the prospect that the faltering of nation-states could open the path for a new form of nationalism is less widely acknowledged. Yet all political organisation, not least in social movements, requires a sense of identity, and identities are generally made from the cultural, linguistic and historical attributes that are most convenient, given the structural context and opportunities.

In nineteenth-century Europe, there was a general consensus among liberal nationalists that a certain scale was required for a valid nation to emerge. Irish claims were not countenanced by Mazzini because he thought the island too small. The reasoning behind the arguments about scale varied, but generally depended on calculations of the need to raise an army capable of defending the nation, institute an education system capable of rationalising the language and create a non-dependent economy with its own currency (Gellner 1973, Hobsbawm 1990). These conditions are becoming less important in those countries integrated into the global economy, especially within the European Union (Bauman 1995: 250), and the opinion has recently become widespread that nation-states are too small for some functions and too large for others.

The mechanism through which these changes are likely to influence sovereign states is through a more generalised awareness that the national state cannot deliver in some of the ways in which it did in the past. Welfare states, once underwriters of national identity (as Jensen and Phillips 2001 illustrates with the case of Canada), are less likely to provide the sense of common destiny and security that they once did. In such a context, protest and participation begin to take the form not of new parties but of a more generalised anti-state, anti-party protest, which the state no longer has the resources to buy off. One of the main enemies of the League was indeed 'the parties', a generalised category of all parties operating in the national state arena charged by the League with failing to deliver.

What constitutes a valid nationalist claim, and its consequences, are not of course timeless questions, but are tied to a specific institutionalised structure for the assessment of claims. The national principle can be traced through its origins in revolutionary republicanism, liberalism and romanticism (Kedourie 1993) through its development in relation to citizenship regimes (see, for example, Brubaker 1992) to the twentieth century principle of self-determination which was itself a contingent event, the result of a compromise between Lenin and Wilson (Cassese 1994). The nineteenth and early twentieth centuries, in Europe, in which that structure for assessing national claims was developed, were a time in which assumptions could be made regarding state sovereignty over the economy and culture, and regarding the scale necessary to constitute a nation (Hobsbawm 1990, Gellner 1973). The process of nation-building led to the development of welfare-type states, which reinforced national interdependence. The current period is arguably the period in which those assumptions and institutions are beginning to break up, due to globalisation, in the economy, culture and political rights (Robertson 1990, Soysal 1994, Sassen 1996).

In such a context, the institutional framework for assessing claims of autonomy should also, we might imagine, shift. This is another reason to doubt that movements such as the League could be easily and convincingly dismissed as 'virtual' nationalism or 'false' nationalism. If the national state is going into crisis as a model and there is a search for new models, it is through movements like the League, however distasteful they may appear, that it will be dismantled. Free from the previous conditions of scale and self-sufficiency, we can expect new nationalisms to resemble the old in some respects (such as in terms of mobilisation strategies and organisation structure) but not all (Bauman 1995: 252). Protests generally take elements of their repertoire from the past, and mutate them in the process to fit new conditions, and nationalism as a repertoire of action will do so too.

The rise (and fall?) of the state-sanctioned, mediated, national, public sphere

If culture is a key medium of nationalism, then surely current identity work in nationalism will be effected by transformations in the media, the cultural infrastructure. Nationalist mobilisation, or what Tilly (1996) called the 'we are a nation' performance, was in the last century performed through print media (as Anderson (1983) and Deutsch (1953) have described) and in political arenas such as mass meetings.[30] But such authors did not go on to attempt to determine what the conditions of national imagining are in the current period. The implications of television and the new media have been analysed mainly in terms of their effects on culture, rather than on the conditions for political mobilisation or political identity construction. (See Morley 1992, Collins 1990, Scannel and Cardiff 1982.) Little has been done to analyse the implications for nationalism of the widely-noted spectacularisation of political action due to the influence of television. If the constructivist approach to nationalism is adopted, however, then the importance of controlling the media agenda becomes obvious. If the nation-as-event consists merely in individual actors enacting their identity (and thus perceiving of their interest) as national, then the achievement of a competing identity and the presence of this competing identity in the media texts that individuals draw upon in making their identities is likely to be very significant for the ways in which individuals constitute their identities and thus political actions. In short, whereas Breuilly (1982) analysed how nationalism as a form of politics operated in the last century, this case study attempts to use the example of the League to examine how nationalist mobilisation works in the era of the sound-bite.[31]

Individual identity

Individuals, we thus assume, construct their collective identities from a limited number of texts available to them, and those identities are recognised and rewarded. Where hegemony breaks up and identities compete with one another (as in the case, for example, of the League membership) there is more scope for instrumental choice of identity. In the current period, individual identity construction becomes more reflexive, fragmented and ironic (Giddens 1991, Lash and Friedman 1992: 7–8). In such conditions, the free play of identity construction that is the characteristic of the League is less problematic. Hyphenated identities, regional identities and other alternatives to the homogenous national identity become more common and may even have some strategic value. Identities are more like clothes and less like skins, therefore, and we might expect a more general tendency to use, change or redefine them strategically.

Those who seek to dismiss the League as a bogus form of nationalism therefore miss the points that current identity entrepreneurs may be developing forms of belonging and solidarity more adapted to the current context, and that their free play and experimentation with solidarities, cultures and allegiances may be a strategy appropriate to the current context.

Identity work, folklore and culture are fundamental, because they alter the very foundations of the habits and rationality of individual political actors. What, we may ask, is real politics? The Festa on the Po, where all of Northern Italy watched the declaration of independence on television, or the attempt of the League to take part in an unworkable government coalition? Clearly there is much to be said for the argument that the Festa on the Po is more fundamental than taking office, since for many Italian citizens it underlined an alternative sense of collective destiny. This is not to imply that it will work, however, or that the League is destined to be a great success. Far from it, the movement may never again enjoy the levels of support it achieved at its peak. But it does signal a clear need to understand the changing conditions of generating support for separatist movements, and the changing rationality of nationalist leaderships. Nationalism should be understood as a way of mobilising, organising and legitimising a movement. The consequences of using such a strategy, and its effectiveness, are revealed by the history of the League, to which we now turn.

2 The movement in context

Lombardy in post-war Italy

Roberto Maroni, Interior Minister in 1994, and the party leader, Umberto Bossi, had been part of a group of friends who started to meet and discuss politics in their hometown of Varese, near Milan, in the early 1980s. The pair and some of the others at these early meetings were to become the most powerful in the Northern League. Even then gaunt and intense, Bossi was a failed medical student and one-time guitarist, and bearded, more cheerful Maroni had been active on the Left in the 1960s and 1970s. Their political argument was simple. They claimed that their region, Lombardy, was being systematically exploited by the corrupt politicians of Rome, who continually increased taxes, using funds squeezed out of the rich North to line their pockets and buy votes in Southern Italy.

From outside Lombardy, the charges of exploitation of Lombardy by the South must have seemed strange. Whereas poverty remains a very real problem in the South of Italy, Varese, a small town nestled in a subalpine valley north of Milan was, and still is, very rich by any standards. During the mid- and late 1980s, when the League was growing fastest, a visitor to Varese would have been hard pressed to see the effects of the 'exploitation'. The streets were littered with new Mercedes. Women paraded the piazzas in furs. Why then was this charge of exploitation by the South not laughed at by the electorate in these towns? Clearly, some background is necessary.

In 1955, the GNP per capita in Italy was $464 compared with $2,310 in the USA and $1,152 in the UK (Clogh 1992). Italy was at that point one of the least developed countries of Europe. The average Lombard's economic position, excluding more industrialised Milan, was not a great deal better than elsewhere in Italy, due to the lack of industrial development and the crisis of the rural economy. In the 1950s, the areas surrounding Bergamo – which later became the cradle of League success – were known as the 'valleys of the white widows' because so many husbands worked abroad. The 1970s and 1980s, however, were to witness a flowering of small industry. The process of development in the valleys of Lombardy was different from the large-scale capitalism already established in Turin and Milan. Firms were smaller, and there was a less marked proletarianisation of the workforce than in Turin, for instance. As well as the growth in productivity and incomes, the number of enterprises also rose. In the province of Como, for instance, the number of self-employed artisans almost doubled from 33,262 in 1951 to 59,469 in 1981, while the overall population remained relatively stable. In Lombardy as a whole, those employed in agriculture declined from 28.9 per cent in 1936 to 6.0 per cent in 1981. At the same time, industrial employment rose from 57.9 per cent to 68.9 per cent (Bull and Corner 1993: 115).

By the mid-1980s, living standards in the medium-sized towns of Northwest Italy had by far surpassed French and British national averages. There emerged an ever larger and ever more prosperous entrepreneurial class. In one generation, Lombardy and the North of Italy more generally had leaped from being a peripheral region in a poor peripheral European country to leading the continent in productivity and living standards. Most residents of Varese will tell you that this was the fruit of hard work, and that the local economy developed despite the Italian government, not because of it.

This leap in prosperity left behind the South of Italy. Although consumption and productivity increased, and there was some industrial development, the Southern economy remained prevalently agricultural, and lacked the North's thriving export-oriented smaller business. Publicly-funded industrial and infrastructure projects became embarrassing 'cathedrals in the desert', often because of corruption and mismanagement. There was increased migration from the countryside into the larger Southern cities, but there were few opportunities there. Emigration from these regions, which had the added disadvantage of high levels of organised crime, remained very high, declining only slightly in the 1970s.

Around the same time, Northern Italy (especially Piedmont and Lombardy) ceased to be an area of high emigration. The uneven development of industry within Italy resulted in a new pattern: from the 1950s onwards (there was little migration under Fascism), a steady flow of migrants went north into industrialising Piedmont, and Lombardy, from the less-developed regions of the South.[1] In the first years these settled in the big Northern cities, and only later in the smaller hill towns, where the boom came later. In the peak year of 1963, a net 287,000 people migrated from the South of Italy to the Centre and North. The annual figure did not drop below 100,000 until 1974 (Ginsborg 1990: 219). As the smaller-scale industrialisation patterns of the towns accelerated, many of these immigrants came to areas that, unlike Turin and Milan, had experienced very little immigration during the previous centuries. Kinship links were institutionalised in local economic and political life, and access to local networks was difficult. The first generation of migrants to the industrialising towns faced stereotyping and exclusion due to their accent, their poverty and their alien customs. But they were eventually accepted, second generation *meridionali* (Southerners) being almost indistinguishable from their Lombard neighbours.[2] In the smaller towns, where the social fabric was thicker, however, integration was more difficult. Although the dominant Christian and communist cultures in the Northern regions advocated acceptance of Southerners for reasons of charity and solidarity, some exclusion from kinship networks, and some residual discrimination against Southerners continued.

After recession and industrial strife in the 1970s, the North of Italy seemed – on paper at least – to be performing excellently in the 1980s. '*Il sorpasso*', a moment when Italy overtook the UK to become the fifth-largest industrial economy in the world, was loudly proclaimed by Italian politicians in 1987. The explanation for this sudden success was found in the social resources of trust and cooperation that remained important in the form of industrial development particular to Lombardy and the North. So Lombardy, geographically, productively and demographically the biggest region in Italy, seemed in many ways to be moving from strength to strength.[3] Why then did a great proportion of its population rise in a sudden electoral revolt against the 'exploiter', and such a huge proportion of voters elect Bossi and friends to power, apparently giving them a mandate to dismantle the Italian state?

A Lombard's eye view

Reading between the lines of Lombardy's industrial triumph, an inquiring mind (perhaps that of a member of the growing number of prosperous small-business owners from Lombardy), might have questioned the glossy appearance. The luxurious boot – newly industrialised, newly wealthy Italy – seemed to have an embarrassingly scuffed sole and heel. In the South, corruption, organised crime and embarrassing industrial performance seemed to threaten the progress that parts of Northern Italy had made, from the European periphery to the industrial core. Successive coalition governments seemed unable to correct the problems of the South, as governments had been for over a century, and many reported that the problems of corruption and organised crime in the South were worsening. When Lombard businessman Signor Bresciani went north to Germany and Switzerland to market his ice cream products in the 1980s, he was met with respect for the quality of '*Il made in Italy*', but sometimes sensed that his customers suspected that Italian economic success was built on shady deals and corruption. Though pleased for his export business when currency markets periodically lost confidence in the lira, he felt ashamed when foreign banks refused his currency. The ice cream producer, who joined the Lombard League in 1987, complained: 'when they don't accept lire any more abroad, you begin to feel a bit nervous'.[4]

Bresciani had emigrated from Italy to Canada in the 1970s. Like the other 93,000 migrants who *returned* to Northern Italy between 1980 and 1985, he had experienced a different system of relations with the state while abroad.[5] When he returned to Italy, and started his small business, he began to envy his Northern European, and North American neighbours. He joined the queues to use comparatively poor public services tangled in bureaucracy, and resented paying for them with what he thought was the highest taxation in Europe. Shortly after he returned from Canada he joined the League: 'It was a moral decision. I was fed up with the falsity of Italy. As an independent businessman I felt suffocated by the lack of openness and clarity in relationships with banks, and with the state.'

Throughout the 1980s economic boom, public scandals concerning Italian business and political leaders filled the press, but did not seem to rock the power base of the Christian Democratic Party, which had controlled governments since 1948. While many outside Italy remarked on the successes of the Italian First Republic during this period, this sentiment was not shared by all Italians. The politicians seemed, to many Northerners, to be getting richer and more arrogant every day, while taxes continued to rise. The Italian state, which in the early post-war years had successfully modernised infrastructure and education, seemed to many to have been turned into a self-serving parasite. Long before the big political bribe scandals broke in 1992, the P2 affair linked banking leaders, politicians, and even the Vatican, to a Masonic group involved in the suspected murder of a top banker.[6] Investigations of politicians went as high as Giuseppe Leone, who resigned as President in 1978 amid accusations of corruption. All this fed the general assumption that illegitimate practices were rife at all levels of the system. The implication of leading figures in a suspected right-wing coup plot (Gladio), undermined already weak trust in the state and the main parties. After the mini financial crisis following the P2 scandal around 1982, and a series of terrorist attacks by the Mafia on public figures, it was easy for our Lombard friend to lose patience and wonder just how permanent his current material success would be. The very structures supposed to guarantee stability and growth – state and political parties – seemed to him to be bent on undermining it.

Like many of the economically successful in the core countries, the new middle classes in Lombardy were increasingly prone to a 'fear of falling': an insecurity born of economic uncertainty in the globalising economy.[7] Given that the economic rise of Lombardy was so recent, and the Italian welfare state so feeble, this uneasy sensation was perhaps even more pronounced in Italy than in other countries. The high standards of living achieved in Lombardy seemed fragile, and many North Italians veered towards what Habermas (1992: 13) called 'the chauvinism of prosperity'.

At the same time, many in Italy became increasingly cynical about party politics. A Machiavellian logic that said 'if it wasn't these politicians it would be another corrupt bunch' prevailed. The prospects for changing things through existing political parties seemed remote. Since the Communist Party (PCI) and the Christian Democrats (DC) began to cooperate in the mid-1970s there had been effectively no opposition apart from the (then still openly fascist) Movimento Sociale (MSI). The ruling parties seemed tangled in a web of *partitocrazia* (the clientelist stranglehold that the party machinery had on public bureaucracy). The exercise of clear, open politics seemed to be in decline, suffocated by the hidden bargaining of political and economic élites.[8]

Although it was therefore accurate in the 1980s to speak of Italy as a 'blocked political system' (Ginsborg 1990: 418), there were in the background some signs of leakage. During the 1970s, Italy had witnessed the gradual erosion of the two faiths: the Christian and communist subcultures that had defined political life in Italy since the war.[9] The share of received votes of the two main parties, the Christian Democrats and the Communists (later the PDS) went down from 67.8 per cent in 1975 to 46.4 per cent in 1990 (Biorcio 1992). New generations began to question the fixed loyalties that had long characterised voting behaviour (Biorcio 1992). The new thinking was not, however, reflected in great changes at the level of party politics. Because of the electoral system, new parties still tended to cooperate with the old. The biggest winner of votes in this period was abstention, which almost doubled, rising from 2,315,570 in 1968 to 4,532,319 in 1987 (Caciagli and Spreafico 1991: 83–4).

In another sense, however, the system remained genuinely blocked. Although every survey pointed to a growing discontent with what is called in Italy the 'political class', there was no political actor to gather together this generalised protest. Commentators spoke of the '*partito che non c'è*' (the missing party) and intellectuals bemoaned the loss of faith in progressive ideologies. The lack of articulation of desires for new alternatives was undoubtedly due to the web of political consociationalism and clientelism: the colonisation of all levels of administrative power by the main parties. Even in the 1980s, many of those at the middle levels in the state sector (local government employees, teachers, services) were tied to the political party system in such a way that they could not easily change political allegiance. Loyalty to a party – having the *tessera* (party card) – was to a great extent a precondition for having a job in the media, education, and anywhere in the public sector. In the country with the largest public sector in Western Europe this involved huge numbers of jobs, and especially the more influential ones. To openly campaign for a new political movement that was in opposition to existing parties would in many cases be to risk career problems. Political alternatives suffered as a result: the very problems that informed opinion agreed justified reform – the lack of 'governability' or a strong executive – themselves prevented any reform.

The inter-party bargaining involved in the *lottizzazione* (carve-up) of government controlled industry and political posts between members of the five-party governing alliance during the 1980s made direct representation of the interests of the growing sector of independently affluent Northern Italians seem impossible.[10] The electoral system, and a political space structured by communism and fear of it, ensured that the only alternative parties, bar the fascists, that were not sucked into the generalised patronage system were the tiny parties representing minority interests such as hunters or pensioners, or locally-oriented 'civic lists'.

As the 1980s went on, this blocked political system faced ever-greater strains, some of which were becoming obvious to the electorate. The integration of European economies put pressure on governments to cut the budget deficit, constraining them to increase taxes in an already labyrinthine and greedy fiscal system. Tax evasion continued, perhaps increased. Many sectors, from environmental law to immigration policies, had to be harmonised with the rest of Europe, and governments did not appear to have the capacity to push through the necessary reforms. Such problems were becoming obvious when columnist Giorgio Bocca entitled his 1990 book *The Disunity of Italy: For Twenty Million Italians Democracy is in a Coma and Europe is Getting Further Away* (Bocca 1990). The population of Southern Italy was the 20 million in question. The message that the South would not make the grade in Europe was close to that of the League, and was one which touched a more widespread anxiety that the Southern problem could undermine the chances of largely Europhile Italy to integrate northwards. But what of the broader political context? Was the League's secessionist rhetoric completely unprecedented?

Territorial politics in modern Italy

The nationalist construction of the League could draw upon a rich pool of references in the party's attempt to divide Lombardy and the North from the rest of Italy. Throughout the history of Italian nation-building, the country has been host to inter-regional conflicts. United in 1870, the young state's early years were marked by competition between local élites, and threats of secession by regions that had previously been separate kingdoms. Sicilian landowners met in Palermo in 1920 to pronounce an ultimatum against the 'Rome government' and threaten secession. The Lombard upper classes threatened on many occasions to revive the Duchy of Milan; and the protesting Sardinian Congress of 1911 calculated how much produce had been extracted from the region by the taxes of the central state since 1860 (just as the League would for Lombardy in 1986). With Fascism, regionalism was suppressed. After the fall of Mussolini, however, Italian politics revived its regionalist tendencies, just as Spain would after Franco. As early as 1946 threats of secession from Sicily had won the island a special semi-autonomous status (Lepre 1986: 70).

If Italy's tendency to regionalism in politics was similar to Spain's, her institutionalisation of it was not. In contrast to Spain's decentralisation in the 1970s, government functions have remained centralised in Rome (leaving aside the five 'special statute regions'), even since the 1970 institution of regional governments in the other fifteen regions of Italy.[11] Although each region has its own parliament, with competencies in education and welfare, finance is largely controlled through Rome. Territorial politics in Italy ranged from local rivalry (dubbed *campanilismo*, which literally means competition over the size of church towers) to *regionalismo* such as the more serious mobilisations of the five regions which gained institutional autonomy under the *statuto speciale* and the claims of other regions to that status.[12] Regionalism would periodically make itself felt in elections: the Sardinian Action Party, for example, had been active since the First World War, calling for the autonomy of Sardinia in a federated Italy, and protesting against the bureaucratic inefficiency of the state (Fadda 1993). But such regional movements, when they did not represent a linguistic irredentism, remained minority enterprises. The proportional electoral system allowed representation of smaller *campanilisti* parties, including civic lists which were generally organised only locally, often around local personalities. These had little organisational capacity to grow beyond the local, even if there did arise a demand for them to do so (Fadda 1993: 175). None of the post-war political manifestations of localism or regionalism seriously threatened the territorial unity of Italy, however. At the elections, Italy divided between the key ideas of socialism, communism and Catholicism, not between conflicting regional interests.[13] At another level, however, *localismo* must be taken more seriously. Much has been written of the economic benefits of the interlocking interdependencies and the strong sense of local belonging of the 'Third Italy' (Diamanti 1996a: 29–33). Indeed the resources of trust fostered by stability and informal networks were involved as the crucial cultural background to the very economic miracle that was described above (Putnam 1993; Bagnasco, cited in Diamanti 1993: 31).

Although state power in the post-war period remained centralised, other institutions retained a clearly local/regional orientation, often dating from pre-*Risorgimento* arrangements. Banks often take the majority of their custom from a single city or province. Universities remain tightly localised, the majority of undergraduates coming from the hinterland, and post-graduates and professors being mainly chosen from this home-grown talent. Newspapers, even the ostensibly national ones, are often slanted to one city or region and take most of their readership there. Dailies such as Rome's *Il Messagero* or Parma's *La Gazzetta di Parma* often relegate national news to the inside pages behind discussions of city politics. In the case of Milan, the newspapers *Il Giornale*, *Il Giorno*, and between 1992 and 1995 the Lega-supporting *L'Indipendente* offer their readers a decidedly Northern perspective on events. Television is also very localised. The 1976 deregulation of television has had two effects on the media geography of Italy. First, because of a ruling that favoured the development of local over national private television, hundreds of local stations mushroomed during the 1980s. Italy now has more television channels per person than any other country in the world, a national total of over 1,300 stations (Ward 1993: 307). Most small towns have a television channel, complete with news events presented in an accent other than the Roman and Milanese, which tend to dominate national television. In terms of prime-time viewing figures, however, it is national television that is most watched, with over 80 per cent of viewer hours in 1990 (Mazzoleni 1992).

The fact that the new broadcasters were concentrated in Milan and the long-obvious fact that Milan was the economic capital of Italy, with flourishing industries and easy access to foreign markets, however, seemed to many to be at odds with the city's peripherality *vis-à-vis* the Italian state. It was widely thought that a higher proportion of politicians and public bureaucrats came from the South. This again raised questions about Lombardy's position in the national state.

Thus, state centralisation was accompanied by a pronounced decentralisation in other institutional spheres. Italians cannot be described as citizens in the same way as British or Germans are citizens: they cannot, for example, claim the same rights to social security in a welfare system that is locally differentiated and fragmented. Rome is certainly not a capital to the extent that London or Paris is a capital. While this institutional fragmentation may have contributed to a more pronounced sense of the possibilities and value of decentralising the state and devolving to the regions, it was only one aspect of the politics of the Lombard or Northern League.

The North–South divide

The *Questione Meridionale* (Southern question) has been an eternal theme in the history of the Italian state. Industrial interests were concentrated in the North even before the unification of Italy, and the resulting conflict of interests has periodically manifested itself at the national political level. In the early 1900s, for instance, the Southern élites sought to protect weaker industrial concerns such as cotton from control by Northern capitalists (Gramsci 1971: 69). Although these conflicts were mainly between élites in pre-Fascist Italy, they also led to regional divisions within the socialist organisations.[14]

The question of customs laws under the new Italian state at the end of the nineteenth century had been another source of conflict. Southerners complained that the new 'customs regime' favoured the North because it led to a domestic monopoly for Northern industrial products and difficulty in exporting the agricultural products of the Mezzogiorno (Salvemini 1955: 183–4). All these factors reinforced a tendency to divide the national interest into different geographical areas. Throughout the post-war years, however, regional inequalities (in development, industrialisation and standards of living) were seen as a problem for all Italians. For the Catholics, at the level of propaganda at least, it was a question of charity and for the communists one of solidarity. Overlaying both of these dominant frameworks was a general identification of the nation-state with modernity and rationality, and regional particularisms with backwardness. The League was to attack that by defining the Italian nation-state, and its ideals of charity and solidarity, as backward, corrupt and corrupting.

To suggest that Bossi's movement *invented* a conflict of interests between North and South would thus be very misleading. The League took a latent conflict and gave it a new political expression. Neither did they single-handedly construct a sense of cultural difference between North and South. Conflicts of interests and cultural stereotypes had long been intertwined as the stereotypes formed an explanation for economic backwardness. As Antonio Gramsci, writing in the 1920s, commented:

> The ordinary man from Northern Italy thought that if the Mezzogiorno made no progress after having been liberated from the fetters which the Bourbon regime placed in the way of modern development, this meant that the causes of the poverty were not external, to be sought in objective economic and political conditions, but internal, innate in the population of the South – and this all the more since there was a deeply rooted belief in the great

> natural wealth of the terrain. There only remained one explanation – the organic incapacity of the inhabitants.
>
> (Gramsci 1971: 71)

Gramsci's 'ordinary Northern man' could easily have been a Northern Italian of the 1980s, the basic arguments are so similar. Thus the structural differences between North and South in terms of industrial development were compounded by a popular conception of the reasons for those differences: industrialisation and modernity in the North were explained in the popular imagination by character traits of rationality, morality, civilisation and the work ethic. The lack of industrialisation in the South was labelled the product of irrationality, immorality, laziness, backwardness – the *stereotypical* attributes of Southern immigrants to Lombardy. The weak national democracy of the pre-Fascist period allowed this to be expressed in inter-élite politics. Under Fascism, and the pervasive national party system since Fascism, this structural-stereotypical cleavage was not politically exploited.

The Second World War projected another painful North–South divide onto the peninsula. Between 1943 and 1945, Italy south of Naples went to the Italian King and the allied forces, and the North to the Germans and Mussolini. After the landings of the Allies in Sicily and Southern Italy in 1943, and the attempted arrest of Mussolini by King Vittorio Emanuele II, the King left German-occupied Rome for Brindisi in September 1943. There, and later in the south-western port of Salerno, he and his advisors set up what later became known as the *Regno del Sud*, to be distinguished from the *Repubblica Sociale Italiano* at Salò that the escaped Mussolini had set up in the extreme North. During the months of civil strife and military occupation until June 1944, the symbolic governments of Italy were at Salerno and Salò. There is little doubt that this further undermined conceptions of national unity, already in crisis in this period. The 'Gothic Line' (*Linea Gotica*) of division between the two occupied territories was to become one among the many symbols in the armoury of the League. This phrase was already a quote from an earlier period.[15]

A glance at a few basic indicators shows the extent of the economic divide in the Italy of the Northern League. In 1993, unemployment ran at 18.9 per cent in the South, and 7.7 per cent in the Centre-North. 20.8 per cent of the population of the South were officially defined as living in poverty, compared to 6.7 per cent in the North.[16] In 1995, the average wage in the Southern regions was 57 per cent of that in the North, and the gap was widening during the recession of the 1990s.[17]

Because of the existence of the special statute regions in Italy, regional autonomy existed as a clear goal and opportunity. Within a rapidly integrating Europe, however, where regional lobbies, the Council of the

Regions and cross-border integration seemed to be increasingly significant, the new landscape offered some scope for redefining the very nature of the nation-state-region relationship, and new ways of legitimising claims that undermined the nation-state. What secession meant within an integrating Europe, where most regionalist movements were pro-Europe (for example the Scottish Nationalists, Basques and those on the European border such as the Slovenes and Czechs) was an open question that the League sought to exploit and explore.

If the economic divide is at least as old as Italy, and the North–South stereotypes are ancient too, it was the effective political use of them by the League in the 1990s that was novel. The League contrasted with previous incarnations of regional politics because the League succeeded in encouraging the various autonomist movements to cooperate with one another. Bossi even attempted to make the League into a nation-wide federalist movement, but public identification of his movement as Northist, anti-Southern, doomed these attempts to public rejection. The League remained an expression of the North–South divide: an assertion of the interests and identity of the North (including Northern industry and exports) in Italian politics.

Unblocking the system

The spoils system of shady financial deals and payments for public contracts was, by the end of the 1980s, beginning to break up, because of its own internal disequilibrium. As some commentators had discerned previously, such systems begin to buckle when they run out of resources to deal in (Bull and Rhodes 1997). It has become accepted that *Tangentopoli* (the bribes scandals of the early 1990s) occurred at the moment when the Italian business class were no longer able to pay: the internal strain on the system must have facilitated the decision of the magistrates to move on political corruption rather than turn a blind eye as many must have done previously.[18] When the Milan pool of judges opened their *Mani Pulite* (clean hands) inquiry in the early 1990s, they did so, it is likely, with considerable support from a local business class that was feeling a triple burden of increasing taxes, illicit payments (to organised crime and to the parties) and the economic crisis. Public outcry generated by the findings of the *Mani Pulite* investigations, in turn, was channelled into support for the League.

The end of the cold war is also surely connected with the shift in the power balance within Italy. Clearly, the Christian Democrats had enjoyed the support of the Americans in the run up to the historic 1948 election, in the face of a genuine possibility that the Communists would win. Any support they may have enjoyed later, however, would have been more clandestine. But conspiracies aside, fear of communism had been just as relevant a structuring device within Italian domestic politics. Bordering on Yugoslavia, and with one of the largest communist parties in Europe, Italy experienced a turbulent period of action of both right and left mobilisation in the 1960s and the 1970s. Fear of communism led to a widespread tendency to support political antidotes that were proven to be effective, such as the Christian Democrats, and to avoid parties that appeared to threaten stability. With class de-alignment as Italy became more affluent, the split and de-ideologisation of the Communist Party from 1987, and the symbolic event of the fall of the Berlin Wall in 1989, however, organised communism and fear of it ceased to structure domestic politics. Both Catholic and communist subcultures had been based on a strong sense of the enemy, and although it was later revived by Berlusconi's party Forza Italia, talk of either fascist or communist enemies sounded increasingly hollow, especially after 1989. Voters were therefore much more ready to seek alternatives to what had in effect been a 'government of national unity'. The League themselves encouraged this and took it further, repeatedly claiming that the left–right distinction was no longer valid.

Increasing international awareness, another shift that helped the League, was caused not only by the new and widespread phenomenon of return migration, but by a more globalised culture industry, a more literate and educated public, immigration and a burgeoning tourism industry. This not only made Italians more aware of the malfunctions of the Italian state and bureaucracy, it made them more aware and critical of the nature of Italian national stereotypes and identity abroad (which it is commonly argued are stereotypes of Southerners, not Northerners).

It was onto this political stage that the Lombard League (Lega Lombarda) quietly stepped, scarcely noticed for the first five years. In 1981–2, Bossi and friends began to meet each week in Varese. Inspired by existing regional separatist movements in Italy, they cobbled together some slogans and a logo and started a campaign demanding freedom of their region (which they at this point insisted was a *nation*) from 'thieving Rome'. The movement at first seemed to resemble the other microparties calling for regional autonomy (particularly the Venetian League(Liga Veneta)), offering a combination of nostalgia for the supposed social stability, democracy and cohesion of the medieval city republics, reluctance to lose the local dialects, protest at the corruption of the 'Roman' state, and a sharp dose of xenophobia in calls for tight controls on immigration into the region. On this platform (discussed in detail later) the movement gradually began to mop up votes in this economically muscular – but arguably politically underrepresented – sector of Italian society.

In the early years the League was to find support among those most free of obligations to the system of party rule. As the Italian parties (especially the Christian Democrats) lost control of the system of loyalties that had kept it in place, however, League support was to come from an increasingly wide span of North Italian society: economic independents with affluence to defend, workers disillusioned by the implication of communists in the corruption trials, small artisans and farmers disgusted by their government, and uncomfortable with the passing of traditional ways of life. For simplicity here I have referred to these people as 'Lombards'. Until the League, however, few of them would ever have thought of themselves as Lombards. If they did, it was simply an empty label. It was the League themselves that offered them that name, told them what it meant and advised them to renounce their allegiance to Italy in the name of 'Lombard Freedom'.

By 1987 the Lombard League had struck upon a large seam of alienated voters in the Italian electorate, and organised some 400 paid up members to meet, protest and campaign for the movement. The propaganda formula it used was not new to Italy. The Venetian League, the self-proclaimed 'mother of all Leagues', had grown out of a tiny cultural organisation founded in 1968, and won around 4 per cent of votes in the Veneto region in the 1983 elections, on a similar platform to that which the Lombard League would adopt.[19] Union Valdotaine had been campaigning on a similar platform in the Northeastern French-speaking areas of Italy, and separatist movements in Sardinia, Sicily and Tyrol had already a long history. With new slogans, however, Bossi's League added a potent dose of righteous anger to the previously inert regionalist cocktail. 'Roman Thieves! – You are Finished!', 'Free Lombardy!' and the most often repeated mantra: '*Roma, Ladrona, la Lega non Perdona!*' (The League will not pardon thieving Rome) were chanted in meeting rooms and daubed onto walls in the small towns around Varese, as the Lombard League began with increasing success to link Lombard nationalism with the pressing political issues of the day.

3 The rise of the League

Umberto Bossi, as he sought broader acceptance for the 'League of Government' in the early 1990s, tried to distance himself from his ethnicist-separatist antics in Varese in the early years. He claimed that the League's folkloric stunts were simply tactics in provocation and publicity seeking (Tambini 1994). A perusal of the movement propaganda of the earlier period, however, confirms that in the early years the 'folkloric' stance was central to the League's campaign. Almost every issue of the movement newspaper contained articles on Lombard history, many going back to the twelfth century Lombard League. Until the late 1980s the movement had thus resembled – or at least attempted to resemble – 'ethno-nationalisms' such as the Basque or Welsh independence movements.

Before founding the Lombard League, Bossi had worked a short federalist apprenticeship campaigning for Union Valdotaine, another regionalist movement in Northern Italy. With Bruno Salvadori, leader of Union, Bossi wrote and distributed a federalist newsletter in 1979–80. Inspired by the older man (who died in 1980), Bossi claims that he attempted during this period to deepen his knowledge of federal theory and of traditional Lombard culture, and that he has worked for 'freedom from the Italian state' ever since (Bossi and Vimercati 1992: 32–4). The Lombard League had its first informal meetings in 1982. As the movement grew, the circle of friends involved in the Lombard campaign widened. Some of these were to become the first parliamentarians of the League. Giuseppe Leoni, Marino Moroni and Roberto Maroni are mentioned as friends of the first hour by Bossi, and it is clear from his autobiographical comments that his relations with these people were based on very close personal links of trust, bonds that would remain important in the movement's organisational structure (Bossi and Vimercati 1992: 40–7, 81–95).

These people, according to League legend, met in Bossi's then girlfriend's one-room apartment in Varese and discussed federalism and Lombard autonomy. In his autobiography, Bossi described his original motivations with his characteristic drama: 'I read a great deal, and became convinced that it was the hour: the class struggle was over, the moment had arrived for autonomy' (Bossi and Vimercati 1992: 40).

Introducing the enemy: slogans and speeches

Bossi and friends' main problem was to publicise the League. While he was confident that his message would mobilise many supporters, he soon became aware that it repelled journalists. The approach of the early years was therefore mainly direct communication, in small meetings in bars, piazzas and homes. After 1985, the media began to take an interest in the movement: not as a serious threat, or as a credible political movement, but as a curiosity (interesting precisely because of its success despite apparent repulsiveness). Sensing that even this form of publicity could feed the movement, the League began to develop a repertoire of staged media spectacle. Bossi was sure that he could convert many if they would come to the meetings, and media coverage, however disparaging, could create the notoriety necessary to attract potential converts.

In 1982, Bossi and a few faithful followers had begun a long round of campaigning: hanging posters, organising meetings, and distributing the movement newspaper. This period also witnessed the unveiling of the most basic and blunt of early League propaganda media: graffiti. The walls of Varese, then Bergamo and other medium-sized Lombard towns, were nocturnally splattered with slogans such as '*Roma Ladrona*' (Thieving Rome) and '*Lombardia Libera*' (Free Lombardy). Place names on road signs were translated overnight into dialect.[1] Bossi himself was not afraid to pick up a paintbrush, it is said, and he regarded it as essential that his early followers be prepared to dirty their hands doing such jobs. He later defended this kind of work: 'A slogan, a poster with just a few words (hard words) is worth a thousand polished, hypocritical messages in politicianese' (Bossi, in Iacopini and Bianchi 1994: vii).

While crude slogans may have turned heads, they alone would not have mobilised the militants that the League needed at this stage. Interviews with supporters reveal that cartoons – perhaps surprisingly – also had a crucial role.[2] The most famous of these is that of a Lombard hen who is laying (with considerable effort) a golden egg promptly stolen by a plump Southern peasant. All the elements of the League stance are there in a simplified, caricatured way: the hard-working Lombard who produces, the stereotypical southerner, a lazy, well-fed, traditionally-dressed peasant who simply waits for assistance, positioned, in the cartoon, where Rome is on the Italian map (see page 108).

The symbolism of the League was not complete without the party symbol which was registered at the official founding of the party in 1984. Bossi himself claims to have designed the symbol, which is based on a statue of Lombard hero Alberto da Giussano: 'Which was the most appropriate symbol?' Bossi recounts in his autobiography. 'Of course, the statue of Alberto, which stands in the Piazza of Legnano. I went straight away to photograph it' (Bossi and Vimercati 1992: 41).

In the early period, the organisational structures upon which the movement depended were personal friendship networks, and also the existing organisations of local dialect networks, in which Bossi and Vimercati (1992) claims to have been active. There was a problem of ensuring loyalty of members, and the siege mentality of the League served well in this respect. The sudden expulsions of leading League members who disagreed with Bossi, such as Pierangelo Brivio and Franco Castellazzi, were cases in point.

The combination of League propaganda and the reporting of the movement in the press resulted in a widespread image of the League, particularly outside Lombardy, as folkloric, racist, and anti-Southern. At this time there began to be a big difference between the images of the League held by insiders and by outsiders. Since the League sought to present Lombardy as an oppressed 'ethnie' (ethnic group) colonised by a foreign 'regime', the propaganda specifically set out to undermine the reporting of the national press, which it argued was the tool of the regime with the single aim of destroying the League.

In Lombardy, ethno-national campaigns were a relatively new phenomenon. Previously, tiny organisations such as the Movimento Autonomista Bergamasco (Bergamo City Autonomist Movement) fielded local council candidates, but the choice of the region of Lombardy as the subject of a popular autonomist struggle was a new idea: a new idea that took off remarkably quickly.

'But the League doesn't have any policies'

This statement was often heard from critics of the League during the 1980s, particularly those who argued that the movement was a purely negative, protest movement. It was true that the League's manifesto was very thin. A fuller elaboration of policies would not appear until 1992–4, although even then it remained unclear, and many movement cadres disagreed with – or were unaware of – official stances. Various programmatic statements were issued between 1982 and 1989. Given that the League had no real legislative or executive power in this period, they served more as propaganda devices than concrete plans, symbolising goals rather than means for achieving them. The 1983 *Political Programme* listed the aims outlined in Figure 3.1.

This programme remained without great changes up until the early 1990s when it repeatedly appeared on the pages of *Lega Nord*, the Northern League

The conquest of the complete autonomy of Lombardy with the consequent right to self-government, self-management of the economy, of finance, of education, of health, of social security, of justice, and of public order. In particular the movement commits itself to work for:

1. The transformation of the Italian state into a confederation of autonomous regions.
2. Direct democracy with popular initiatives and referenda.
3. The decentralisation of political power to the provinces (cantons) and to the local councils.
4. Public sector employment on an ethno-regional basis.
5. Government housing and subsidised buildings in general in Lombardy reserved for Lombards.
6. Effective health service, social security and pensions on a regional level.
7. Fiscal policy at regional level.
8. Industrialisation proportional to the availability of local labour.
9. Guarantee of work for Lombard workers, or returning Lombard emigrants before those coming from other regions.
10. The creation of an economic climate that favours the return of immigrants to their country of origin.
11. The support and provision of incentives to Lombard agriculture with the defence of agricultural land from large industrial powers.
12. Particular attention to small business due to its productive nature.
13. The recuperation of the cultural and linguistic inheritance of Lombardy and its diffusion through the school system.
14. The conservation of the hydrological equilibrium of the territory, through environmental policy that does not conflict with the citizen, and industrial policy that is limited to the availability of local labour.
15. To stop the use of Lombardy as site for the '*soggiorno obbligatorio*'[1] and for the sending away ('*l'allontanamento definitivo*') of immigrants that commit serious crimes and get involved in kidnap, extortion or drug pushing.[2]

1 The system through which those involved in organised crime in the South would be rehabilitated in the North. The League argued that this simply imported crime into Lombardy.

2 Printed in *Lombardia Autonomista*, anno ii, no. 14, September 1983. For a similar programme from the same period see Vimercati (1990: 153).

Figure 3.1 The manifesto of the Lombard League

Source: This material appeared repeatedly on the pages of the newspaper *Lombardia Autonomista* after 1983. It was also used on handbills and posters during campaigns.

newspaper. The programme, and the elaboration of it that accompanied it, speaks also of broader goals. They are not modest ones. On defence, for example, the League 'holds that . . . to realise stable peace . . . it is indispensable to create a new international political and economic order, founded on the self-government of peoples and on their co-operation'.

The League in the 1980s

The early years in Lombardy and Veneto 1983–7

If Bossi was to find himself at the head of a party in government by 1994, his party was already proclaiming an electoral earthquake back in 1987, when they had just a handful of MPs. Though in 1987 the earthquake metaphor was premature, it is hard to find European rivals for the League's rise in the North of Italy between that year and 1992. Commentary on the electoral rise of the League has been concerned with better understanding the new movement through discerning the geographical, social and political composition of its support, and patterns in the development of the movement. In a later section I analyse the changing social and political composition of the electorate. Here I will limit myself to a descriptive account of the vote, covering its numerical and territorial growth.

Although parliamentary candidates do not have to pay a deposit in Italy, hopefuls must collect a petition of signatures in order to be included on the ballot papers. In the elections of 1983, the Lombard League had not even managed that. Candidates were fielded under the symbol of another party, the Lega per Trieste, a local group based far from Lombardy in the Venetian town. These League candidates stood only in Mantova and Varese, reflecting the limited spread of the movement at that time. Where no League candidate was available, Bossi advised his followers to 'annul the ballot paper, by writing "Free Lombardy" across it'.[3] While we will never know how many times ballot counters were bemused to come across this slogan (which at that time would have sounded something like 'Free Essex', or 'Free New Jersey'), we do know that in 1983 the League received a total of 3,652 votes, and no seats.

East of Lombardy, however, the Venetian League made a breakthrough in 1983, polling 4 per cent of valid votes. In the provinces of Vicenza and Treviso, where the party had been better organised, the League's vote was as high as 6–7 per cent (Diamanti 1992: 226; 1993: 43). (These provinces in central Veneto, along with Verona and Padua, were to remain the stronghold of the Venetian League vote into the 1990s.) By 1985, the Lombard League had the organisational capacity to field candidates in its own name, but only in the area around Varese, where the League's leaders were based. In the 1985 local elections the party was still very small, however, candidates being limited to a few town halls in the province of Varese (Fusella 1993: 4–5). With 2.5 per cent of votes, it won one seat on the provincial council and two on the town council (Mannheimer *et al.* 1991: 85). (See Table 3.1.)

Conspiracy theories about hidden interests secretly funding the League were heard consistently throughout the campaign. It is perfectly conceivable that funds were received from private sources: indeed a League officer went to court in 1993 accused of receiving bribes (see Chapter Five), but in the early period much of the finance seems to have come from the grassroots. Apart from the sporadic and amateurish newsletter, and the rental of offices after 1985, there was little in any case that would have cost the League a great deal in this period. Their use of the media was relatively cheap since they never bought space. They preferred to provide spectacular events and soundbites that journalists thought would sell newspapers, and thus got coverage free. The spectacularisation of politics staged by the League, however, began a kind of inflationary spiral: although in the early years it was enough to use a dialect word, strike a thuggish pose or make an outlandish nationalist claim to get reported, it was always necessary to make more exaggerated threats and claims to grab the headlines, and eventually, to seek ways of making the threats credible.

The first League candidate to take office was Giuseppe Leoni, who became a town councillor in 1985.[4] He made his maiden speech in the elegant, frescoed Varese Town Hall in the local dialect. All the councillors of the other parties left the council chamber in protest (Vimercati 1990: 27).

Breaking the mould 1987–9

The 1987 elections were a genuine breakthrough for the Lombard League, sending the first League MPs to the Italian parliament, although the Venetian League vote declined. Table 3.2 places the rise of the Lombard League in

Table 3.1 Results of local elections in Varese, 1985

List	*Votes*	*Per cent*	*Seats*
Christian Democrats	22,336	36.7	16
Communist Party	11,907	19.5	8
Socialist Party	9,324	15.3	7
Social Democrats	2,500	4.1	1
Italian Republican Party (PRI)	3,697	6.0	2
Liberals	2,419	3.9	1
Italian Social Movement – DN	4,275	7.0	3
Proletarian Democracy	1,026	1.6	–
Lombard League	1,841	3.0	1
Pensionati (pensioners' party)	1,534	2.5	1
Others	256	0.4	–

Source: after Fusella 1993: 4.

electoral context, showing that the electoral gains of the League were part of a more general 'search for alternatives' evidenced in an overall rise of new parties, and the decline of the traditional ones, especially the Christian Democrats. The League also seems to have been more than simply the beneficiaries of a few floating voters, however. It took the lion's share of the vote for 'new parties' (50 per cent in 1989 and 65 per cent in 1990 (Natale 1991: 89)). This was still not enough to convince Italians that a broader movement was underway. The League sent one MP and a senator to parliament in 1987, but the national and international press were more interested in another product of spectacular politics: Ilona Staller, a porn star who became an MP at the same time. The national press generally greeted the early League victories as curiosities for the gossip pages rather than political news. Only in the local press around Varese and Bergamo did the coverage begin to change, though it would be five more years before the League had any, however brief, support from the mainstream national media.

The League therefore grew steadily after 1985, both in terms of number of militants and number of voters. Offices were opened first in Varese and then in Milan, with a combination of contributions from supporters, militants' subscriptions, and the first contributions of government party finance which arrived after 1987. Private contributions, according to the League, were small, and often took the form of

Table 3.2 Results of elections in Lombardy, 1987–90 (percentage of registered voters)

	1990	*1989*	*1987*	*Diff. 87–90*
Proletarian Democracy	1.0	1.3	2.1	–1.1
Communist Party	16.2	18.7	21.1	–4.9
Socialist Party	12.3	12.6	15.1	–2.8
Social Democrats	1.4	1.6	1.9	–0.5
Italian Republican Party (PRI)	2.2	3.4	3.6	–1.4
Liberals	1.2	—	2.0	–0.8
Christian Democrats	24.6	25.4	29.9	–5.3
Italian Social Movement – DN	2.1	3.5	4.3	–2.2
Total. 'traditional parties'	61.0	66.5	80.0	–19.0
Verdi (Greens)	4.6	5.3	2.9	+1.7
Antiprohibitionists	0.9	0.8	—	+0.9
Republican Party (PR)	—	—	2.6	–2.6
Lombard League	16.4	6.5	2.7	+13.7
Pensioners' Party	1.5	—	—	+1.5
Others	1.5	1.4	1.0	+0.5
Total 'new parties'	24.9	14.0	9.2	+15.7
No vote	14.1	19.5	10.8	+3.3
Total	100.0	100.0	100.0	—

Source: after Mannheimer *et al.* 1991: 88.

Note: Traditional and new parties gaining less than 0.5 per cent of the total vote are not listed; hence totals are not the sum of this list, but are totals of precentages of votes cast.

contributions in kind, such as the loan of an office or a printing press. The organisation remained tightly controlled by Bossi, as evidenced by the expulsions of challengers such as Castellazzi. The leader monopolised the platform at public meetings and no other leaders were routinely quoted in League propaganda. A question that was to echo down the entire career of the League began to be asked: should this movement simply be ignored, be denied the publicity that it needed to prosper, or should it be taken seriously since it represented a danger?

The League and the media

The League had in the first few years the capacity to support candidates only in a small area around Varese and Bergamo.[5] In the local elections of 1985, the League vote was concentrated in Varese, the hometown of Bossi. The League received 2.6 per cent at Varese, 1.1 per cent at Sondrio, 0.7 per cent at Bergamo, 0.6 per cent at Brescia and Cremona, 0.5 per cent at Pavia and 0.4 per cent at Mantova. These towns were to remain the hub of League support in Italy. The 1987 and 1989 results show how the League's support began to grow away from its traditional centres. This reflects the increase in media attention, together with organisational changes within the League, such as the formation of the Alleanza del Nord to organise cooperation between northern regional movements. Table 3.3 shows that support for the League indeed spread continuously over the period covered; and became more uniform over the region as a whole. In 1987 the League candidates in Bergamo received almost three times the votes of their colleagues in Belluno, the twelfth strongest voting province, and

Table 3.3 League support by province, 1987–92 (percentage of valid votes)

National 1987		*European 1989*		*Regional 1990*		*National 1992*	
Bergamo	7.3	Bergamo	12.4	Brescia	24.2	Bergamo	26.7
Varese	7.2	Varese	9.5	Bergamo	23.1	Vicenza	26.4
Como	6.3	Como	9.4	Como	19.7	Varese	25.9
Torino	5.5	Sondrio	7.9	Sondrio	19.7	Vicenza	24.9
Cuneo	5.1	Cremona	7.7	Cremona	19.7	Como	24.9
Vercelli	5.0	Pavia	7.0	Varese	18.7	Treviso	24.5
Sondrio	4.7	Brescia	6.9	Pavia	15.2	Verona	23.7
Vicenza	4.5	Milano	4.1	Mantova	12.4	Belluno	21.9
Verona	4.1	Mantova	2.8	Milano	12.1	Sondrio	21.9
Treviso	3.8	Verona	2.0	Vicenza	9.7	Pavia	21.3
Asti	3.4	Vicenza	1.9	Verona	9.3	Cuneo	20.6
Belluno	2.7	Asti	1.9	Savona	7.0	Vercelli	20.7

Source: after Diamanti 1993: 31.

Note: Included under 'League support' are votes for the Lega Lombarda, Lega Nord and Liga Veneta and all associated Leagues.

in 1992 Bergamo's candidates received 26.7 per cent compared with twelfth-placed Vercelli with 20.7 per cent. Milan, the capital of the Lombard region, would wait until later to give any significant electoral support to the League. In 1990, the breakthrough year for the party in Milan, the League received 14.6 per cent of valid Milanese votes.

Before 1987, the League received little coverage in newspapers and television. The attention they did get was uniformly negative, judging by a collection of press cuttings from the earliest period.[6] There is almost no notion in the early years of the League as an anti-party, anti-state protest. As Bossi had predicted, what made news in 1985–6 (the first years in which the League began to attract press coverage) were the polemics against Rome and Southerners. Guido Passalacqua, a columnist from the national newspaper *La Repubblica* remarked characteristically:

> The European summit has just finished, one speaks of Milan as a city of Europe, but for these people the Lombards are a nation that has had the misfortune to have been invaded by Southerners . . . But how do they expect to get votes . . . it is the same old mess of barroom banalities that in Veneto brought success to the Liga Veneta.
>
> (Guido Passalacqua, *La Repubblica*, 2 July 1985)

Not only does Passalacqua demonstrate the preoccupation of the press with the movement's more extreme slogans, he neatly sums up the identification of regionalism with backwardness that dominated the early commentary on the movement. It was only much later, as the League became more successful, that it began to receive more sympathetic coverage. Daniele Vimercati of *Il Giornale* was the first journalist on a national daily to move closer to the League, with the only vaguely positive report on the congress of the Lombard League (10 December 1989). Vimercati, however, was exceptional in that he subsequently became very close to the party, and wrote Bossi's biography.

During the late 1980s, the League perfected its tactic of using showcase events to capture media attention by fitting some sensationalist elements into the otherwise mundane events of the congresses and rallies. The first congress of the Lombard League was held in Milan in December 1989, following the 1988 European elections where the League received over 8 per cent of votes in Lombardy, and a local poll at Seveso where they received 11.2 per cent of votes.[7]

This set the pattern of subsequent congresses, and fitted the general tendency in liberal democracies for party conferences to resemble rallies rather than genuine policy discussions. Much of the media coverage of this conference reflects the shock effect of the League's style of presentation. The stadium atmosphere was criticised by politicians more accustomed to restrained dialogue, and at least the semblance of discussions and votes on policies. The music and stage managing were rather primitive in this first congress compared to subsequent ones, but the basic elements were all there: a tightly-controlled podium and programme, with speakers approved by Bossi; no questions; votes for leadership positions restricted to a handful of approved candidates; and policies and candidacies mandated by applause (‘*per aclamazione*’). For those allowed to speak, however, there was some room for manoeuvre, since there was no direct link between speeches and the statutes of the party, nor the ‘official’ programme of the League. Speeches were spectacles, for the function of militants at these congresses was not to participate in policy formation, but more like that of a football audience. Indeed, the press referred to militants as the ‘fans’ of Bossi.

The first rally at Pontida took place in April 1990, and it had a similar function. Taking place at the site where the twenty cities of the original Lega Lombarda swore their allegiance in 1167, there was a strong dose of nostalgic folklore, and plenty of chain mail for the photographers. Stalls sold regional food, and books on local history. In some ways Pontida was similar to the *Festa dell' Unità*: the town fairs organised by the Italian Communist Party and now the PDS. Unlike such events, however, the party leadership took centre stage. The climax was always a speech by Bossi. One of the frequent chants of the crowd attempted to link folklore and politics by likening Umberto Bossi to a hero of the twelfth-century Battle of Legnano: ‘Umberto da Cassano = Alberto di Giussano’.

Alongside these showcase events were a host of minor events, ranging from the threatening to the ridiculous. Curious stories about the League printing currency and passports, or about local councillors calling for the teaching of dialect in schools, did nothing to convince the electorate that the League was a credible force of government, but they kept the party at least on the inside pages of the newspapers. The League had achieved an affectionate notoriety in the eyes of many who would never admit to voting for the party, and the press needed a consistent character like the League to brighten political news that in the 1980s was still frustratingly blocked.

Performing politics: League policy

As I have shown, the conferences and programme of the League were symbolic, given the scant opportunity that the League had to implement its policies during this period. Those who gained access to administrative power in this early phase also committed mainly symbolic actions, aimed more at gaining publicity and legitimacy for the movement than at achieving practical goals. Indeed, it would be repeatedly shown that the

League was happier in opposition than in power, precisely because it preferred posture to policymaking, since the latter is divisive.[8]

The League tended to focus on issues that threw their caricatured view of Italian problems into clear relief. The *soggiorno obbligatorio*, the practice of sending those involved in organised crime to regions distant from their own (sometimes in the North) was a favourite campaign issue around 1986–8. It was this practice that the first MPs of the League, elected in 1987, sought to overturn by introducing changes to the legislation. The abolition of the *soggiorno* had been part of the programme since 1983. The League argued that its aim was to keep out of Lombardy 'immigrants who commit grave crimes or are implied in kidnapping, extortion and drug pushing'.[9] A change in the law was eventually achieved.

In May 1989, Bossi made a parliamentary speech concerning a dump of industrial waste in Apria, Lombardy. He said it was a danger to the citizens and called for it to be moved.[10] In November 1988, Franco Castellazzi made a tough speech in Pavia town hall about the case of 'a young citizen of Pavia', who was kidnapped for extortion (a type of crime often associated with the Calabrese N'drangheta gangs). Castellazzi claimed that the state was responsible for the youth's continuing captivity through its lack of response to organised crime. Through 'intervening' on such cases, the League constantly reiterated its stance. Above all it attempted to reinforce a feeling of an in-group of honest Lombards threatened from the outside, by an inefficient state apparatus or by crime, or, ideally by a combination of the two.[11] Lombard actions remained mainly symbolic at least until 1992, when the League won extensive power in local government in the North.

Like many parties, the League protested against high taxes. League leaders went further than most, however, in making open threats of a fiscal revolt (Bossi and Vimercati 1992: 129). Until late 1993, League leaders such as Miglio made calls for a tax strike, and the League published a 'manual of fiscal resistance' in 1996. The fiscal question has been a linchpin of the programme, given the Lombard claims of 'exploitation'. On one hand it demonstrated the benefits of greater fiscal autonomy. A poster from 1988 read: 'Petrol at 337 lire per litre. Like in Val D'Aosta. Why do the Lombards have to pay such absurd taxes to Rome?' On the other hand the League continually published figures to illustrate a supposed Southern 'welfare dependence'. The threat to suspend payment of taxes, however, was never carried out. It is likely that it had been made to gain publicity for the League, not as a genuine threat (though there is some evidence of a boycott of television licences).

The early period thus set the pattern for later protest. Several fundamental patterns of action and identity construction had already emerged. First, the League came to know the contradictions between maintaining a protest stance and exercising executive power.[12] As ecological parties have found, taking office entails compromise and realism, which can dilute and delegitimise protest. This was eventually what led the League to bring down the government in 1994 in order to renew its protest stance. Second, the flexibility, instrumentality and playfulness of League identity construction was already in evidence by the end of the 1980s. The first posters and symbols were openly plucked from the array of possible histories, and used to define and underline the economic aspect of the protest. Third, the position of the leader, in a tightly-controlled organisational structure, was undisputed, and with the passage of time became more unquestionable. Fourth, the notoriety of the movement and its leader was established as a prominent aspect of the unfolding drama of Italian political life. As long as Bossi remained a caricature, the Northern Italian public had a great deal of affection for him.

Above all, the League's peculiar relationship with the media had taken shape: the hot internal politics of mass meetings, graffiti, chants and propaganda organs contrasted with the cool dismissal of anything reported by the external 'regime media'. This helped totalise the movement and consolidate a space of League discourse. The media coverage served mainly to arouse interest in the movement. Journalists may have attempted to ridicule the League, but it was the experience of coming to meetings, working with other militants, and seeing their pictures on television and in the press that gave militants, many of whom were political novices, a sense of identity and self-worth. These militants, seeing themselves as the 'Lombard work ethic' embodied, set up the network of offices and officials that were the foundation of the huge growth of the League in the following years.

The patterns of the League's peculiar uses of nationalism were thus already set: a particularly flexible use of 'ethnic' constructions linked to the political issues of the day; the use of a paranoid nationalist 'enemy logic' to justify a hierarchical and centralised organisation; and a switching between sincere and ironic use of nationalist spectacle. One day the League gathers on a stage to sing the Lombard national anthem, the next day it issues a press release which says the performance was merely a posture to trick the regime media. It became clear, however, that nationalist identity logic is not infinitely flexible.

4 The dilation

From Lombard League to Northern League

Umberto Bossi's political aspirations, like those of the *Risorgimento* nationalists Mazzini and D'Azeglio, drew inspiration from 'abroad'. While Mazzini looked to England and France, Bossi's example came from Bruno Salvadori's independence movement in French-speaking Northwest Italy: Union Valdotaine. Working with Salvadori in the years before he set up the League, Bossi learned that the key to success was to cooperate with other regionalist movements for common goals. Previously, Italian regionalists had occasionally reached a high level of votes in a given region, but had had little impact on national policy. As soon as he had the necessary fame, and the organisational capacity to do so, Bossi began to extend his operations outside Lombardy.[1] Preceding a full merger of the various Northern regionalist leagues, the Alleanza del Nord (Northern Alliance) was founded in 1987 in an attempt to bring together those regional movements which had a common aim in wresting power from the Italian government at Rome. The first elections in which the members of the Alleanza cooperated were the Euro elections of 1989.

The Northern Alliance was at first, however, mainly symbolic. As it involved only regional parties, with candidates in a limited area, there was no need for an electoral pact. During the years 1987–9, the Lombard League leadership had met with leaders of autonomist movements outside Lombardy to discuss the modalities of cooperation.[2] They found common ground in a call for less fiscal pressure from Rome, and in their similar constituencies among small business owners and alienated workers. The movements that were eventually to make up the Northern League developed a more uniform approach to the economy during this period, based on the Lombard League's Thatcherite championing of small entrepreneurs.

Taking the region of Tuscany as an example, it was the Movimento per La Toscana that, among various Tuscan regionalist movements, succeeded in joining the Northern League. Prior to linking with the Alliance, the movement had 'little to do with real politics' according to Riccardo

Fragassi, who was to become the first Lega Nord-Toscana MP in 1992. It was a cultural, debating and historical society rather than a protest movement. Florentine and Tuscan history, including the period of 'domination by the Habsburgs' and the joining of the Kingdom of Italy, were debated by a small group of Florentines and university historians, according to Fragassi. The discussion of history is probably inherently politicising, however, in ways which seem to have been overlooked by scholars of nationalism. The mere act of reading about massive changes in the exercise of administrative power over time can only loosen the legitimisations of existing state arrangements, and tempt the reader with the heady responsibility of taking charge of history.

Fragassi and friends discussed the fact that in the 1860 plebiscite to join the Kingdom of Italy only 1 per cent of Tuscans could vote. Historical descriptions of the 'administrative genius' of the Grand Duchy of Tuscany gave these local history enthusiasts a flush of pride. The step to political aspirations was small, and in the mid-1980s the Movement began to present candidates at some of the elections.[3] It takes more than an interest in history to make a movement, however, and votes received were negligible before the Northern League became successful. In May 1990, in the first elections under the banner of the Lega Nord, the Tuscan 'dynasty' (the first parliamentary candidate – Riccardo Fragassi – was the son of the leader of the party, Tommaso Fragassi) still received less than 1 per cent of votes. In the elections to follow, however, fortunes would rise, though less than those of the other partners in the Northern League. The Lega Nord-Toscana eventually sent two deputies to Rome in 1992, and only one, Simone Gnaga, in 1995.

In Tuscany, as elsewhere, the transition from independent autonomist movement to rigid central control by Bossi was not easy. A fraction of the Movimento per La Toscana resigned over the issue of joining the Alliance, and similar splits appeared in the Piedmontese and Venetian Leagues. The southward expansion caused loud protest within the Lombard League, too. The implicit decision to include Tuscany in 'the North' was quite controversial at the time. Many Lombard Leaguers thought that the southern limit of the North should be the Po River, or Bologna.[4] It was clear that the previous construction of Lombard identity as an ethnic and cultural phenomenon was, for some League members, incompatible with the extension of the movement far beyond the borders of Lombardy, whatever Bossi's ambition. There is also evidence of ideological disagreement. Joining the League was seen as a move to the right by many in the Venetian League, which had previously been more leftist (Diamanti 1992: 250). A faction refused to cooperate with Bossi and eventually broke away from the movement to form another party. The resulting group, Lega Autonomista Veneta, was to receive 4.9 per cent of the votes in Veneto in

1992, compared with the Northern League who scored 17.3 per cent (Mazzette and Rovati 1993: 74).

While the leaders claimed that the resulting Northern League was an alliance between the existing movements, the reality was that Bossi's more dynamic Lombard League effectively swallowed smaller groups from other regions, and augmented its power in the process. The League newspaper *Lombardia Autonomista* was renamed *Lega Nord*, and redesigned, but still edited and printed in the Milan offices of the Lombard League. Bossi was president of both Lombard and Northern Leagues until 1993. When the Northern League moved into its new HQ in Milan in 1992, it continued to share its offices, and many of its officers, with the Lombard League.

The Northern League (representing the complete merging of the various Northern autonomist movements) was officially founded in 1990. During the first subsequent rally at Pontida, the movement was blessed in a solemn oath by Bossi:

> Today at Pontida, the years of our commitments for the freedom of our peoples join together with the sacrifices of our ancestors who chose this place to swear to do their duty, to make the utmost sacrifice. I make my sacrifice one with that of our ancestors.
>
> (Quoted in Fusella 1993: 44)

At the first Northern League congress, in February 1991, the constitution of the movement was 'approved'. In the Federal Council, which would coordinate the various movements that made up the Northern League, there would be fourteen members. The primacy of the Lombard League was guaranteed, since they would have, in addition to the presidency, six members against the three of the Venetian League, two of Piedmont, and one each of Tuscany, Emilia-Romagna and Liguria.[5] The role of the Federal Council within the movement remains vague, however. It is likely that participation has been for mainly symbolic and communication reasons and that policy/strategy decisions are effectively controlled by Bossi. Such guarantees of control for Bossi must have been very unpopular with the leaders of the more established Leagues that the Lombards thus, in effect, disempowered (such as Rocchetta of the Venetian League). They were in no position to bargain, however, since *Leghismo* had become – for the public and for the media – one single phenomenon, and that phenomenon was owned by the best performer, Bossi.

The ethnic discourse was not completely abandoned with the formation of the Northern League. Where possible, it was adapted to the new context, and the first hints of the formulation of a Northern 'ethnicity' were made. In the first party congress, a speech was delivered entitled 'The

Ethno-Cultural Affinities of the Northern Peoples'. Although the dialect as an issue was dropped at this point, Bossi continued to use historical references in speeches and rallies (though not in policy, or written propaganda), and the symbol of the League remained the warrior of Legnano. If the 'other' to Lombard separatism was 'underdeveloped', 'corrupt' Southern Italy, there was an attempt to change the identity references of the League in the 1990s. The South remained the key concept, but it was increasingly linked to the Third World. During the run-up to the founding of the Northern League, the League (undoubtedly at Bossi's command) removed from their propaganda any references to Lombardy as an ethnic entity. It replaced them with references to immigration. The League became most prominent as a protagonist in the debate on *extracommunitaria* immigration and in particular the 1990 Martelli Law.[6]

The League continued to grow during this period, not only in terms of its vote, but in terms of numbers of militants. The number of militants was estimated at 18,000 in December 1989.[7] The vote for the League reached its all-time high in 1992. In the heartland of the League's support, however, there was already some sign of decline and reversal. In Brescia, for example, the share of valid votes declined by 2 per cent between 1990 and 1992 (Mannheimer 1993: 90). (See Table 4.1.)

The League's dramatic success and growth put some pressure on its organisation, and generated competition from other parties. A rival organisation, Unione Federale, was set up at Mantova, which began to gather together defecting League officials under a less anti-Southern, more conventionally federalist banner. According to *Il Giornale* (25 July 1991), twenty-three local councillors left the League to join the splinter group in July of 1991.

The formation of the Northern League also brought changes to the political programme. Professor Gianfranco Miglio joined the fray on the side of the League in May 1990 (Miglio 1994: 15) and made the new proposal of the 'Three Macrorepublics' (Poche 1995).[8] This suggestion,

Table 4.1 Votes for the Lombard/Northern League, 1990–2 (by percentage of valid votes per region)

	Regional election 1990	*National election* 1992	*Difference*
Piemonte	5.4	19.4	+14.0
Lombardia	21.4	25.1	+3.7
Veneto	5.7	18.9	+13.2
Liguria	5.2	15.5	+10.4
Emilia-Romagna	3.0	10.6	+7.6
Toscana	0.7	2.8	+2.1

Source: adapted from Mannheimer 1993.

a proposal for a federation of Italy into three macroregions, North, Centre and South, began to replace the old policy of autonomy of the existing regions. Agreement was never reached on this within the League, however. Franco Rocchetta, for example, then president of the Northern League, and secretary of the Venetian League, was publicly opposed to it (Tambini 1994). Given that, first, there were no congress votes on any of these policies, and second, the programme remained at the level of symbolism, as a kind of campaign flag, it was never clear which of the two was official League policy. *Repubblica del Nord* (Republic of the North), however, became a crucial campaign slogan, and it appeared on stickers attached to buildings, road-signs and cars all over Northern Italy. Clearly there was a sense that the new subject of national awakening for the League was the North, not Lombardy. In a later section the reasons for this change in strategy will be examined. It will become clear that one crucial factor to take into account was the symbolic construction of identity of the movement. Because the Lombard identity (based on stereotypes of work, honesty and affluence and the historical legend of the Lega Lombarda) had taken the 'South' as the other against which to construct an identity, and not other Northern regions, the dilation was feasible. This was also true of the other Leagues: where they had developed a clear sense of identity as in Veneto and Piedmont, they did not take as an enemy other regions of the North, but rather the South. The next attempted expansion of the League, however, proved more difficult.

1990–4: From Northern League to National Federalist League?

It may appear surprising that the League also made an attempt to expand into the South of Italy. This, however, has to be understood in relation to the wave of protest that swept across Italy in the early 1990s, and the shifting political landscape due to the collapse and reform of the main parties. Between 1992 and 1994, the League more than any other party received the votes that were released by the profound crisis of the ruling parties. Apart from the long-term decline of the two major political subcultures, there emerged a severe political crisis centred around accusations of corruption and links between politicians and organised crime. From the first arrests of politicians in February 1992, the highly publicised *Mani Pulite* (Clean Hands) inquiry fed the League with discontented souls as the extent to which corruption was routine in Italy was revealed. By the end of 1993, over 200 MPs had been informed that they were being investigated, and the League's share of the vote had reached 30 per cent in some Northern constituencies. Bossi saw this as his moment to break with provincialism. Despite the Italy-wide fame of his movement, the vote for the Northern League had been negligible outside a clearly delineated geographical area: Lombardy, Veneto and Piedmont. In order to expand beyond the North, and capitalise on the votes released by the scandals, the League had to make a jump comparable with that they had made in 1990 with the foundation of the Northern League. They had to become a national federalist party (Bossi 1995: 25–6, 36). They would find this difficult, however, and their failure to do so reflects how their instrumental use of regional identity had come to restrict their options.

In the local elections of 1993 for the first time, and subsequently in the European and national elections of 1994 the League vote ceased to grow, and votes received declined in some areas as the wave of protest faltered. In Lombardy as a whole, the League received 22.1 per cent of votes in 1994 in the national elections (down from 24 per cent in 1992). In Italy as a whole the League received 9.7 per cent of votes in the April 1994 national elections and 6.6 per cent in the June European elections.

Two factors transformed the political landscape late in 1993. In August it became apparent that the next elections would be fought under new electoral laws. Three-quarters of parliamentary seats would now be elected using a simple majority (first past the post) system. Given that this system would favour those parties that came first in each constituency, many argued that this reform was bad news for the League, who had previously won a lot of seats as second or third party. Before the League could make a definite change of strategy to cope with the new circumstance, however, a second new condition emerged. By the end of 1993 it was clear that Silvio Berlusconi was going to join the political fray, and it was also clear that he intended to ally himself with Alleanza Nazionale, the ex-fascist party then clawing back some respectability by burying its ideology. The League's monopoly on 'the new' appeared broken, and Berlusconi boasted both a structure to rival that of the League and nationwide potential, since his support would be strongest in the North, and that of the Alleanza Nazionale/Italian Social Movement would be strongest in the South. Bossi clearly felt that he had to respond to this challenge, and thus plans for a national federalist party were effected in months.

The idea was not entirely new. The League had previously received some votes in the South, but numbers remained negligible: no seats were won, they never won more than 1 per cent of votes cast in any constituency, and League candidates outside the North were fielded as ad hoc independents rather than as part of a coordinated campaign. Bossi began therefore in the early 1990s to be more proactive, arranging meetings with the Sardinian separatists, for example, and trying to set up a 'Southern League'. In April 1993, Bossi made his best publicised attempt to go national, announcing that from the coming administrative elections onwards, League candidates South of Tuscany would stand not under the Northern League emblem, but as candidates for Lega Italia Federale (Italian Federal League). A poll by the weekly magazine *Panorama* reported that under this name the League would receive 15 per cent of votes in Rome, in Naples 9 per cent, and in Bari 8 per cent.[9] Bossi was at the same time trying to open diplomatic links with regionalist movements outside the North. In April 1993 he was discussing an alliance with Efiserio Serrenti, the leader of the Sardinian Action Party.[10]

The results of the 1993 local elections in November and December (the last elections before Berlusconi's Forza Italia fielded candidates) confirmed to the League that the period of intense growth in their support had indeed stalled. Perhaps sensing that the League was hitting some kind of ceiling, and aware that movements generally run into problems when they cease to grow, Bossi repeated an announcement he had first made the previous April: he wished to change the name of the party to Lega Italia Federale. In November 1993 he launched a newspaper of the same name, with the plan that it would replace the existing paper *Lega Nord*, thus continuing a strategy that he had begun to toy with in 1990. The objective? To go national before it was too late. He sought to unite the League with existing autonomist movements in the South and islands, to stimulate new federalist movements where they did not already exist, and thus consolidate a larger national power base. Such a move would, Bossi hoped, widen the support for the League even in the North, since its appeal was curtailed by a widespread sense that it was an anti-Southern movement.

This represented a deep shift in the League's campaign strategy, and confirmed to commentators that Bossi himself would respect no frontier in his attempt to keep his movement growing. Since the formation of the Northern League and the first proposals for the three macroregions, the League had been appealing for the spontaneous organisation of Southerners into a federalist movement to mirror the North's. League propaganda showed a map of Italy with three symbols superimposed: that of the Northern League, and also of a supposed Lega Sud (Southern League) and Lega Centro (Central League) (Figure 4.1). Although the Central League and the Southern League mainly remained wishful fictions, various attempts at inventing Southern Leagues were made, with no direct intervention on the part of Bossi. In 1989, the Lega Meridionale (Southern League) was set up – in Milan. It consisted of a small group of Southern immigrants in the North who organised to oppose the Lombard League.[11] Ignazio Insisa's Southern Star movement with its journal *Southern Wind* was closer to what Bossi had in mind. The movement had emerged in 1988 as the first movement 'mirroring' the League, trying to

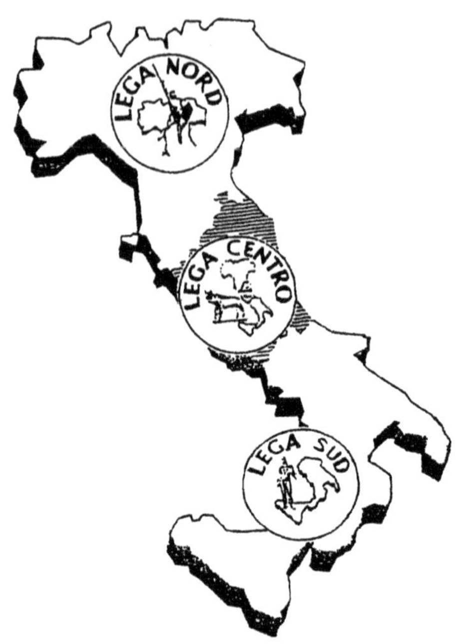

Figure 4.1 Lega Nord, Lega Centro, Lega Sud

Source: This figure appeared repeatedly on the pages of the newspaper *Lega Nord* after 1992. It was also used on handbills and posters during campaigns.

Note: Translation: With the Leagues for Integral Federalism.

capitalise on the attention any form of League now attracted in the media. Nothing of any substance emerged from these enterprises, however, nor from the Lega D'Azione Meridionale, which received 2.5 per cent of votes in Puglia in the national elections of 1994, and 3 per cent in 1996 (Ceccarini and Turato 1996).[12]

Throughout the early 1990s the Northern League enjoyed a new respectability, reining in the extreme elements and publicising the movement's more palatable individuals such as ex-EC official Formentini who became Mayor of Milan in June 1993, and respectable, Catholic and camera-friendly Irene Pivetti. The response of the media was a general warming to the League. For the 1993 elections they enjoyed the support of Montanelli (director of *Il Giornale*). Columnist Giorgio Bocca summarised the ambivalent feeling of reformist Italy towards the League: 'Grazie Barbari' (Thank you barbarians) was the title of his report on the 1993 local elections in which hundreds of new local League administrations were elected.[13] Bossi and his followers were barbarians, it was argued, but they should be thanked since they were the only effective tool to unblock Italy's political system (Fusella 1993: 130). From around this time, Bossi and Miglio were given more newspaper interviews, while the previous coverage had taken much more distance from the content of their discourse. New Mayor Formentini announced that his election showed that 'the League has gone beyond the ethnic phase'.[14] But although the ethnic discourse was less prominent, the movement continued to use threats and extreme statements to get into the news. They made a series of remarks about planning a coup in April 1993, and continued threats of taxpaying strikes.

This was the background to the announcement by Bossi that he planned to change the name of the Lega Nord to Lega Italia Federale. It was a move calculated in reference to the political opportunities of the day; there was a scarcity of well-organised, well-known political alternatives with 'clean hands', and a deep pool of disaffected voters looking for new politicians to replace those whose corruption was now coming to light. The League fuelled this by encouraging people to identify competitor protest parties, such as Leoluca Orlando's Rete (network) party, with the 'regime' or with the South, which for the League amounted to the same thing.

Candidates were not, however, to stand under the name Lega Italia Federale. After a protest from the '*puri e duri*', the separatist wing of the League in Lombardy under the leadership of Gianfranco Miglio, Bossi shelved the idea (Fusella 1993: 146). Miglio, who had continued, along with Venetian League leader Rocchetta, a more anti-Southern stance, saw Bossi's Southern campaign as an attempt to transform the party into a national political force and gave interviews damning the move. Grassroots members of the Varese and Bergamo old school also protested loudly to the press, threatening a revolt (Miglio 1994: 48–9).

This must be seen as a consequence of 'playing the nationalist card'. Had the movement in its earlier phases used means other than its separatist-nationalist stance and 'enemy politics' to mobilise and organise its support, the North–South divide would not have presented such a significant obstacle. The cultural tools of the movement had come to define its very identity, its political trademark, and thus the identity of the North could not be abandoned. The Sardinian Action Party and other regionalist forces in the South were wary of making an alliance with a party that they knew was hated by their constituents for its rough anti-Southern slurs. They thought it would lose them votes.[15] The South had therefore been excluded by the nationalist constructions of the League, and it would be left to the Italian Social Movement and Forza Italia to collect votes in the South. Thus, the League leadership was clearly unsuccessful in its attempt to form a national league and attract support in the South. Bossi himself accepted that this failure was in part due to the identification of the League as an anti-Southern party:

> The League did not manage to penetrate, because of its organisational limitations, because of the economic and cultural backwardness of the South, and because of the campaign of the press who accused us of racism and prevented the people of the South from understanding the Southern Question.
>
> (Bossi 1995: 25–6)

Bossi could hardly complain, given the anti-Southern statements that he had been publicly making for some years. Even in the North, the spread of the vote was limited. Was the territorial limitation of the vote the direct result of the separatist form that the movement had taken, and in particular the movement identity mobilised in the early years?

There are, of course, other potential explanations for the failure of the League to expand south of the Po. As Bossi pointed out, there was the League's limited organisational capacity. The League would have received votes, but it simply did not have the capacity to support candidates all over Italy. This was true of some areas and some elections, but not all. Clearly in the very early years the headstart that Varese, Brescia and Bergamo had was due to the fact that the centre of the organisation of the League was in those areas. Once the movement was gaining extensive coverage in the national media, however, these organisational limits were largely superseded. In the 1992 elections, for example, League candidates were fielded, albeit as Independent-Lega candidates, in many areas south of Tuscany. The campaign in Rome, to take an example, was well organised, and had high profile candidates, but the vote simply did not take off. Further, this limited organisational capacity itself needs to be explained. An efficient network of League offices manned with committed militants mushroomed overnight in Liguria but not in Lazio. It could be asserted that the limited reach was due to the organisational style of the movement, the reliance on small public meetings, direct contact with militants and so on. This is not sustainable, however, since the movement did manage to get wide support in areas where no previously existing regionalist movement existed (such as Liguria) very rapidly after the formation of the Northern League. It could also be asserted that the vote was limited to the areas where owners of small and medium-sized businesses had interests; these were the people whose 'objective class interest' was best represented by the League. The geographical spread of the vote does not conform to that pattern, however (there were few votes from the entrepreneurs of Lazio, for instance), and neither does the class profile of League voters, many of whom were workers.

Thus it appears that the movement remained limited to the North because of its previous use of Northern nationalist themes. Whatever their claims to be anti-Mafia agents of change, the Lombard, and later the Northern Leagues were hated in the South. When Bossi attempted to address an electoral meeting in Catania, Sicily in May 1991, he was greeted by a crowd shouting, 'Bossi, racist, you are first on the list', 'Bossi, get out of Sicily', and threatening him with violence (Bossi and Vimercati 1992: 171). Excluding the protestors, about twenty people came to the meeting, at a time when the party was pressing to become the most popular party in Northern Italy. Notwithstanding Bossi's protests that the League's proposed shock treatment would be good for the South in the long run (Tambini 1994), the League at this point was better known in Sicily for its anti-Southern posturing than for any positive plans or even as a vehicle for protest. It should be noted that this limited spread of the vote had both electoral and strategic advantages, particularly before the 1993 electoral reforms. Just as the electoral system rewarded concentrated support, so concentrated support meant that movement resources were used in an efficient way.

A generalised awareness that the movement represented the identity and interests of Northerners must therefore have been the decisive factor in explaining the persistent territorial limitation of the League vote and the impossibility of finding support outside the North.[16] The objection could be made that it was a question of timing, that the League would have managed to spread sooner or later, had it not been for Forza Italia, a new political force that emerged in 1994 and competed with the League for votes, and the makeover of the Italian Social Movement by Fini. This could have been the case, especially given the polls that painted a bright future for Lega Italia in the South. The fact remains, however, that Forza Italia and the Italian Social Movement were preferred in the South. The League did have time before the emergence of Forza Italia to develop in the South, but failed to do so because its campaign was identified as anti-Southern. Between the rejection of a campaign in the South by League cadres and the rejection of the League by the electors and potential militants in the South, the possibility of Southern expansion was closed. Further, the Italian Social Movement vote in the Centre and South definitely revived *before* the arrival of Forza Italia, thus showing that the Italian Social Movement was chosen over the League as a force for change.[17]

The route to the South blocked, and with a lack of other federalist/autonomist movements prepared to ally with the League, Bossi was ready for other suggestions of alliances, though keen to avoid open associations with the traditional parties. The electoral pact that he eventually did make for the 1994 elections, however, was always going to be awkward. Defined more in terms of what it was against than in terms of what it stood for, the pact with the ex-fascist Italian Social Movement and Berlusconi's Forza Italia was a pact with the League's most direct competitor, and with the most anti-federalist party on the spectrum, two parties that the League had accused of being a restoration of the First Republic. Despite claiming a shared commitment to neo-liberal economics (this was less convincing in the Italian Social Movement), the coalition government was, as Bossi himself later admitted, a 'government of numbers' based on seats and control of power rather than a shared programme.

There may have been an element of panic in the decision to go into government. There were, as I noted, the first signs of a decline in support for the League, and there was also a serious public scandal in December 1993 when Alessandro Patelli was arrested, suspected of receiving a bribe of 200 million Lire. Clearly, this affair tarnished the League in the eyes of the public (Bossi was called as witness on 5 January 1994), although neither Bossi nor Patelli was charged. Bossi claimed that the affair was a set up to trap the League, and that the money was never banked, since it was stolen a few hours after it was received. Besides, he said, in a statement that echoed so many of those made by the accused in the *Mani Pulite* trials, 'the money was a gift, not a bribe. A contribution to the campaign' (Bossi 1995: 18).

On 26 January, however, a larger problem caught the attention of the League. Silvio Berlusconi made the long-awaited announcement that he would stand at the elections 'to prevent the Left taking power'. A media entrepreneur based in Milan, and chairman of its most successful soccer club, Berlusconi claimed to stand for precisely the constituency that the League had declared its own. In political terms there was little choice for the League at this moment: ally with Berlusconi's Forza Italia or be killed by it. There was also the matter of the electoral system. If the League chose to compete against Forza Italia under the new majoritarian system, but came second, as seemed at that point likely, they would have received far fewer seats than the proportion of votes indicated, and would have faced a future on the margins.

Berlusconi's courtship of Alleanza Nazionale leader Fini came earlier than his approach to Bossi, and the resulting relationship was to prove more durable. Even before he had founded Forza Italia, Berlusconi made overtures through the press throughout 1993, openly supporting Fini's candidature for the Roman Mayor's office against the Green Rutelli. After Berlusconi formally announced the formation of his party on 26 January, a public statement was made in February announcing the formation of the Polo della Libertà, the coalition with Bossi and Fini. The name, which means the Pole of Freedom, was an attempt to stake a claim to a broadly Rightist space on the wide-open political landscape of Italy. Both Fini and Berlusconi advocated a neo-liberal package of privatisation and flexible labour markets, and many hoped that there was potential for a deeper coalition between these two and the League, whose supporters would, it was argued, have had an interest in such a package. Commentators hoped that this pole might become one half of a stable two-party system, with alternating governments and a genuine opposition. Such a scenario was not foremost in Bossi's mind, however. When asked why the League allied with Berlusconi and Fini, Bossi answered in his usual graphic terms,

> because they were very powerful, and could squash us. I have to do what Machiavelli teaches: ally myself with the enemy who is too powerful, hug him like a boxer does his opponent when he is in difficulty. And then, when they trust us and drop their guard, bang. In with the right and down he goes.
>
> (Bossi 1995: xiii)

But coalition politics, particularly that involving bedfellows as strange as these three parties, is much more complex, subtle, and symbolic than boxing. A key event in the period leading to the formation of the coalition was the anniversary of the 1945 liberation of Italy which is celebrated every year on 25 April. In 1994, this date was particularly poignant for two reasons. First, the occasion was taken up as an attempt to rally the anti-fascism that had shaped Italian politics for so long against Italian Social Movement/Alleanza Nazionale and thus their coalition with Forza Italia and the League. The PDS (Democratic Party of the Left) organised a series of commemorative processions, and Fini, the leader of Alleanza Nazionale, was again asked to make an apology in the Jewish ghetto of Rome and a statement to distance his movement from its links to wartime Italian fascism. (He refused, as he had done in the past.) Second, only weeks before, previously secret films taken by the US Army during the days of the liberation of Milan were released by the US government. The films were shown on several television channels, and, since they graphically detailed the violence of the crowd's treatment of suspected fascists, encouraged a revisionist mood, and ultimately the acceptance of Alleanza Nazionale. The post-war oppositions were certainly over. Not only would politics no longer be conducted in terms of Catholicism versus communism, but the anti-fascism that those two had in common was no longer an over-riding political cleavage.

Like many of Bossi's strategy shifts the decision to go to the 1994 elections in coalition with Berlusconi and Fini proved unpopular from the outset with the League militants, who had of course not been consulted. 'In many provinces of the North, letters and phonecalls were pouring into local party offices, protesting that it was unacceptable that we ally with parties that stank of recycling of the old parties' (Bossi

1995: 45). The electoral pact was relatively simple: Fini would have candidates in the Southern constituencies where his newly renamed Alleanza Nazionale had most strength, Forza Italia would mobilise mainly in the Centre, and the North would be divided in a ratio of approximately seven League candidacies for every three Forza Italia candidacies: a winning formula.

The General Election, 27–8 March 1994

The March elections mapped out a complex new political topography in Italy. Pre-election alliances polarised parties into two main groups: the Pole of Liberty and Good Government, and the Progressives, two poles that approximated ideological oppositions between right and left, however much the League claimed that such divisions were outmoded. Within the Pole of Liberty, the League had candidacies only in the North, and the newly renamed Alleanza Nazionale (formerly Italian Social Movement) was more strongly represented in the South. To underline the new geographical divisions, the Pole of Good Government was the official name of the coalition between Forza Italia and Alleanza Nazionale in the South, and Pole of Liberty was the Northern coalition, between Forza Italia and the League. The central 'red zones' continued to be dominated by the left. In practice 'Good Government' was dropped and the coalition was referred to as the Pole of Liberty.

The League, contrary to the fears of its leaders, was rewarded by the new electoral system. In the Chamber of Deputies, they polled 3,237,000 votes, compared with 5,202,000 for Alleanza Nazionale and 8,119,000 for Forza Italia. But the League received a total of 117 seats, compared with 109 for Alleanza Nazionale and 99 for Forza Italia. Similar overall voting patterns were repeated in the election to the upper house: the League won 60 seats, compared with 47 for Alleanza Nazionale and 32 for Forza Italia. Thus, while polling considerably fewer votes than their coalition partners (in the complex mix of proportional and majoritarian systems), the League clearly had a great deal of power in the coalition, although no party had an overall majority of seats, and Berlusconi formally remained leader and became Prime Minister.

The evolution of the League vote, in comparison with the 1992 elections, showed a pattern of stabilisation and the first hints of decline. The pattern of retreat to the geographical area that Diamanti (1996a) was to call 'Pedemontana' was beginning: as the more moderate and less separatist voters in Milan and elsewhere began to vote for Berlusconi, the League was increasingly reliant on its original base in the subalpine regions stretching from Piedmont in the west to Veneto in the east.

The rise of the League had shocked all observers, including the movement's leaders. In the mid-1980s, even the most fervent believer would not have predicted that the movement's high point would be forming a government with Berlusconi and the post-fascists. The separatist/nationalist rhetoric which strengthened and motivated the movement was still there and still strong (Tambini 1994), but it became increasingly difficult for Bossi to satisfy the hardline separatists in the movement.

5 The League in government, 1994

Carroccio in Cabinet

The League's post-election rally, held in the fields around Pontida on 10 April 1994, was billed as a victory rally, but the mood was not wholeheartedly festive. There was little genuine celebration going on in the marquees or around the stalls manned by party activists. The centre of attention was the stage, where all 180 new League parliamentarians were to appear, and the lucky few chosen by Bossi would make speeches.

This meeting was quite different to the previous Pontida rallies. Not only was it larger, with a stronger international media presence to reflect the fact that the League was now a force of government, but there was a distinct sense of unease at large. Hardened militants of the League, sitting on the long benches and eating polenta before the speeches began, were not chanting the good old League chants. Some of them were even ready to discuss how they would have to reconsider their support for the League should it stay in government.

A huge statue of Alberto da Giussano dominated the view from the food tents. The statue, 10 metres tall, was the colour of bronze. On closer inspection, however, it turned out to be made of papier mâché, and was swaying gently in the wind. There were some stalls, including one with a mechanical scaffold, offering the chance to hang a dummy representing a 'thieving politician' by throwing a tennis ball at a target attached to a lever. Lunch facilities were stretched to the limit by a crowd that seemed to have outgrown the small field. Other stalls were selling the usual range of local products with Lega Nord stickers. Emilia Romagna were selling *Lambrusc* (dialect for Lambrusco) wine and vacuum-packed local cheeses with a Lega brand. The Ligurian Nation hawked '*Ce L'ho' Duro*' underpants to celebrate Bossi's macho slogan. League currency, complete with pictures of Bossi, keyrings, dialect wristwatches, badges, and all the usual fundraising paraphernalia were on sale.

The speeches were shorter than previously, perhaps because of the threat of rain, perhaps because the League's personnel had grown, or perhaps to leave more time for Bossi. The crowd is subdued. What would Bossi say? Could he get out of this one? Could the League go into government in Rome, and join those corrupt politicians that Bossi had been criticising for so many years? Would the League risk alienating the hard-line separatists and form a government with the neo-fascists and Berlusconi? Where was the Lombard nation in all this?

Gianfranco Miglio, who had brandished the word 'insurrection' in a newspaper interview published the previous day, said in his speech that the League would use only legal methods to achieve federalism. He further claimed that he had already completed the constitution for a federal republic. A new slogan, 'fiscal federalism', circulated in the crowd, and appeared in Miglio's speech and the newest League pamphlets.

League MPs, if they were to form a government, now faced the prospect of making positive, constructive contributions, voting with the government, and being obliged to '*indossare il doppiopetto*' (wear a double-breasted jacket, or in other words find a leadership style). This would be a shock, since most of them had previously sought and achieved only notoriety in parliament. At the height of the Tangentopoli scandals, League deputies had brandished a noose before television cameras during a parliamentary debate on corruption. And Bossi's harsh style had outdone even these backbenchers. He had never got beyond the use of shock tactics to gain headlines, and the *doppiopetto* would feel more constricting on him than on his deputies.

There were of course the doves of the movement, such as Roberto Maroni and the Catholic fundamentalist Irene Pivetti, among the leaders on the stage. They were much more comfortable with the prospect of government and had been making cooperative overtures to the other coalition parties (to the disgust of the hard-liners). In the days before Pontida, the mere prospect of forming a government had already created new fissures in the protest machine of the League. Whereas Bossi the protest leader was worried about being tainted by association with the corrupt state, many in the League were prepared to compromise such questions of image in order to consolidate their privileges, and Bossi the power-broker was eyeing the ministries.

This explains the tension in the air on that blustery, changeable Pontida day in 1994. How was Bossi going to get out of this one? How could he take up the seat in government, engage in the process of bargaining about who would get which 'armchairs' (ministries), and carve up the political bureaucracy in precisely the manner which they had so loudly criticised? How Bossi did get out of the corner was a classic display of nationalist identity work and use of crowd sentiment, which he had perfected over the previous years.

The challenge for Bossi's speech was to sustain the image and identity of the movement, while making an argument in favour of forming a government in Rome, in alliance with people that his own propaganda have identified as very suspect Italian nationalists. His speech consisted of a characteristic appeal to popular sentiment, uniting against an enemy, claiming that 'today we decide if we will go into government', that 'the League remains a popular and revolutionary force' and that the League had to remain constantly alert in this key moment because 'They want to buy Us'. Bossi's claim was that the League must go into government to battle for federalism, and to control Berlusconi it must become the critical conscience of the government and a guarantor of governability: 'We will be the guarantors of democracy and legality', 'not afraid to go into government'. Bossi called upon the League to continue the battle in the belly of the beast.

Bossi ended the speech with a series of 'votes': on whether the League should go into government, and with whom it should ally. In a characteristic display of the working of the internal party democracy of the League, all motions were built into the whirlwind of his speech, and passed by applause, with no chance for debate. The audience was given each clause for the first time at the moment in which it had to 'vote' for it. Clearly the intended effect was to give the members of the League the impression that they were being consulted, without incurring the danger that they might in fact be consulted. The 'people of the League' had approximately one second to think about each point, before being carried into a wave of the crowd's applause, which was itself prompted by the cadence, more than the content of the speech. 'Do we go into government?' 'Hurrah!' 'In a coalition formed with Berlusconi and Fini?' 'Hurrah!' These were the forms of decision-making that Bossi later described as 'consultation with the people of the League'.

The relationship between Bossi and his audience was one of deep trust and identification, however, far from the norm of a conditional, mandated link between party cadre and party leader. League supporters knew that their leader would change his mind and do exactly what he wanted, but they identified with him, and trusted that he would do the right thing, because he was, fundamentally, 'one of us'. He had, his supporters accepted, to be clever and strategic, because he had to defeat the 'octopus' of occult power. Open, democratic parties are simply not equipped to wage such a battle, according to the League's own paranoid conspiracy logic. The closing music of this, as of every Pontida rally, was Verdi's dramatic *Và Pensiero.*[1] The rally began to empty as soon as Bossi left the stage. The sagging papier mâché Alberto was dismantled, and joined the other 80,000 or so militants on the tiny road out of Pontida.

Coalition cramps

Behind the scenes, of course, the decision to go into government had been made long before Pontida, leaving only the negotiations over offices. When these were complete, one month after the rally, and the League had its ministers in their 'armchairs', the League faced a new and somewhat uncomfortable role as party of government. Their approach was cautious. Federal reforms were clearly not high on Bossi's list of priorities in government. He appointed ex-flight technician Francesco Speroni as Minister of Institutional Reforms, thus completely alienating constitutional theorist Professor Gianfranco Miglio, who had coveted the position. Miglio, a committed federalist, soon left the League in protest.

The policy programme of the new government did not dominate political news in Italy, which was still filled with revelations about what the League continued to call 'the regime'. On 28 April Sergio Cusani, financier for parastatal company Feruzzi-Montedison, was sentenced to eight years' imprisonment, and then on 10 May former director of the Health Ministry Duilio Poggiolini was arrested, and police searching his apartment uncovered hidden works of art and furniture stuffed with cash amassed in a racket involving bribes from pharmaceutical companies.[2] As for the other party leaders in the government, the priority for the League was to retain party unity and the level of votes in these turbulent times, while waiting for new political opportunities to emerge.

The agenda of the new government was set by Berlusconi's inaugural speech of 18 May in which he presented a standard 1990s neo-liberal package of liberalisation, deregulation, privatisation and fiscal policy 'to favour investment'. This represented a compromise for the old corporatists in Alleanza Nazionale who had long opposed privatisation and were only now being led toward a slightly more libertarian stance by Fini. The League's calls for devolution and federalisation were high on the agenda during the talks to form the government, but quickly sidelined into the Commission on Constitutional Reform which would take many months to report. Points of conflict and disagreement between the coalition parties loomed on the horizon, however. No one wanted to take responsibility for the necessary but unpopular pension reforms, and the continuing problem of bringing to justice corrupt politicians was another potential stumbling block.

Taking office cramped the flamboyant protest posturing style of the League, and they were yet to find a new repertoire. In his first interview after becoming Minister of the Interior, Maroni cautiously announced that he would not be an 'instrument through which the League would make party politics' but would simply seek to improve the efficiency of the Ministry.[3] No use of his position, then, to begin a process of decentralisation, for example by reforming the Napoleonic system of centrally-appointed local prefects, and no anti-immigration crusade; two areas where the League may have been expected to act first. The suggestions for reform that were made by the League during this period generally came from the less powerful echelons of the party, and were as ever relatively simple, and regionalist, such as the idea of having representatives of the regions on the Council of the Bank of Italy. Given the brevity of the period of government, and blocking from Alleanza Nazionale, however, little was put into practice.

To be fair to the League, neither they, nor anyone else in the coalition had the power to push through drastic reforms. The government was in almost permanent internal conflict, since there was the constant threat of elections, and continual competition and electioneering between the League and Forza Italia. At every step the League tried to present Berlusconi as the old regime in disguise, and it was difficult to enter productive debate and negotiation over reform when the coalition parties were involved in zero-sum battles for the same votes. When traps could be set, they were set (though rather less by Fini and Berlusconi). Bossi and the League joined the opposition in criticising Berlusconi's control of the media, and called for new anti-trust laws to avoid conflicts of interest between his huge business empire and the public good. Berlusconi countered by accusing the League of being an untrustworthy coalition partner and obstructing the government.[4]

Bossi, throughout the government, was openly worried that the League was losing its 'identity'. He subsequently admitted thinking that every cooperative act, and every photographed handshake with another coalition leader, tarnished the brand image of the League. The leader later complained that Maroni began early in the period of government to speak of a united party with Forza Italia, which would mean a 'renunciation of the identity of the League' (Bossi 1995: 85). He also reflected that 'at the end of June, after the European elections, I brought the League to a loose consensus precisely in order to protect its identity' (Bossi 1995: 86).

It was over the aspects of the government programme most likely to affect polling between the governing parties that the League and Forza Italia came most often into open conflict, especially regarding the media. Although the country faced the urgent problems of meeting the European monetary union convergence criteria, the budget deficit and pension reform, it appeared that Berlusconi's own more pressing problems were in legitimising his own government. Apart from the anti-trust law supported by the League, emergency legislation regarding political content of broadcasting and media ownership was called for. The control of public television, which had previously been divided between the ruling parties, became an issue because of Berlusconi's near-monopoly of the control of private television. After the board of public broadcasting corporation RAI resigned over the issue of appointments on 30 June, Berlusconi was directly responsible for 90 per cent of Italian television.

The League's position within the government was relatively strong, since they would have been difficult to replace in the coalition given the position of the other parties. But the movement did run into problems of party discipline, many of which emerged because the party had grown so quickly. Some parliamentary candidates had been selected by the 'national secretaries' (leaders of the component regional leagues), and many of these candidates had had little or nothing to do with the League before the elections. In many cases, the normal procedures of vetting and apprenticeship (see Chapter Six) had not been applied in candidate selection. Apart from the resulting problem of the inexperience of MPs (Bossi 1995: 62), it also created a problem of loyalty, as Forza Italia immediately made it clear that they would accept League defectors with open arms. This only compounded the problem of ideological disagreement within the League, as the true believers in federalism and autonomy clashed with newly-arrived rightist reformers who sought to deepen the alliance with the Polo partners.

European elections on 12 June revealed a swing from the League to Forza Italia. Bossi, in an interview with *Il Giornale* published on 18 June, complained that Berlusconi was pressurising to unify the parties, and governance took a back seat while the political manoeuvring continued. The next day Bossi announced in another interview that 'the League has to break away from the stifling and deadly embrace of Berlusconi'. Not a right hook, but a shift to the left was announced. It remained unclear if this was made in order to attempt to distinguish the League from Forza Italia, to threaten the Polo with withdrawal, to take away the support of the PDS (Democratic Party of the Left), or to prepare for an alliance with them.

In another rally at Pontida on 19 June, the formation of two factions was announced as a device to give voice to the two conflicting souls of the League: the pro-government federalist faction and the 'Independentists'. More a means of appeasing and controlling than of mobilising such groups, there were even reports of a Labour faction organising itself, indicating that Bossi was having increasing trouble steering the movement. He was more concerned with conflicts within the coalition and within his own party than with conflicts with the increasingly well-organised opposition parties on the left (Bossi 1995: 82).

Arrests continued, and the debate about Tangentopoli began to take a new turn. After the initial period of the corruption trials, in which public opinion was shocked and indignant enough to support severe punishments of politicians and public-sector managers, harrowing stories of suicides of familiar public figures and a sense that the magistrates held huge and unaccountable power, began to put the brakes on the revolution. People began to ask when this would stop, and whether an entire business class could be found guilty when informal practices, legally definable as corrupt, were rife and had arguably long been necessary for business survival. Public opinion shifted: had the previous general acceptance of bribery and 'occult politics' now become the tool of an opportunist group who merely used it to serve their own purposes? Berlusconi, who may himself have had a hand in orchestrating such shifts of opinion, must have been relieved that his own polls revealed such a shift, for the judges were getting closer to him. On 11 July, his brother and Fininvest colleague, Paolo Berlusconi, was committed for trial on charges of bribery.

The Prime Minister's allies had meanwhile been working on a reform in the Laws governing detention of corruption suspects, and on 13 July Justice Minister, Alfredo Biondi, issued a decree to alter the system of pre-trial detention. The scandal surrounding this so called '*decreto salvaladri*' (thief-saving decree) was the most obvious external sign of problems within the coalition (Bossi 1995: 90–1). It seems that Berlusconi and Biondi had overestimated the degree to which public opinion had shifted against Di Pietro and the magistrates running corruption investigations. A public uproar ensued when 2,137 prisoners (189 facing corruption or bribery charges) were released the morning after the decree was signed and Interior Minister Maroni, who had signed the decree, was asked to explain himself.

On 18 July, several Milan magistrates resigned over the decree (they later withdrew their resignations), and Maroni threatened to resign, claiming he had been tricked into signing a decree containing amendments made without his knowledge. The decree was withdrawn, and the climate of animosity within the coalition worsened. On 21 July, coalition MPs from Forza Italia and the League traded insults and even blows in the Chamber as the decree was debated. The League thus claimed to represent the 'new' against this return of the corrupt 'old'.

The identity solution

Constrained by the straitjacket of government, the League did appear to be losing momentum. Polls reflected that infighting in the coalition was costing both Forza Italia and the League support, and the Pontida meeting in June was as subdued as, and worse attended than, that of April. Perhaps this explains Bossi's sudden and outrageous claim – albeit made to journalists from a beach during the silly season of late August 1994 – that he had turned back 300,000 armed citizens of Bergamo who were ready to march on Rome in the mid-1980s. Bossi, we can only imagine, must have felt the need to issue a rallying cry, and give the League back their gloss of notoriety, or perhaps he could not resist claiming a few of those undersubscribed August front pages. For the claims themselves are beyond refutation: there are barely that many people in Bergamo.[5]

It was at the end of June, Bossi later recalled, 'that I became aware of some foreign bodies within the movement, and of a mechanism that began to break up the parliamentary group' (Bossi 1996). In an effort to get his movement in order during the summer, Bossi deposed Franco Rocchetta, president of the League and his most vociferous critic within the movement, and some of his supporters.[6] Bossi then announced a summit of the League leaders to meet at Ponte di Legno after the close of the parliamentary session. In an attempt to rally his own leadership within the party he threatened to resign on 2 September, though his resignation was never accepted.

Meanwhile, Bossi and Berlusconi had also negotiated a tense peace in an attempt to rescue the government. The terms of the agreement were never made public, and no agreement was reached on the crucial issue of media ownership and control: on 18 September Bossi complained that no League nominees were accepted in the new RAI appointments and threatened to introduce antitrust legislation to overturn them. Apart from the obvious aim of limiting his main competitors' campaign resources, Bossi's aim was to gain access to media space for the League. In the campaign to generalise the identity work of the League, more access to broadcasting would be crucial. This was never achieved, however, and Bossi was further frustrated as his movement appeared to be breaking up before his eyes.

In October a new split emerged within the League as Gipo Farassino, leader of the Piedmontese League, left and took seven rebel MPs with him. Bossi reached around for any tool possible to reunite the League, making an invitation for Miglio to return to the League in late October and rally the League around its supposed project: federalism. Miglio, it was reported, refused, saying, as did Farassino, that he would return if Maroni became leader.[7]

Despite the turbulence within the governing coalition, the Council of Ministers reached agreement on 28 September for a draft budget for 1995. It announced, as expected, the privatisations of ENEL and STET, the public energy and telecommunications companies. Also as expected, the investigations of corruption continued to knock on the door of the supposedly 'clean' Polo Della Libertà. In early October, in a *Corriere della Sera* interview, senior *Mani Pulite* prosecutor, Francesco Saverio Borrelli, appeared to hint at a forthcoming investigation into Silvio Berlusconi.

The Northern League's annual conference at Genova on 6 November was one in which the strategy and identity of the movement were often more important than policy debates. MP Roberto Ronchi underlined the necessity that the League had a 'strong project' and was 'the protagonist' without detailing exactly what that project should be. Bossi spent most of his speech arguing against those rallying for the unification of the League with Forza Italia (Bossi 1996: 77–81).

Despite these distractions, the government could not avoid the problem of pension reform. This was a politically costly operation, however necessary experts agreed it was, as millions of Italians had been looking forward to generous, early pensions, and their desire to have them was not to be tempered by platitudes about the 'broader national interest' in the spending and deficit cuts necessary to satisfy the criteria to join European Monetary Union. A half-day strike against pension reforms was held on 14 October. Approximately 3 million people demonstrated in ninety demonstrations, which were followed by another huge strike on 15 November.

It is no surprise, given these difficulties, that the first stage local elections on 20 November saw Berlusconi's vote cut to below 10 per cent. In municipal elections on 4 December, Berlusconi seemed to be experiencing further losses of support, whereas the League recovered slightly. Clearly the prospect of an election began to look more interesting to Bossi, and on 12 December he made a speech at Milan announcing his decision to leave the government. (Interior Minister Maroni continued to argue publicly for support of the coalition.)

On 21 December, one day after the Budget was approved, a vote of no confidence in the Berlusconi government was passed. Three no confidence motions were tabled, one of them by Bossi. On 22 December, the same day that his brother Paolo was sentenced to seven months' imprisonment for an illegal payment to the Christian Democrats, Berlusconi resigned. The decision to bring down the government was clearly not popular with the pro-government part of the League élite, but militants were largely in favour. Bossi made his speech in favour of the motion of no confidence in the government on 24 December. The speech he made inveighed against the government for its failure to achieve its objectives on fiscal policy, bureaucratic efficiency or standards of living. There was no mention of the League's own role in that government. 'Signor Berlusconi,' Bossi closed, 'you are not the state. The League hereby takes away your mandate' (Vimercati in Bossi 1995: viii). (See also Bossi 1995: 141.)

Despite Bossi's grandiose gestures, December 1994 and January 1995 were very difficult times for the League. Maroni was not alone in his opposition to the decision to break up the government, while others were still smarting that the League had gone into government in the first place. (The fact that hard-line separatists such as Miglio and Rocchetta had parted company with the League did not help rally the old-school nationalist extremists.) Many League deputies, perhaps as many as a third, shifted allegiance at least temporarily during this period. Even Luigi Negri, until only months previously darling of the League, and elected as the secretary of the Lombard League, departed acrimoniously. Forza Italia continued to court League deputies with offers of positions and candidatures within Forza Italia, and for a time the parliamentary party was rife with accusations of spying by those who had made the change but not yet made it public.

Once again, the League were in uncharted territory. How was it to understand its position, and what could be its next move? In general, social movements seek to become institutionalised when they reach the end of a protest cycle, or a peak in power. There were many calls for the League to do so, in the period 1992–4, not least the call, made by Maroni, to merge the party with the others in the coalition. Bossi's preferred goal (if he had one beyond the maintenance of his own position in the leadership) was still clearly to construct a national federalist party in order to fend off the challenge from Forza Italia. But even if this objective were to have been reached, it seems unlikely that he would have renounced his grip on the hierarchy of the League and permitted the institutionalisation of a more conventional, democratic internal structure, particularly after the experience of mutiny during the government. What in fact happened was that Bossi left the government in order to save his movement and his power within it. It was only too clear to him that a few more months would bring increased pressure for a merger with the other coalition partners, and the end of his League. He saw that the movement was breaking up. Long-time militants were defecting, and, as he so often commented during this period, the very identity of the movement was under threat.

In the next chapters we return to the question set out at the beginning: what explains the nationalism of the League? Why the folklore? To answer that question we first analyse the structure and motivations of the League as a movement, and then reveal the role of the nationalist-separatist stance in mobilising, organising and legitimising it.

6 Leaders, activists and organisation

As we saw in Chapter One, the League was labelled variously as a nationalist, populist, communitarian, and as a protest organisation. Movements are normally easy to categorise because they have an agreed central text or creed and represent a clearly defined interest (as with green movements, working-class parties, and so forth). At times of change, however, organisational structures, ideologies, memberships, and identities part company, shift, merge and develop. To understand movements such as the League, one must always have in mind this shifting configuration. Reductionist views, which I began this book by criticising, tend to take one aspect of the movement (the opinions of the leader, of voters, or perhaps the content of propaganda at any one moment) and say that this represents the essence of the movement. I argue that all these must be taken into account, but that the League cannot be understood if reduced to the sum of its parts. In this chapter I take a tour of the League, examining the membership, organisation and leadership, on the assumption that no element of the League is stable, or reveals the essence of the League. Voters, personnel, leadership, and propaganda are all constantly renegotiated, in tension with one another. In Chapter Seven I reconstruct what holds these various aspects of the movement together: the identity of the movement and its uses of nationalism.

The leadership

Umberto Bossi

Biographies of charismatic political leaders often begin with a constitutive psychological event in the childhood of their subjects, a shaming failure perhaps, or a trauma, a peculiar relationship with a parent, or some other means to explain the subsequent political obsession. Bossi has been no exception. A biography thus concluded:

> The portrait of Umberto Bossi that emerges from this work is that of

> a person with a strong personality and a great sense of self esteem, thanks to a good relationship with the mother, but a lack of models of authority, because of the lack of a father figure.
>
> (Castellani 1996: 244)

Bossi's autobiography constructs its own narrative of Bossi's federalist awakening, his determination born of years of hard work, poverty and debts as he dedicated himself to the federalist cause. But the autobiography is of course more of a campaign tool than a useful historical source, and psychological analysis is too often impressionistic and anachronistic. We know most about Bossi the man and Bossi the politician by tracing some undisputed facts about his background, and following his actions since he entered the public view in the mid-1980s.

Bossi, like many of his friends who were to take on leadership roles in the movement, came from the new middle class in a small town north of Milan. He was born on 19 September 1941 in Cassano Magnago, near Varese. His father had a management position in a factory. After failing to complete a degree in medicine, Bossi married, remarried, and had three children. He has had no professional life to speak of outside politics. The League's undisputed leader is often described as a charismatic figure, and indeed many of the League's inner circle do appear to have been mesmerised by him. In certain periods, however (for instance during the 1994 government), this source of Bossi's power was revealed to be fallible. Clearly, in the early phase of the movement's mobilisation, direct personal relationships with the leader were central, and this aspect of his authority was the key. This explains why Bossi remains first in the movement, and not first among equals. According to Bossi's long-time deputy, Maroni, 'Ours is a political movement that was born neither around a project, nor a particular interest. . . . One could say that the League, like Forza Italia, was born around a leader' (Maroni cited in Castellani 1996: 213). Similarly Formentini, prior to being elected the League's Mayor of Milan, refused, without recrimination, to accept a journalist's suggestion that he was third in command of the League: 'In the League there is Bossi,' he stated, 'then there is the League. There are no number twos, nor number threes, nor fours' (Formentini, cited in Cantieri and Ottoviani 1992).

As the League began to depend increasingly upon the media to communicate with its supporters and potential supporters, this source of his charismatic authority was gradually transformed; Bossi's star status consolidated his power. The remarkable intensity of the personal relationship between Bossi and his followers is partially explained by identification. Bossi, wearing not sombre suits, but patterned cardigans, even on television, still living in a small hill town, and still speaking in the blunt idiom of the local bar, is widely perceived by his supporters as 'one of us', while the Italian political class could hardly be more distant. Supporters claim that he looks very Lombard, and many of them, since they feel that in some way he embodies their best qualities, thus experience the adventure of the League in a vicarious way, as *their own* battle with Rome. The personal fascination with the leader is no doubt amplified by the gloss that regular television appearances add. Indeed, while Bossi's authority with his inner circle was cemented early in the campaign, the media's embrace of the League and Bossi has added to his standing within the movement. While Bossi may have been a leading figure in the early years, he could only be in one place at a time, and address one meeting at a time. Television and the press remove such constraints, and, despite fleeting attention to the likes of Miglio, Pivetti, and Maroni, the media are interested only in the leader of the League. This reinforces the man's aura with his followers, and his power over possible challengers for the leadership. Rivals have no means to reply to the public smear campaigns Bossi launches against them: they simply cannot get the airtime. Like many party leaders, Bossi plays his deputies off against one another, and uses them to execute the most politically costly tasks. Patelli was the public fall guy for the 1992 bribe scandal, and Maroni for the 1994 '*Decreto Salvaladri*'. When members of his own party contradict him, he will go so far as to insult or publicly humiliate them, or, as in the case of Rocchetta, Castellani, and a series of others, to unceremoniously oust them.

Although Bossi's memoirs have been useful in this study as a window on Bossi's changing preoccupations and opinions, future historians are unlikely to treat them as reliable sources of facts. In his writings, speeches and statements Bossi was not worried about such abstractions as truth or consistency, knowing that contradictions and inconsistencies are lost in the general noise of mediated politics. The League leader's political statements, when they are read side by side, reveal many contradictions. In his book of 1996 he claimed that Maroni had been proposing a unification of the League and Forza Italia. In an interview in 1997 he denied that. Policy documents (such as Miglio's 1993 proposal of the 'three republics') were issued with support from Bossi, and then withdrawn only days later (Tambini 1998b). Bossi was little interested in debate, perhaps guessing that such processes, especially when carried out in public, tend to cost, rather than attract, votes.

Does Bossi use the identity constructions of the League in a strategic way? Is he cynically using nationalist themes simply to keep his political machine running? Clearly Bossi is involved in identity work, and we have seen that he often reflects on the identity of the movement and the need to protect and foster it. We have also seen that he is sometimes prepared to play down identity themes (such as the dialect) when they prove to be politically costly. But to claim that this is cynical would be another point entirely. As regards his personal ideology, Bossi is an impulsive, intuitive politician, and his discourse betrays allegiance with few of the main ideological arguments that divide others. He claims that his own position is 'post-ideological' (Bossi 1995: 57–8) superseding previous oppositions such as that between left and right. Maroni has often commented on his admiration for the intuition of his leader and long-time friend: 'He has an extraordinary capacity to intuit future developments, he always says that the true politician is someone who predicts phenomena, not someone who follows them' (Carraro, Maroni and Diamanti 1996: 47). We could disregard this as deliberate flattery on Maroni's part, but it is revealing in that Bossi is not being flattered for being a rational, or instrumental leader, but for being an intuitive one. Bossi is primarily a tactician. His explanations of political processes are invariably accompanied by scrawled diagrams that resemble hybrids of electronic circuit diagrams and military battle plans. Internal League memos by Bossi are similarly covered with these strategic plans, complete with large arrows representing the League's plan to 'penetrate' opposing coalitions.

Bossi does not drop his rough, soapbox style, even in private interviews. The voice is raised, and fists are clenched in an embodiment of the righteous anger that fuels his party. The man is swarthy, a touch threatening, and Bossi takes none of the opportunities offered by one-to-one interviews to strike up a sympathetic rapport. Indeed, there is very little evidence of a private Bossi that differs from the public leader apart from the odd joke at the expense of the 'regime', Bossi's interviews read as a catalogue of defensive sparring, and there are no cracks in what clearly is a performance.

What motivates Bossi? It would be tempting to say that Bossi the leader has been driven more by the joy of the political chase than by concern for a particular view of justice or Utopia. His experience of politics has been of a difficult, but astounding, rise to power, and he had known relatively few setbacks before the mid-1990s. He is clearly very interested in power for its own sake: as we saw, values and goals such as independence and federalism or the protection of a given culture or community tend to be sacrificed to the broader aim of simply achieving the highest possible vote at a given time, and consolidating the leader's power over challengers. As the movement faces difficulties, it is interesting to speculate how he would react to the scenario of an isolated, declining League, or what would be the limits of actions that he would take if the League was reduced to a rump of extremists. When publicly questioned on these issues he is enigmatic (Tambini 1998b). It is likely that Bossi would ideally like to remain within the rules of liberal democratic politics, but has devised his own set of criteria regarding when civil disobedience might be justified.

Given the hold Bossi has over his movement, it might be tempting to reduce the politics of the League to the opinions of its leader. This is not feasible, however. A glance at the history of the League shows that Bossi does not simply dictate his wishes to his followers, but 'rides the tiger' of the changing humours of the movement as new political opportunities emerge.

While Bossi comes from the new industrial middle class, others among the leaders come from farming families. None of the inner circle comes from an aristocratic family. Unlike the electorate and the militants, the leadership of the League did not go through great changes during the period 1990–4. This was because (for reasons discussed in the section on the League's organisation later) the leadership protected its position within the League.

The parliamentary party

Judging from the data gathered by Cantieri and Ottaviani (1992) members of the parliamentary party of the League are mainly of middle-class origin, and a little better educated than their electorate. In 1992, almost all senators and more than half the deputies were educated to degree level. Most of those without such qualifications were business owners or professionals (Cantieri and Ottoviani 1992: 100–41). We have seen that there were sudden influxes of new faces in 1992 and 1994, and also that although candidates were drawn as far as possible from among the established membership, they were not all long-standing members. As we saw, this sudden expansion of the League took on many MPs who had not been fully integrated into the world-view of the League, and many soon defected. Just as the parliamentary party becomes more moderate as it expands, it – at least so far – tends to become more extreme as it contracts, and the longer-standing members are selected (ultimately by Bossi) for the safer constituencies.

Supporters of the League

Voters 1982–90[1]

The conventional account presents those who supported the League in the early years as macho hooligans, who were briefly joined by more respectable voters and activists during the 'revolutionary years' of 1991–4, before the League was again left to the hooligans. The analysis that follows reveals such a picture to be exaggerated, as League support changes much more slowly in terms of social composition and attitudes, and the supporters are more average and moderate than such a picture would imply.

Unlike competitor Forza Italia, which used the offices of Berlusconi's Fininvest Corporation to mobilise a ready-made network, the League had to start from scratch. Bossi was addressing meetings of only twenty or thirty people until 1985. Local groups sometimes failed to attract any people to their meetings (Bossi and Vimercati 1992: XII; Vimercati 1990: 30). In the first months, the four-page campaign newsletter was distributed to 13,000 addresses (Bossi and Vimercati 1992).[2] The target group was those most alienated from the existing *partitocrazia*: small business owners, and those among the lower middle class and working class who owed nothing to the clientalism of the parties. In the following section I focus first on those who voted for the League and second on the militants.

Various studies have analysed the social class, previous affiliations and attitudes of the electorate of the League for the years after 1990. Unfortunately, however, there was no systematic study of the very early years. For that period we have to rely on impressionistic accounts, many of which were coloured by the media reception of the early League. Given that the greatest expansion of the League electorate occurred between 1989 and 1992, the 1989 data are the best available guide to the profile of League activists in previous years.

Social characteristics

Ilvo Diamanti (1993: 112) characterised the typical voter of the League between 1983 and 1987 as 'male, with a low level of education, probably private sector middle classes or workers in small business, mainly Christian Democrat'. Vittorio Moioli (1990) also argued that League supporters had a low level of education.[3] The earliest study of the electorate of the League, however, suggests that their level of education was not low when compared to the population at large.[4] The average League voter was relatively young, male, prosperous and educated. In Mannheimer's analysis, it was found that there was indeed a slight preponderance of males amongst the League voters in 1989 (over 10 per cent more than females). Voters were also more likely to be aged between 45 and 65 (Mannheimer *et al.* 1991: 126–7) than were voters of other parties. Mannheimer's data suggest that the League was supported by more educated and professional people (the classic middle classes) than Diamanti or Moioli had suggested (ibid.: 128–9).[5] In comparison with the population at large League supporters tended, according to 1990 data, to be less likely to have no qualifications, though also less likely to have a university degree (ibid.: 129). There was a preponderance of business owners in the League's electorate compared to the population at large, and also a slight preponderance of wage workers. The social profile of the electorate was in fact fairly average.[6]

Political profile

From which parties did the League poach its voters? What was the political past of League voters? On the previous political affiliations of League supporters, data are again scarce for the early period. The general consensus is that the League took votes from all major parties, but more from the Christian Democrats than from others. According to data from the Lombard regional statistical office, 7.1 per cent of all Christian Democrat voters in Lombardy in 1987 voted for the League in 1990. This compared with 2.1 per cent and 2.2 per cent of the Communist and Socialist votes respectively (Natale 1991: 110) (see Table 6.1).

Past allegiance does not predict current attitudes, however. Writing in 1989–90, Vittorio Moioli argued that you could find in the League 'a bit of everything' when it came to attitudes (Moioli 1990: 87–8). The consensus of studies confirms that in the period up until 1990 the supporters of the League did not show a particular leaning towards either traditionally left-wing or traditionally right-wing attitudes (Mannheimer *et al.* 1991: 133–7). Diamanti attempted to isolate five ideal types of League voter on the basis of an attitude survey by the Lombard regional government with a sample of 1,816 respondents living in Lombardy.[7] Of those who expressed a clear preference for the League, he specified five main types of League supporter according to their main political motivations: the disenchanted (42 per cent); the particularists (13 per cent); the intolerant (16 per cent); the localists (15 per cent); and the efficiency-oriented (10 per cent). The 'disenchanted', he argued, showed only a limited intolerance of immigrants, but above all a very high measure of scepticism about politics. The other categories speak more or less for themselves, the efficiency-oriented being those driven by a lack of faith in the public sector and strong faith in the private.

Table 6.1 Previous voting of 1990 Lombard League voters (in Lombardy)

	1987		*1990*
Christian Democrats	7.1	->	L.L
Communist Party	2.2	->	L.L
Other *'laici'*	2.1	->	L.L
Socialist Party	1.8	->	L.L
Others	1.9	->	L.L

Source: Servizio Statistico Regione Lombardia, quoted in Natale 1991: 110.

Note: In 1987 the League vote was 2.7 per cent of all valid votes in the Lombard region; in 1990 it had reached 17.4 per cent.

League voters after 1990

Diamanti's categories were not the only way that the support of the League could have been categorised. In the period 1990 until 1994, there would have been a great deal of change to account for in whatever categories were chosen, however. The great expansion of the League electorate that took place over that period involved a change in the social and political profiles of voters. The conventional understanding was that during this time, to parallel the increasing moderateness of the parliamentary party, more of Diamanti's efficiency-oriented voters joined the movement, while those driven by particularist or intolerant motives became a less significant proportion of League voters. There are two problems with this reasoning, however. The first is that individual opinions are assumed to be constant, and the second is that they are held to be singular. It is perfectly imaginable that individual supporters hold several of these opinions at once, and that they change over time, especially as they undergo political socialisation by the League.

The accepted account of the 1990–4 period is that during this time the League broadened its base of electoral support to include social groups it had not reached before, as the League became the principal vessel of the rising wave of protest at the government corruption revealed by the *Mani Pulite* inquiry from 1992 on. This widening of support was encouraged by the gradual 'coming out' of a number of public figures behind the League. The conventional story ends with the League losing the more respectable bank of voters it gained during this period when Silvio Berlusconi's new party, Forza Italia, emerged in early 1994. It would appear that there is some truth in this account, which is accepted by Bossi (Tambini 1998b), but that it should not be exaggerated. There was a great deal of continuity over time.

After that of the formation of the Northern League, 1990–4 was the period in which the geographical spreading of support for the movement was most marked. Before this period, there was some support for the various autonomist movements in the North that were to ally with the League, but all such movements experienced a boost in votes after merging with the League. Many argue that in addition to the geographical and numerical growth there was also a social and attitudinal broadening.

Social characteristics

Mannheimer (1993: 253–74), the same author who analysed the 1990 data (discussed earlier) has gathered comparable data on age, profession and level of instruction. A comparison of the data reveals that the

League expanded its appeal between 1990 and 1992 to include slightly more wage workers, and a very slightly higher proportion of voters with university degrees. It seems that if a significant change in the social composition of the League did take place, it was not until after the elections of 1992 (Diamanti 1996a: 117).

Political attitudes

Here of course we return to the problem that respondents to attitudinal surveys generally repeat the party line. It may be that the movement propaganda during this period came closer to the values of efficiency and private enterprise than to ethnic particularism. The media presentation of the League, however, largely ignored this, continuing to present the League as an ethno-national party. Between 1990 and 1994, the League's propaganda machine, which as I have noted was highly developed by that point, indeed moved away from the previous position of localism and intolerance, and towards a broader set of goals. It should not be assumed however that voter motivations changed accordingly. To present the opinions of League voters as independent of this propaganda machine (as though the League was somehow reducible to the opinions of those that support it) would be a serious mistake. The shift in opinion is not merely the result of new supporters being attracted by a new political line; it is the result of the existing membership being persuaded by the leadership to hold new opinions or at least to express a new 'party line' in an interview situation. Thus again we see that accounts of voter motivation are confused if they are not incorporated in a model of the movement. Mannheimer's (1994: 263) data are reproduced in detail in Table 6.2. They are based on a survey taken of voters in the April 1992 elections.

The stimulus statements represent points of League ideology on federalism and decentralisation and permit us to understand which in the armoury of League themes resonate best with League supporters. Number 3, a protest statement, received a very positive response, with 65 per cent in strong agreement. Statement 5 was a very succinct caricature of the League's programme of 1992. This was strongly agreed with by 51.2 per cent of those who had been identified as League voters, although statement 1, on fiscal federalism, was strongly agreed with by the same proportion of Leghisti as the 'protest' statement. Thus the data reveal a complex picture: strong agreement both with protest and with federalist/autonomist motivations. The motivations of League voters were complex and fragmented, and that many 'protest' supporters were also supporters of increased autonomy.

Ricolfi also found that League supporters had a rather low commit-

Table 6.2 Attitudes of League voters, 1992

	Per cent declared 'in strong agreement'		
Stimulus phrase	*League voters*	*Potential League voters*	*Others*
1 'The taxes which we pay in our region should be used mainly here.'	65.9	57.3	36.5
2 'It would be better if teachers in schools in our region came from here.'	40.2	32.8	22.0
3 'The traditional parties argue among themselves, but they are basically all the same.'	65.9	52.1	46.6
4 'Third World immigrants do not integrate well because they are different to us.'	18.9	20.8	12.6
5 'North, Centre and South are very different from one another; it would be better if they were more autonomous.'	51.2	34.9	17.2
6 'It would be better if people married people from their own area.'	14.0	7.3	8.0
(N)	(164)	(192)	(564)

Source: Mannheimer 1994: 263.

ment to Catholicism: 'Only the priest-eaters by definition (the Radicals and ex-Communist party) present levels of secularisation higher than the League' (Ricolfi 1992: 58). After 1992, however, this may have been reversed by the very visible presence in the League of Irene Pivetti (a devout Catholic), and the institutionalisation of Catholic sections within the party.

Returning to that favourite pastime of political scientists (putting the League on a spectrum from left to right), Ricolfi made an analysis of 1992 survey data comparing the opinions of the electorates of all major parties on solidarity, welfarism, corporatism and economic liberalism. According to his results the electorate of the League belonged squarely with the economic liberals (Ricolfi 1992: 59–61). However, in 1993 Corbetta agreed with the League that it would be impossible to put it anywhere on a left–right continuum. This is not of course to suggest that the attitudes of League voters shifted between 1992 and 1994. What is revealed is disagreement over how to operationalise the left–right distinction.

To summarise, the claim that the electorate of the League broadened (socially and politically) and became less attached to regionalist goals between 1990 and 1994 has been hard to support conclusively through

Table 6.3 Membership of the Northern League by region and membership category (ordinary, supporters, youth and pensioners), 1993

Region	*Ordinary members*	*Supporters*	*Youths*	*Pensioners*	*Total*	*Per cent total*
Lombardia	3,026	13,955	5,308	4,045	26,334	60.81
Piemonte	1,067	5,340	1,389	816	8,612	19.89
Liguria	164	490	136	139	929	2.19
Trieste	31	94	20	10	155	0.36
Trentino	35	468	170	53	726	1.68
Veneto	946	1,285	102	149	2,482	5.73
Romagna	160	391	105	52	708	1.63
Emilia	177	870	227	100	1,374	3.17
Toscana	487	812	261	123	1,683	3.89
Friuli	0	197	44	22	263	0.61
Aosta	0	18	10	14	42	0.10
Bolzano	0	5	5	0	2	0.02
Total	6,093	23,920	7,772	5,523	43,308	100
Per cent of total	14.07	55.23	17.95	12.75	100	

Source: Northern League, office of organization internal report.

Note: The totals do not add up. This is as in the original League document.

analysis of available data. It is clear that there has been a broadening of the geographical base of the vote, of the socio-economic position of the electorate, and that the male bias was corrected. However, data are not sufficient to reach conclusions on the degree to which the electorate identified with the federalist/autonomist goals of the League, or where it stands on a left–right continuum.[8]

Active members: the 'tesserati'

Huge events like the Pontida rallies, the Festa on the Po and the referendum on secession require a great deal of manpower in their organisation and execution. In the League, such work is done by volunteers from local offices, and they have proved crucial to the League's success. Alessandro Patelli estimated the number of paid-up members of the Lombard League at around 10,000 when he took up the post of officer of organisation in 1989, and the number had grown to more than 26,000 in the Lombard League and 43,000 in the Northern League by 1993.

For the 1980s few data exist on the social background of the militants. The relevant information was not gathered by the League, and the only studies that date from that period were on the electorate, not active members. The League has kept relatively detailed data on membership numbers by region and province, however. The regional totals are reproduced in Table 6.3, and show the weight of the Lombard League within the movement. (It is likely that any error in these figures tends to exaggerate the number of militants, since the League needs to appear strong.)

Previous political experience

There is evidence that the higher echelons of the League have a more left-wing past than the grassroots. Segatti interviewed thirty-three local candidates of the Northern League in 1990 to ascertain their previous political experience. In contrast with Natale's earlier findings on the electorate of the League (already discussed), he found a greater number (thirteen of the thirty-three) had experience in the Italian Socialist Party. Only six said they had experience with the Christian Democrats.[9] (There may of course be a selective memory effect at work here. At the moment of the study, the Christian Democrats were the arch enemy of the League, identified with the South and corruption. League militants may have been tempted to forget any past involvement.)

Political attitudes of militants will not be examined in detail. Unlike voters, militants tend to have their opinion formed quite strongly by the party propaganda machine, and to be loyal in their public statements of political attitudes to the central canons of the ideology. Of those interviews with League militants done for this study, most simply repeated the most recent line of the League.

The League: a male party?

Umberto Bossi's most famous slogan was uttered in 1991 in a speech to his party, which was praising the arrival of large numbers of women into the membership of the Northern League. 'The women are arriving' he said, happy that the male bias in membership and voting figures appeared to be in decline. In the next part of the speech he returned to the main thrust of his speech: searching for new metaphors to describe the irresistible nature of his movement's assault on the old regime. 'La Lega c'è l'ha duro' he rasped into the microphone in his most infamous ad lib: 'The Lega has got a hard on(e)'.

Was the League a male party? Clearly there were women members and voters, though women are better represented as activists in the other leading Italian parties, particularly the PDS (Democratic Party of the Left). And Bossi was correct in noting that the League needed to improve its appeal to women voters (Mannheimer *et al.* 1991: 126). The picture in the parliamentary party was less clear-cut: seven of eighty League MPs in 1992 were female, which in fact was a higher proportion than the overall ratios of female to male MPs in Parliament. But numbers aside, the macho traditionalism of the League offered little support for women's issues. There were no women's committees, and such leaders that did emerge did not explicitly take up gender relations as a political issue. The most visible of the League women, Irene Pivetti, who became speaker in the Chamber of Deputies at the age of 31, was firmly traditionalistic in her views of gender roles in Catholic society.

The League in phases

Many commentators responded to the apparent disorder of the League – its shifts in membership, strategy and goals – by dividing the movement's history into several phases, stressing the discontinuities in the League's electoral strategy, its forms of action, and its support. Ilvo Diamanti (1993), for example, divides the rise of the League into four phases: ethno-regionalism (1983–7; socio-economic regionalism (1987–90); anti-state protest (1990–2); and party of government (1992–).[10] This version of events was also shared by the leaders of the League themselves when they found it useful.[11] Conceptions of phases are useful as introductory guides, but by stressing the sudden changes in strategy that the League makes, they may distract our attention from deeper continuities in the organisation, identity and membership of the League, and from understanding why the changes in political strategy were made.

Most analysts see the movement as an essentially political phenomenon. Diamanti's model relates the motivations of voters to the political programme (*proposta politica*) of the League. Thus the motivations of voters appear as intentionally rational, directed to an unproblematic political offer made by the League. Whatever the division into phases suggests, the movement could not have existed without at least some continuity in key ideas. Like a product in a competitive market, the League needed a clear identity in order to sell. A movement that changed quite as much as Diamanti's periodisation suggests would surely lose its appeal to voters, appearing contradictory and unstable. League sympathisers in fact see the League leaders as embodying determination, constancy and resolve. The key question therefore is what was it then that united them, and linked the various stages.

The charisma of their leader and the rigid organisational structure are the answers given most often. There was also, however, a good deal of consistency in the movement's propaganda. It seemed that on some levels it had quite clear, if rather simplistic, common ideas, and had no problem in communicating them. If Diamanti, Rovati and others paint a picture of League history as marked by discontinuities and ruptures, it is because the areas in which the League shows more continuity fall outside the scope of their analysis: these are the organisational aspects of the League, and the movement's identity.

League organisation

The internal structure of the League

Given the lack of political experience of the leadership and the militants, and the fact that the League emerged as a grassroots movement rather than as a splinter of an existing party, there was no obvious blueprint for the internal structure of the movement. With only a few exceptions, there was little expectation among militants that they should have a role in policy formation, or even election of a leader. That Bossi has been able to maintain such an undemocratic internal structure has been due to his vigilance with challengers and personal identification with the movement, which I have argued was due in part to his successful use of the media. That it is tolerated by the grassroots is due to Bossi's use of enemy logic creating a siege mentality framed in nationalist terms.

Political commentator Giorgio Bocca argued as follows:

> (the) miracle of the League . . . is that they understood that localistic roots, the feeling of belonging to territory, to history, customs and language, can be easily transformed into a political network, and into a political organisation more solid, more agile and less costly than those of the traditional parties.
>
> (Bocca 1990: 25)

While Bocca's statement would need a great deal more evidence to be accepted, he has intuited that the localism and nationalism of the League was not 'mere folklore' but underpinned the very organisational structure of the movement.

The importance of the construction of identity to the mobilisation of collective action was discussed in Chapter Two. This was the League leadership's problem as much as that of any other movement trying to persuade people to invest time and money in political action. Did the movement use an existing form of 'communal solidarity' to organise its action? Yes and no. On the level of day-to-day organisation, it could be argued that it certainly benefited from existing networks (such as the dialect clubs and local bars), especially in the period before it received mass media coverage. On the level of collective identity, however, there was, prior to the movement, little pre-existing sense of collective solidarity or identity, and the movement had to start more or less from scratch, using scraps and patches of existing cultural stereotypes, aspirations, and habits to construct an identity.

In the early period of the movement, the newsletter *Lombardia Autonomista* provided the movement with structure, as a great deal of

League activism consisted in the production and distribution of the newspaper (Bossi and Vimercati 1992: 42). Prior to the formation of the Northern League and its first congress in 1991, the movement lacked formal organisation. The Lombard League, with only five permanent staff members as late as 1989, and offices in a four-room Milanese apartment, was a 'do it yourself' organisation, according to Patelli. In the years following 1985, the Lombard League remained an informal ad hoc arrangement, held together by the stern leadership of Bossi and his demand of personal sacrifice and loyalty, as evidenced in the stormy departures of Castellazzi (Piccone 1992: 9) and others in the late 1980s. The organisation was small enough for meetings and congresses to be organised in an ad hoc way, and for the few MPs and MEPs to be in regular contact with their leader, who maintained his power through close personal trust. Initiatives for campaign issues came from the top of the movement, and were approved by the membership by applause at rallies and meetings. (Pontida was symbolically used in this way by the League.) On the site where representatives of the cities of the Lombard League swore loyalty to the League of 1167, the 1980s League supporters would swear loyalty to the decisions of the leaders of their movement.[12]

As the League grew, however, a structure was required that would be simple to understand, and, for the leadership, enable it to retain control of the rapidly-growing movement. It also needed legitimacy, since Bossi had attracted criticism for his reluctance to introduce democracy into the movement. The formation of the federal structures and the first steps toward realising the plan outlined in Patelli's diagrams in Figure 6.1 coincided with this period of growth.

> Until 1990 there were four or five secretaries who did a bit of everything. Then by about 1992 the total went up to ten. At this point we had a great success in the elections, getting eighty MPs and therefore we had more financial scope. We took a larger office, we augmented the components of the federal secretariat, and started to institute the national secretariats.
>
> (Bossi, speech to conference, 1991)

The League moved, first to the double-fronted building in Via Arbe, where around fifteen staff worked, and then in 1993 to Via Bellerio, where the hundred or so Northern League staff members shared over 7,000 square metres with the 'national' staff of the Lombard League. The sheer size of the movement necessitated the formalisation of authority in the League. At the first congress of the League in 1991, Bossi announced some big changes. Apart from the peripheral organisations such as the new 'Autonomist Trades Union of Lombardy' (known as SAL) and the

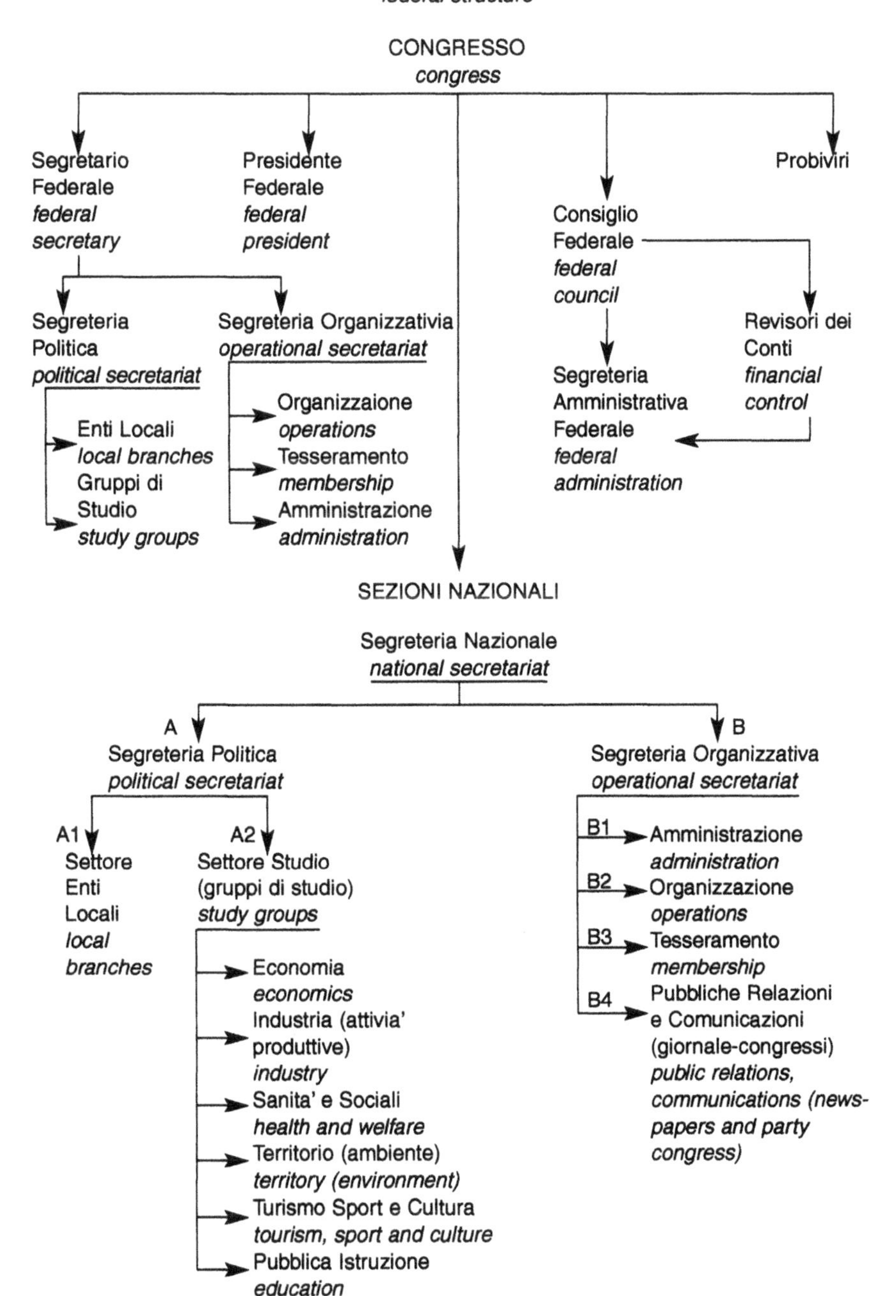

Figure 6.1 Internal organisation of the Northern League

Source: Northern League office of organisation.

acquisition of two radio stations in Lombardy, he changed the rules concerning membership. New members would have to wait a year before being elected to local office, and two years before election to the provincial council.[13] These, and the three-year delay before being able to rise to the *consiglio nazionale*, and four years to get federal responsibilities, would ensure that there was great continuity in the leadership and control and surveillance of rising stars.

Nationalism is symbolically inscribed in the organisation of the League, as the regional offices are known as the 'nations'. Alessandro Patelli, executive secretary of the League from 1989, introduced the doublespeak:

> Be careful not to confuse matters. For us, national is regional and federal is national let us say. So, the federal congress issues the political line. The national congresses in fact have the power to design who in that nation will be responsible for bringing forward the political line of the movement.
>
> (Interview with Patelli, 1 August 1994)

Is this purely a matter of appearance? Or do the nations (the regional sections of the League such as Veneto and Piedmont) have genuine independence? The short answer is that they have little independence, and little influence in the highly-centralised policy formulation process of the League. The longer answer is a little more complex. Because of the underdeveloped policy discourse of the League, councillors and mayors have considerable independence on the local level, and in some instances, such as over the Venetian Eight in 1997, the leadership has bowed to grassroots pressure.

The official line within the League was that democratic reforms had been instituted with the setting up of the 'federal structures' of the Northern League in 1990. Alesandro Patelli insisted that the federal structure in which the ultimate power rests with the Northern League congress (delegates elected by each 'national' congress) was up and working by mid-1994:

> The ultimate power rests with the federal congress. The federal congress elects the federal secretary and the federal president . . . this is the already existing structure. Currently, the congress gives the political line to the movement and – as well as giving the political line to follow in the next years – it decides who will be the personnel who bring these into practice.
>
> (Interview with Patelli, 1 August 1994)

Patelli has been responsible for instigating the institutionalisation of the League. It is worth examining his description of the internal structure of the Northern League. The control that Bossi exercises within the movement is clearly based not simply on centralised bureaucracy, but on a combination of informal control, personal trust, and use of the media.

The official description of the League structure is outlined in Patelli's diagram (Figure 6.1). This official description of the structure remained stable in subsequent years. In practice, however, the democratic format is overridden by the informal use of central powers. Whereas most party structures at least pretend to have an internal democracy, the League simply inverts the model. It does not allow the grassroots to delegate leaders, but gives the grassroots centrally selected officers and the political line to follow. The federal structure, which at that point had just moved into the new headquarters of the League in Via Bellerio, Milan, sits on top of the seven 'national' structures, and 'gives the political line to them'.[14] It is not accountable in return, since candidate selection (both for election and internal office) tends where possible to be controlled by Bossi or his clique. The main functions of central office are under the management of the federal secretary: Bossi. These are divided into the political secretariat, the 'think tank' of the movement, and the organisational secretariat, which provides the bureaucratic support for that. Within the political secretariat, the main activity is research, divided into policy working groups for each sector. It is here, not on the grassroots level, that League policy is made, and issued in pamphlets. The 'federal president', like the federal secretary, is elected by the federal congress. The position has no managerial functions. This position was created after the founding of the League to contain the then Venetian League leader Franco Rocchetta.

The federal council's functions are obscure, though it appears to work mainly on the financial control of League administration. It is supposed to nominate the federal administrative secretary and others responsible for managing electoral campaigns, finances and so on. The twenty-four members are elected by the federal congress, which comprises the 'national' secretaries, plus elected delegates from each of the nations, weighted to favour the biggest 'nation', Lombardy. The 'national' structure consists of a similar division between political and organisational functions. There are study groups on the political side, although in the case of the smaller 'nations' Patelli admits that these are virtually nonexistent, simply because the 'national' secretariat is smaller:

> How many were on the staff in 1992? About fifteen in the federal secretariat and a couple in each national secretariat. Now there are about fifteen permanent staff in each of the three bigger national

secretariats, and two or three in the smaller nations. Bit by bit they will get bigger.'

(Interview with Alessandro Patelli, 1 August 1994)

Apart from the general problem of internal democracy, the main controversies concerning League organisation are the position of Bossi and the position of the Lombard League more generally within the Northern League. Judging from observation of congresses and the relationships between Bossi and the other leaders of the League, it appears that the movement is yet to achieve the structure outlined in Figure 6.1. Patelli's scheme is designed to deflect accusations that Bossi is a dictator within the League. The scheme leaves out many aspects of the day-to-day running of the League. It fails to take account of the massive power of Bossi to sway opinion within the League, and of the barriers that are in place to prevent challengers from rising quickly within the League.

The pronouncements of leaders of the League on the organisation of the movement must be analysed at a critical distance. One of the chief criticisms directed at the movement throughout its history has been that it is authoritarian, with all power concentrated in the hands of one man. Statements from the victims of that power suggest that the 1993–4 democratic reforms in the League were not what the League claimed them to be. In an interview in July 1994, for example, Franco Rocchetta, then federal president of the League, said that Bossi 'wants to transform the League into a party like those in Eastern Europe; the votes [in the Venetian League congress] were worse than Romania, worse than Russia. A political force that negates democracy is digging its own grave'.[15] There may be a dose of sour grapes here of course. Bossi had spoken against the re-election of Rocchetta as secretary of the Venetian League and Rocchetta had lost the vote. By August 1994 he had also lost his position as president of the Northern League. The accusations are, however, very similar to those made by other League leaders deposed by Bossi. Castellazzi made claims along these lines when he finished his career with the League in 1989, and so did Gianfranco Miglio in 1994. Anyone who has witnessed the League convention's 'votes by acclamation' in the stadium atmosphere whipped up by Bossi will know that there is something to Rocchetta's claims. In the congress of December 1993, when Bossi finally gave up the position of secretary of the Lombard League (he had been secretary of the Northern League as well since 1991), the congress elected his successor. There was only one candidate, Luigi Negri, then a staunch Bossi supporter, who was elected 'by acclaim' (applause) by the assembled delegates.

The League leadership defended the concentration of power in their hands with the use of slightly paranoid enemy reasoning. According to Bossi,

> In the first phase, the main danger that the League faced was to prevent external infiltration. For the Christian Democrats or the Socialists, it would have been enough to buy 100 members to buy the movement. It was not possible to open the doors straight away to everybody . . . we needed a small, protected leadership with strong unity and agreed leadership.
>
> (Bossi in Vimercati 1990: 118; see also Bossi 1995: 114–15)

Rocchetta's failure to be re-elected as national secretary of the Venetian League in July 1994 shows how Bossi's power has worked in practice. The vote was made at the end of the conference after the usual closing speech from Bossi, in which he not only openly gave his support to the candidate that supported him, but also gave damning speeches about Rocchetta and the other candidate.[16] The vote no doubt was free (if not secret), but Bossi has much more effective influence on voters' decisions than do most party leaders, because there is a sense that the leader and the movement are synonymous, and that without Bossi the movement would lose its unity and power. The power over opinion also applies to the middle management of the League, and thus Bossi and his loyal supporters will be able also to influence candidate selection. Bossi's almost paranoid message, 'unity at all costs', was heard at the various levels of the League.

The organisational structure of the League is designed to delay the entrance into positions of power and parliament of all except those who have worked at the central office of the League. Candidate selection is controlled at the level of the federal secretariat, which is a way of ensuring the loyalty of the parliamentary party. The majority of candidates has either worked in central office prior to being elected, or has been in the party for many years. The latter route is due to the complex membership system. At the time of writing there are basically three types of members. First are the 150 élite *soci fondatori*, the founding fathers of the movement, all of whom are from the Lombard League, and who are used to consolidating the power of Bossi. They have ad hoc powers such as being able to sanction a change in the statutes of the League, if two-thirds support it. The other two main types of member are the *soci ordinari* (ordinary members), 6,093, in 1993, and the *soci sostenitori* (supporting members), 23,920 in 1993.[17] Other types of members are the youth members and pensioners. The three main types imply a hierarchy, with the ability to become *soci ordinari* only after a period of duty (and surveillance) as *soci sostenitori*. Only then can they be considered for more responsibilities.

Aside from this, Bossi as federal secretary has other ad hoc powers, such as the power to 'temporarily suspend' anyone in the movement whenever it is deemed opportune, and such decisions remain good until the next meeting of the federal council. Clearly, the organisational model introduced by Patelli remains something of a fiction, unless it was meant to represent the conduits through which initiatives from the summit of the party are transmitted to the base. The League's internal design symbolises its professed intentions regarding federation, but in practice permits very little genuine devolution of power.

Nationalism and League organisation

In approaching concrete, bureaucratic problems, such as the arrangement of decision-making within the movement, the setting up of offices, and putting out propaganda, the nationalist approach had clear advantages over other potential action repertoires. By taking a position above and beyond the wheeling and dealing of Italian party politics (or beneath it as the League's competitors might have said), the League was permitted access to the personal networks that existing political parties were denied. This was particularly important in the first phase of League organisation between 1982 and 1987. During that period, the crucial conduits of information were local bars, football clubs, and cultural organisations such as dialect clubs, which enabled the League to have a much more streamlined and cheap central organisation than any other political party in Italy, especially during the first years.

The intense loyalty resulting from a clear sense of the enemy was a crucial organisational resource. It could be used to override internal splits, which could be dismissed as media exaggerations designed to destroy the League, and to legitimise the necessity for the tight control and unaccountable manoeuvring by the League leadership. The sense that the enemy was 'foreign' to insiders, and that the insiders represented a larger group of people sharing a unique world-view, certainly sustained this crucial us–them mentality. An – albeit constructed – sense of Lombard, and later Northern, pride also enabled Bossi to rally the audience behind him, as it became his trusted rhetorical device for gaining the support of his people. The 'historical' sense of mission of the League, augmented by the League's flags and paraphernalia, added to that and arguably elicited a particularly high level of commitment among militants. The flags, anthems, and paraphernalia also gave the audience something to do at League meetings, given that they were not involved in major decisions. There was no circulation of motions in writing, no prior discussion, and no chance for questions from normal delegates. The emerging culture of League conventions in the 1980s, which would last well into the 1990s, involved militants not in debate but in clapping, flag-waving, chanting and even bell ringing. Many remarked at the time that it seemed more appropriate to the stadium. Thus as well as helping ensure loyalty, the partisan enemy logic of League conventions gave supporters a ready-made script for action, and arguably distracted them from concrete political questions that were likely to prove divisive.

All these organisational resources could have been provided by discourses other than nationalism, of course, but it was nationalist frames of reference that the League used. The resulting compactness and motivation of support was clearly a key factor in the success of the League. In the next chapter I investigate a related aspect: the identity work of the movement.

7 The uses of nationalism

Identity, interests and action

Identity work is crucial to any attempt to redefine political interest and mobilise protest. We have seen that much of the League's campaign can be understood as an attempt to persuade individuals to reassess their identity and therefore interests, in particular by undermining the previously stable framework of their common Italian national identity. In a situation where class identities were not strong, and in the face of the decline of comprehensive and compelling political ideologies, the League's identity constructs became crucial. In order to generalise these identity constructs, however, and to undermine Italian nationalism, the League needed access to the ears of Northern Italians. With none of the media resources enjoyed by their opponents, they had to find a way to gain free publicity. Their method was to engage in spectacular politics: providing editors with colourful news in exchange for a constant, however negative, media presence for the League.

By the mid-1990s, the League had in effect regular, almost daily columns in the national newspapers. *La Repubblica* had a regular feature entitled 'La Sfida della Lega' (the challenge of the League), which they ran above the latest news of League antics, together with the League's 'warrior of Giussano' logo. *Il Corriere della Sera* printed the new Padanian flag in the corner of the pages containing League news. The League made Italian politics more entertaining, and helped sell newspapers. As a result, it created a fully institutionalised running story. All the dailies had reporters whose responsibility was to follow the news of the League and the League alone. Television could hardly ignore the League, and despatched crews to all the major League events, thus helping keep the momentum of the protest going. Clearly, if the League wanted publicity for their identity contestations, they had found an effective way of getting it.

By 1995 a debate began to emerge on whether this gift of media attention to the League was justifiable, particularly since it was made at the expense of public-sector television. Just as the Thatcher government in Britain had banned Sinn Fein spokespeople from television news in order to deny the movement 'the oxygen of publicity', so there were renewed calls in Italy to shun the League, not from the government but from journalists wise to the League's game. In contrast to the situation in Britain, however, a media blackout could not be formalised in Italy: the 'national interest' in the face of 'terrorism' could not be used as a justification of political influence on television news, and League stories ran and ran.

The newspapers had clearly been dancing to Bossi's tune for some time. Reflecting on the early years of the League, Bossi claimed that

> we decided to exploit the anti-southerner sentiments diffuse in Lombardy, as in other regions of the North, to attract the attention of the public and of the mass media. We threw in a few coarse keywords and put at the centre of the propaganda the question of the dialect – both to create a bit of hype and to distract the Roman parties who dismissed us as folklore during the first years.
>
> (Bossi 1992: 42)

Despite the 'mediatisation' of the party after 1987, Bossi never tired of talking directly with his followers in rallies and public meetings. But like most astute politicians of the age in which most people form their political preferences in front of a television, he was soon aware that most of his followers and potential followers would not hear the hour-long speech, but would listen to a ten-second sound-bite from it. The extreme simplicity of the League's nationalist-separatist position was well adapted to such a context. This chapter will discuss the nationalist identity constructions that the League mobilised, analysing when and why they were changed, the links between the identity constructions and policy, and the political and organisational aspects of the movement.

The discourse of the League

How to research the identity constructions of the League? It is not as simple as analysing the League's 'official' propaganda. In May 1989, *Il Giornale* reported that copies of a Lombard League leaflet had been circulating in Pregnana Milanese, near Milan. According to the article the leaflet read: 'One, ten, one hundred, a thousand Southerners dead. All told, what difference would it make? They are destroying our precious race, that is the race of Northern Italians.'[1] This is strong stuff, and the pamphlet was in fact quickly disowned by the League who said it was not their work. A similar episode occurred three years later, when a similar pamphlet was printed by League activists in Veneto. This time the message was: 'Southerners, go home. Your people need you there to help fight the Mafia.' This time the League leadership asked their local group to issue a statement claiming responsibility for printing the leaflet on their own initiative. Whether these episodes were, as the League claimed, 'set-ups' by journalists or the covert work of a competitor party will probably remain a mystery, but such cases do illustrate the hall of mirrors in which one finds oneself when trying to summarise the League's propositions. Apart from the multiplicity of possible readings of the propaganda, there were multiple sources of propaganda, and how they were heard depended on the internal organisation of the League and the selectivity of the media.[2]

Those authors who have tried to summarise the political programme of the League (Allievi 1992) have generally used the official newspapers and pamphlets of the League as a source. The official propaganda of the League is probably a good guide if the analyst wishes to make a comment on what is contained in the official propaganda of the League, but if the aim is to summarise what the public image of the League is, or what League voters were attracted by, official propaganda is only a starting point, and a limited one at that. There are several reasons why we need sources other than League propaganda.

First, the League's newspaper represents the opinion of only a small part of the leadership. As long as the movement was growing, the gagged factions within the League did not make themselves heard openly. The tight control of Bossi kept them in line. This does not, however, mean that they were motivated by the Bossi line of the day (be it jobs for Lombards, the Republic of the North, or forming a government with Forza Italia), or that they did not use other agents in their local meetings. Second, the propaganda can be given a wide variety of readings. For example, one cartoon which was supposed to represent the melting pot of the multiracial society had a particularly graphic and alarming image, and seemed to be based on ideas of racial purity. The slogan, however, was in defence of democracy, claiming that multiracial society brings authoritarian states rather than that it is a problem in itself. A speech on sanitary conditions of *extracomunitari* (non-EU immigrants) made at the first Northern League congress in 1990 called for screening of immigrants for diseases.[3] The speech could have been seen as a call for health care for immigrants and it could have been seen as a way of labelling immigrants as diseased, and the Lombards therefore as threatened.

The League was aware of the value of the various interpretations of such images and slogans, however, in mobilising support and getting publicity, and made little effort to correct the anti-immigrant and anti-Southern sentiments that they elicited. Whether the anti-Southern politics are to be viewed as a part of the genuine intention of the League as a whole is not clear. Indeed, it seems that for Bossi at least they were merely a means of getting media coverage for his movement. Even damning headlines such as 'In the Trenches of Racism', and 'Wives from the South? No Thanks' were publicity for the League. They were invitations for the curious to attend one of the public meetings, where the leaders were sure they could convert many, and they were reminders to rethink the question of national identity.

For the analysis that follows, therefore, I have used not merely the League's newspaper, but a variety of data sources to interpret League public discourse: interviews, official newspapers, leaflets, speeches of conferences, interviews with militants, and books and videos sold at League offices. On the basis of analysis of these sources, the following kinds of questions can be addressed: What emerged from the identity construction of the League? How do movement members understand Lombard/Northern/Padanian identity? What determined changes or shifts in the identity discourse (for example, the fluctuations in importance of language or race)? To what extent were boundary constructions controlled by the leadership?

The various sources, taken as a whole, do reflect in general terms the dominant, leadership-sanctioned line. We saw in the analysis of the organisation of the League that it is generally accepted that the leadership of the League generates a 'political line' in relation to each emerging issue, and that these lines are transmitted quite quickly to the grassroots. Because sources are not available on the changing political line, and because the motivations and opinions of many League members diverged from it, I will take an overview of the discourse. In order to focus on the question of the changes and development of the identity discourse, and how it relates to political opportunities open to the League, we are concerned to find not only the overall picture presented by the identity discourse, but shifts, disputes and challenges in the identity work of the League.

The next section examines the communications strategy that the League used. The focus will be on how nationalist themes were used in a tactical way, as was convenient in relation to given contexts and opportunities.

North and South: the world according to the League

The League's great propaganda success was in anthropomorphising and territorialising Italian political problems. While Thatcherism sought to roll back the 'nanny state', Leagueism attacked the '*stato padrone*' and said that the state was anti-North and the embodiment of the inefficiency, criminality and backwardness of the South. All political problems were seen through one very simple prism, which refracted every issue into two distinct wavelengths: North and South. The South stood for all that was wrong with the Italian state and the North stood for its cure. This simple opposition rendered the League both flexible and inflexible at the same time: flexible in that this was a catch-all framework and the details could be changed constantly to fit federalism and separatism, and inflexible in that, as we have seen, the framework ultimately prevented the League's expansion to the South.

We can see that the media-fuelled 'politics of the spectacle' favours extreme stances. Communications theorists argue that novelty and transgression are elements that are most likely to generate news (Wolf, cited in Mazzoleni 1992). Challenging the very rules that structure politics around a given state and national public space is one simple way of providing both novelty and transgression within that public space. It could, at the risk of exaggeration, be argued that the League did not 'push' the North towards separatism, but that editors and readers demanded ever more, and ever more colourful news of the League, and thus that the extremist separatism of the League was a projection of the media. Further, looking at the propaganda over time we can confirm that there is indeed a 'ratchet effect' at work here. News values pushed the League towards ever-more extreme positions. Making an intervention in dialect was news yesterday, but it is not news today; to make the front pages today, we actually have to make a speech in Parliament threatening secession. At some point tomorrow it may be necessary to take actions that lend our threats credibility.

In any political movement, as in any advertising campaign, there must be some order among the confusion of slogans, so that spokespeople do not contradict one another and the public think they know what they are getting. I noted in Chapter Three how such a system of values can structure and organise a movement. For the League, the North–South opposition, or rather a mythologised version of it, provided the movement with order, values and goals, and ensured its continuity over time.

The Northern League rejected the division of politics into left and right. In League propaganda and speeches, the master oppositions were between a supposedly modern, developed, efficient, transparent, hard-working and democratic North, and a Byzantine, inefficient, occult, lazy, corrupt South. This masterframe was not confined to comment on differences within Italy, but symbolically placed Italy in the wider opposition between her neighbours, Germany, Austria and Switzerland to the North, and North Africa to the South.[4] They argued that Lombardy belonged with the developed North and with Europe, and that Southern Italy, because of the area's history, economy, political culture and traditions, did not.[5] Given the core idea that the North of Italy has been colonised by the 'Southern mentality', there is also the latent threat that the South will 'drag the North down' to its own underdeveloped level.

Politicians singing the praises of efficiency, democracy, and honesty are by no means new. The League's 'achievement' was to identify those values – in a stereotyped social naturalism – with the Lombard (and later the Northern) people as a whole, and their opposites with Southern Italians, who the League argued were running the Italian state.[6] According to the League, the way to avoid the evils of this Southern mentality and mode of organisation was to exclude the South and Southerners from affairs in Lombardy and the North. The League invented a new term, 'southernisation', to describe their enemy, which, they insisted, was not the people of Southern Italy, but the way of life that they had imposed on the national administration. The political traditions and culture of 1980s Rome did not evolve from the efficient, honest, democratic principles of the Northern Italian city states, they argued, but the Bourbon domination of the South.[7] Take this quote from Bossi speaking about an opponent in the Milan mayoral elections of 1993:

> It is unbelievable that they would put a man like Nando della Chiesa up against the League, a man who is in a party which has its political head in Palermo. There is a cultural battle going on in this country: between the efficient, transparent European culture of Milan, and the culture of institutional inefficiency and collaboration between Mafia and politics that is in Palermo.
>
> (*Corriere Della Sera*, 28 April 1993)

Bossi here is appealing to – and reinforcing – a stereotypical idea of the South and Southerners; Milanese people should not vote for people who have links with the South. (Della Chiesa was the candidate of La Rete (the Network), a party that campaigned on an anti-Mafia ticket.) Such a confrontational strategy can be risky if taken too far: Bossi was later fined for accusing the same candidate of Mafia connections, referring to him as 'Nando della Cosa Nostra'.

North–South inequality is 'natural' for the League, but not, in general, because of the biological, phenotypic or racial characteristics of the populations. The reduction of North–South differences to biological race in the League's propaganda and in interviewees' statements is rare. Some supporters refer to climate differences as the root of North–South difference, but the dominant reasoning is overwhelmingly historical and cultural. Lombardy, I was told by League supporters, is civic because it had a culture of political responsibility forged in the free medieval communes, and modern and rational because it was part of the Habsburg empire. The South by contrast was dominated by 'Arabs', 'Africans', 'Byzantines', and 'Bourbons' depending on which League supporter you speak with.

The League embraced rationalisation and modernisation, but lacked a sophisticated economic or ideological programme with which to foster them. The movement's propaganda therefore argued, through naturalising supposed differences in civic culture as products of history, that the best way of protecting Lombard modernity and affluence was through liberation from domination by a 'naturally' anti-modern group. A 1989 headline in the movement newspaper summarises the link between the supposed ethnic identity proposed by the League and the mobilisation for political grievances: 'Lega Lombarda: For politics "alla Lombarda" – transparent and honest, like the tradition of our people has taught us.'[8] The individual elements of this framing of Italian problems can be disputed, of course. The argument about the benign effects of Habsburg rule in Northern Italy 130 years ago, for instance, seems to be based on a stereotyped idea of what Austria is like *today*. The linking of Arab dominance with Southern problems seems to be linked to a stereotyped view of Arab countries today. The very idea that such historically distant cultures and traditions could have such a deep contemporary effect might not convince every sociologist, but this picture was feasible and resonant for many people living in Lombardy. Further, it played on the anxieties of a group who were enjoying the first benefits of industrial wealth, but looking over their shoulder at poverty, deprivation and underdevelopment still evident in the South of their own country. This fear of falling was fuelled by a national media system (the centre of which was quite definitely in Milan) that suddenly during the 1980s began to focus on problems of organised crime and poverty in the South.[9] Before then, the media and public awareness in general had overlooked organised crime.[10] The 1980s saw a fad for television documentaries on the South. Ostensibly they were designed to attack by publicity the Southern problems of corruption, organised crime and poverty. These programmes, however, perhaps had the effect of 'orientalising' (Said 1979) the South: rather than rushing to support the South's journey into inevitable progress, wealthy, law-abiding Northerners recoiled at the sight of overcrowded, under-funded prisons, schools and hospitals, and at their southern compatriots hiding from cameras and microphones.[11]

Nationalism, we must bear in mind, is a political phenomenon. Construction and politicisation of regional, cultural 'ethnic' markers occurs as people come together in a political movement and find new ways of conceiving of their interests as common with those of their fellows. The nationalism of the League is no exception. Between 1982 and 1994 the League faced the practical problems of how to mobilise support, and best communicate the goals of the movement. Throughout the first years of the campaigns (roughly 1982–7) Bossi's readers and audiences met with a barrage of devices to inspire them into action, as voters or activists. The results were unusual in modern party politics. Interview research reports that those who 'climbed onto the *carroccio*' (joined the League) in the early years experienced something comparable to a religious revelation: the truth and light of the League's reasoning was so appealing and simple (Diamanti 1992: 234).[12] The decision to join a political movement, like most decisions, cannot however be reduced to a single type of motivation (such as economic self-interest). Joining the League offered many other participation benefits: it offered a new source of self-respect, it offered new social circles and cultural-political events, and in the context of the corruption trials of the 1990s it could be expressed as a principled stand for honesty and against crime. The idea that it might be in the interests of Northern Italians to support the League was not simply a question of individual calculation. It was entwined with, even presumed, a sense of identity that was also fostered by the League's discourse.

Contesting interests: a lesson in League logic

The speeches, propaganda and slogans of the League were not principally concerned with expelling outsiders from Lombardy, or building ancient Lombardy into a nation-state. They were concerned directly with the current problems of the Italian state in the 1980s and 1990s. The first lines of the first issue of *Lombardia Autonomista* are instructive

> It does not matter how old you are, what work you do, of which political tendency you are: what is important is that you are – that we are – all Lombards. It is as Lombards, in fact, that we have a fundamental common interest to which our division into parties has to be subordinated. Italian parties exploit us and divert us from our duty to defend our interests so that we can serve other interests (and theirs, first of all).
>
> (*Lombardia Autonomista* 1, 1982)

The language is of common interests, not cultural nostalgia. In the text of this first issue and the second, there are few references to a Lombard tradition. The thrust of the argument is based on goal-oriented rationality, regarding the material benefits of independence from Rome, and not the endangered folklore and dying dialect of Lombardy, issues taken up only later.

The material benefits (to Northerners) of the autonomy of the North of Italy would be great, according to basic League logic. It was well known that the North, and particularly Lombardy, had of late been one of the most economically buoyant regions of Europe. Without the drain of resources to Southern 'welfare dependants' and state inefficiency and corruption, said the League, taxes could be lowered and infrastructure and services improved. The flow charts reproduced as Figure 7.1, taken from 1986–7 campaign newsletters, exemplify this attempt to demonstrate that Lombardy constitutes a community of interest. The logic is clear. Lombardy should awaken and dam this bleeding to the South, by claiming autonomy. However if the charts were too complex to grab the attention of the potential League supporter, cartoons such as the one in Figure 7.2, showing the fiscal manoeuvres of the government, were clearer.

Other potential advantages of independence were added. Freedom from corruption and criminality was one, and cartoons on this theme were printed in the League newspaper and leaflets from 1985 onwards. The Mafia, identified with the South and with 'Southern' power in Rome, was also presented as an economic 'exploiter' of the North. A weaker version of the same argument focused on the bureaucracy in Rome, simply saying that it was inefficient.

In the early years, then, the League began to argue that *Lombardità* (Lombardness) was crucial. Neither Bossi nor his supporters, however, appeared to know what Lombardità *was* during this early stage. Lombardy was presented mainly as a community of common interest, defined by its economic robustness and its goal: freedom from exploitation by the corrupt political centre in Rome.[13] A plot without characters. Perhaps that was why the League soon began to dedicate such a lot of space to other types of argument. The 'rational', goal-oriented arguments were increasingly interspersed with folkloristic, nostalgic references to the historic *Popolo Lombardo* (Lombard people). After exploring the first designs of Lombardness, I will argue that the shape of the identity that emerged was a not so much a product of pre-existing cultural characteristics of Northerners, but reflected identity constructions that resonated with the current political debate.

At the same time, like all nationalist constructions, League identity work was also a means to provide individuals with self-respect, in particular by ridding Northerners of a much disliked Italian national identity. This is one

Figure 7.1 (opposite) Flow charts: material interest and the appeal of the League

Source: This flow chart 'circular models of cash flow' appeared repeatedly in copies of the newspaper *Lombardia Autonomista* between 1985 and 1989.

Note: Translations:
Fig. 1: Circular model of the flow of cash
Fig. 2: Circular model of the balance of income and expenditure
Fig. 3: Balance of resources produced and resources consumed
Lombardia = Lombardy, transferimento di risorse = resource transfer, verso = towards, Stato = the state, circa # miliardi = around # billions of lire, cessione di risorse = return flow of resources, entrate = income, uscite = expenditure, Sud = South, risorse prodotte = resources produced, risorse consumate = resources consumed.

Tutte le cifre della rapina di Roma

Schiavitù lombarda

La problema economico che vede la Lombardia come la Regione piu importante, per Roma, dal punto di vista del gettito fiscale è centrale al fine della nostra lotta per la libertà. Lo Stato centralista teme soprattutto che i Lombardi spezzino questo legame di stampo coloniale conquistando la libertà

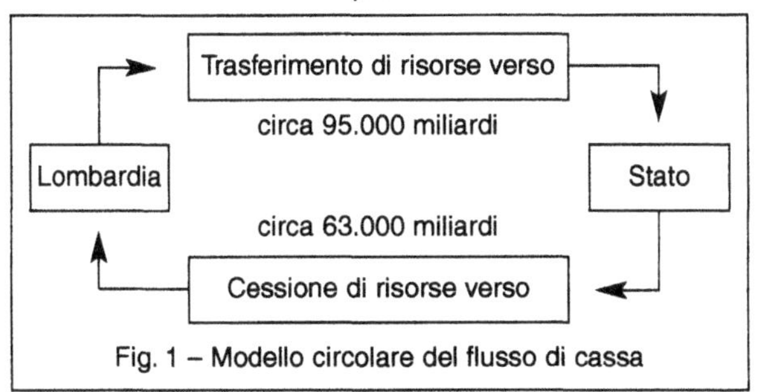

Fig. 1 – Modello circolare del flusso di cassa

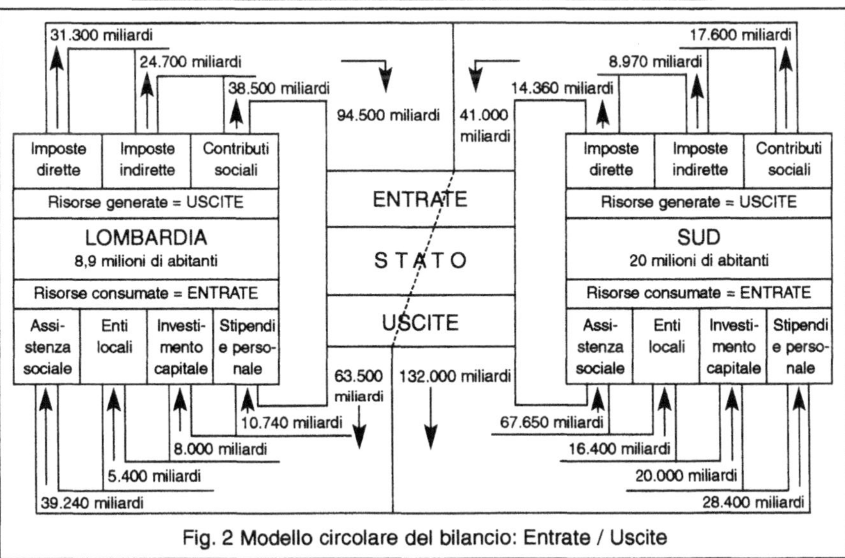

Fig. 2 Modello circolare del bilancio: Entrate / Uscite

Figura 3 – Bilancio risorse prodotte/risorse consumate

Sprechi e mangeria ci salva solo l'autonomia

of the deeply personal aspects of League involvement, underlined in several speeches in League congresses. Signor Mainini, an emigrant returned from London, made a speech in the first congress of the Northern League in which he described his experiences abroad, saying 'I don't accept that abroad they treat us all as *Mafiosi*'. The Mayor of Chiavari claimed in his speech to the 1994 Genova conference of the Northern League that he joined so that he did not 'have to feel ashamed of being Italian when abroad'. The redefinition of identity clearly provides important symbolic and emotional goods, as well as serving mobilisation and interest redefinition.

Figure 7.2 Cartoon: the Lombard hen lays

Source: This figure appeared repeatedly on the pages of the newspaper *Lombardia Autonomista* after 1982. It was also used on handbills and posters during campaigns

Note: Translation: 'Shut up and pay, Lombard Ass. The Lombard hen lays golden eggs for Rome and below. They all get fried and never come back! And you Lombards just get accused of racism.'

Identity work: a lesson in League art

League logic – the communication of common interests – is therefore simple enough. The point was to encourage Lombards and Northerners to perceive of their interests as separate from those of other Italians and served by independence. But how are we to make sense of the long articles on medieval Lombard history in the Lombard League's newspaper, the poems printed in dialect, and the repeated reference to the roots of the 'Lombard people'? How do we interpret Northern League supporters' sense of cultural incompatibility with Southerners, their sense of their work ethic and honesty, opposed to the 'Southern mentality'? The short answer is that identity and interest go hand in hand, and that this interplay was at the centre of the League's nationalism.

The identity constructions of the League are similar to those isolated by Anthony Smith (1971; 1979; 1981; 1991a; 1991b) as general features of nationalism. Language, history, culture, historical myth, and descent/race were some of the themes with which the Lombard League and later the Northern League attempted to differentiate Lombards from the population of Southern Italy, within the master opposition of Europe versus Africa, and First versus Third World. The degree to which each theme was stressed varied depending on context and opportunities.

The discourse of the Lombard separatists during the 1980s, I wish to reveal, involved the constitution of an identity not cynically invented, as was suggested at the time, but negotiated between the movement and its public. The identity work was always closely linked to the political context in which the movement moved, the material interests of Lombardy's residents, and the pressing political problems of the day. In the 1980s, the 'essence' of *Lombardità* was under negotiation. The search was on for ways of marking out the specificity of Lombardness.

What emerged from this surge of creativity that was the construction of *Lombardità*? I will present an analysis of the principal themes, and show how they are related to the exigencies of the League's mobilisation. In particular I will show how what may be described as 'primordial' or 'irrational' elements are interrelated with the goal-oriented elements. Then I will address the question of the legacy of the League's mobilisation of Lombardness, and Northernness. References to language, 'race', 'shared history', high culture and everyday culture are classically nationalist tools for symbolising boundaries, and the League leadership made attempts to gain support on the basis of all these themes. The following is based on an analysis of ten years (1982–92) of League newspapers, interviews with militants from 1993, and newspaper coverage of League demonstrations and meetings. There was a good deal of continuity between the identity constructs of the Lombard League and those of the Northern League, so I will not make a distinction except where (as in the case of the dialect, for instance) there was a clear break.

The question of movement identity remained of primary importance throughout the campaign years. Two months after the 1994 formation of the government, when League Interior Minister Maroni suggested merging the party with Berlusconi's Forza Italia, Bossi admonished him for compromising the identity of the League: 'There is the League which represents the small interests, the small and medium sized enterprises, the people who work. We will pay if we don't stick with our identity, we will leave it in the hands of the private monopolists.'[14]

Miglio, in turn argued that Bossi had betrayed the identity of the League:

> Bossi tried to extend the movement to the regions of the Centre and the South. I had to tell them the costs of such a strategy, and tell them that the League counted because it was a phenomenon of the North: that we would change Italy only by staying to the North of the Gothic Line.
>
> (Miglio 1994: 48)

The stereotypes of Southerners that I mentioned earlier had been one crucial League resource in the creation of that identity. Stereotypes alone, or a sense of cultural difference, do not however automatically result in the construction of collective identity, but they can be used to construct a politically consequential collective identity in certain contexts and under certain conditions.[15] This is what occurred in the mobilisations of the Lombard League during the 1980s. Here I will sketch in broad strokes the boundaries of League identity.

Race 1: Northerners as Celts?

In Italy, more than in other Western European nation-states, there is a diffuse conception that there are phenotypic differences between the populations of the various regions: that there is a difference of descent between regions, and particularly between North and South. Lively, if confused, conceptions of the various so-called 'ethnies' (the Celts, Etruscans, Venetians, Romans and so on) that inhabited the peninsula in pre-modern times lurk behind many stereotypes. In the early 1990s, a distinguished Turin professor of biology was conducting DNA experiments in villages near Siena, Tuscany, to prove the thesis that the inhabitants were descendants of Etruscans. The fact that this drew more media attention from abroad than within Italy reflects the normality of such a proposition in Italy, where movements of population were small before the recent period of industrialisation. In Italy, leaving aside South–North migration, industrialisation has not resulted in internal homogenisation on the scale that it has done elsewhere.

Although race or descent was sometimes used as a marker of difference by the League, it was never the central theme of League propaganda. Propaganda did, particularly during the formation of the Northern League and again after 1995, attempt to specify the particularity of Northern Italy in its Celtic inheritance. Although some references appear to be based on a notion of biological race, most in this category seem to refer to cultural difference between North and South. In speeches and articles in the League newspaper, Lombard dialects and place names were said to have Gaelic roots, which signal the existence of a '*sostrato celtico*' (Celtic substratum).[16] Elsewhere, the construction of Lombard history could only have been said to have meaning to Lombards (as 'our' history) through an idea that today's Lombards are the descendants of those of the twelfth century, and for some, of the sixth-century *Longobardi*.

Given that Celtic identity promotes and attempts to naturalise a boundary between the entire North and the South, this convention can be seen as politically convenient given the timing: it came at the time of the founding of the Northern League, when the movement had to begin to surpass previous constructions of Piedmont, Veneto and Lombardy as separate regions, and stress what the North had in common. Further, the Celtic argument fitted perfectly with the Northern League's slogan, 'Più lontano da Roma, più vicino all'Europa' (Further from Rome, closer to Europe). The Roman–Celt opposition is familiar to any reader of Asterix.[17] The fact that at the first congress of the Northern League the leaders felt it necessary to have a detailed speech on ethno-cultural affinities between the peoples of Northern Italy reveals the importance of such constructs at this time.

Point four of the 1983 political programme of the League says that applications for public-sector jobs should be made 'on an ethnic-regional basis'. Deliberately vague, the programme does not say directly that Southern Italians and immigrants should have no right to work in Lombardy, but it is implied. There is a continuity between the anti-Southern stance, which characterised the early years of the mobilisation, and the criticism of Third World immigration that predominated after the formation of the Northern League in 1989.

In League cartoons and propaganda, the stereotyped 'Southerner' always has dark skin, and invariably long black curly hair. Whether it is possible to detect racial stereotyping in this depends on interpretation. The League quickly, however, became notorious as an anti-Southern, racist movement.

Race 2: 'Extracomunitaria' immigration

The Lombard League was also known for a different type of racial construction, however. It has long been accused of racism towards immigrants from outside Europe. The construction of this boundary also came about at the time of the foundation of the Northern League, and the planned national expansion of the League, and might be interpreted as an attempt to widen the ethnic identity of the League accordingly, or at least distract attention from the previous focus on Lombardness.

Immigration only became a central point in League propaganda when the issue became central in Italian public debate with the Martelli Law discussions in 1990. Immigration controls had, however, been on the statutes of the Lombard League since 1983. A speech approved by the Northern League in 1990 called for the vaccination of immigrants 'to the same level as Italians'. This could be seen as a call for equal health care, but seemed also a deliberate incitement of fear of 'disease-ridden' immigrants.[18] The speaker saw the solution as repatriation for those who were not *in regola* (up to legal standard). The same logic was invoked in 1993, when League MP Mario Borghezio made an 'urgent request' to Parliament that Third World immigrants have a 'health passport' issued on entering Italy, after cases of leprosy were reported among recent immigrants.[19]

Whereas there is no doubt that among League supporters there have been many motivated by racism, Bossi himself has long defended himself against claims from what he calls the 'regime press' that he is racist. He calls repeatedly for the movement of capital instead of labour, and says that immigration leads to social chaos, as well as putting pressure on weak social services (Bossi and Vimercati 1992: 144–50). Here he draws on popular memory of treatment of Italians as they sought work abroad. He does not criticise such treatment, however, seeing it as inevitable. The League repeatedly exaggerated numbers, referring to 'millions' of illegal immigrants entering Italy. The intensity of anti-immigration sentiment varied over time, and according to the political opportunities faced by the movement. And the populist slogans of the League were deliberately ambivalent. The questions 'What is the League?' and 'Is the League racist?' are thus very difficult to answer.[20] The slogans were indeed racist when in the hands of racists, but could be defended by the more politically sophisticated leaders of the League who referred to rights to culture and difference.

Race was a convenient tool as a boundary marker for the League, in the sense that existing conceptions of racial difference were close to hand; in the sense that it could be used to convene groups on a Lombard, Northern, or Italian level; and in the sense that it was a tool-of-convenience, disposed of when no longer useful. It provided a sense of pride and distinction, within a racist value system based on ideas of ethnic purity; it encouraged the use of local and kinship networks, and provided the sense of timeless identity that is so crucial for collective action. Costantini (1993) reports that at certain times during the campaign, League activists would target their actions by choosing particularly Lombard surnames, such as Brambilla, from telephone directories. At the level of movement legitimisation, however, as reported in public discussions in the Italian media, the race constructions served increasingly to discredit the League. As the League attempted to broaden its appeal after 1990, and take more votes also from the left, the boundaries of race therefore became inconvenient for them. Racist stereotyping became less prominent in the propaganda until after 1999, when it became much more prevalent.

Culture and religion: neo-Weberian Leghisti: the work ethic and Lombards as Calvinists

Whereas other nationalists can often draw on a wealth of cultural identifiers, habits, and ways of life, and inflate them into 'national' characteristics, the League had a relatively thin habitus to draw upon.[21] Dialect, and the work ethic were the main reference points, but even Lombard cuisine, especially polenta (claggy cornmeal porridge) was taken up as an aspect of Northern pride.[22]

I have mentioned the general notion in League propaganda that Lombards have a strong work ethic. This was linked to the story about the economic divide between Northern and Southern Italy. Where some had explained the increasingly apparent North–South economic divide in terms of a Marxian notion of uneven development, and others had blamed the climate, the League said the difference was due to Southerners' lack of a work ethic (Bossi and Vimercati 1992: 174), and in extreme cases extended this to an argument about religion.[23] Bossi claims to have read Weber, and there is a distinct echo of his *Protestant Work Ethic* in the League's reasoning concerning the comparative success of capitalism in the North and South of Italy (Vimercati 1990: 7). In various articles, attempts were made to sell the idea of a Calvinist tradition in the North of Italy and Lombardy, in contrast to the backward Catholicism of the South and Rome. Granted, this reasoning never formed a central pillar of the movement (Catholic sections were later incorporated), but it had a place. A two-page article in *Lombarda Autonomista* in July 1990 made the argument that political federalism was incompatible with Catholic centralism, and that Catholicism was the root of corruption problems in Italy. In 1993, then League intellectual Gianfranco Miglio explored the boundaries of credibility in describing contemporary political changes in Italy as a 'Calvinist' revolution, and referring to Calvinism as a tradition of North Italy.[24]

The League's valorisation of honesty as a criterion of purity, and the identification of criminality with the South, played upon existing conceptions of the South as the centre of organised crime, but deepened this into a claim that the Northern 'peoples' are free of the criminal nature that Southerners have. This cluster of themes was played out in the course of the long League campaign against the *soggiorno obbligato* (forced removal of Mafiosi to the North), and against organised crime and corruption more generally, which it dismissed as a Southern problem. The theme of criminality was particularly prominent in the early years of the campaign, but became less so when the League had some success in restricting the practice, and when the Lombard capital Milan emerged as *Tangentopoli* (Backhander City) the centre of political corruption in 1992. It received wide support with a Lombard public who were tired of foreigners seeing organised crime as typically Italian, and for whom it was a distant phenomenon. An extension of this idea of a distinctive Northern habitus was clear in the media debate surrounding the publication of Robert Putnam's (1993) book on civic traditions in Italy. The book's central hypothesis was close to the League's line: the divergent histories of North and South Italy had resulted in clearly different civic traditions, the South's a pale shadow of the North's.

Summary

What are the links between these identity themes and the making of a political movement? As a criterion of purity, the work ethic certainly provides individual approbation, as does the idea of Lombard honesty.[25] These attributes have a feasibility provided by the undeniable reality of an economic divide between North and South, for which cultural reductionism is a simple and accessible explanation. The idea that Northerners work harder is very widespread, especially among League supporters, and is a longstanding (and therefore conveniently close to hand) stereotype, long predating the movement itself (Gramsci 1971). At the *organisational* level, such habitus-type references do not provide the strong and uncrossable boundaries necessary for collective identity-formation.[26] By acquiring the cultural attributes members can presumably 'become' Northern or Lombard. This is precisely why many felt that habitus attributes had to be combined with others such as race or history, to provide the cultural differences with the social naturalism of a given boundary. Public debate of the habitus of the North offered some *legitimisation* for the claims of the Lombards that their culture was incompatible with rule by a 'Southern' mentality.

A disposable tradition: the 'Lombard dialect'

A mass rally of the Lombard League in 1989 was closed with a song in dialect. Bossi (a dialect poet himself), appeared to weep as he led the singers.[27] League supporters had for the past few years been rallying to the defence of their dialects, and getting a great deal of publicity as a result. Young *Leghisti* defaced road signs to render place-names in dialect, leaders made speeches in local government in dialect, and called for teachers to use the idiom in schools.[28] The front page of *Lombardia Autonomista* was, as late as 1989, emblazoned with the scare-mongering headline *'Senza Dialetto Non Piu Radici'* (Without dialect, no more roots). The subtitle read 'the state language is a conventional instrument of communication between different peoples. The regional language is the cultural expression of a people, indispensable and unsubstitutable for a complete relationship between man and society.' This was the standard line, not only of the Lombards, but also of the Venetian League. Through using dialect as a medium of mobilisation, the Leagues had discovered, like many movements before them, that direct, vernacular communication could hit potential supporters like a splash of cold water in the face.

Two years after his emotional dialect performance however, Umberto Bossi made a commentary at the congress of the Lombard League which he called 'The Impossibility of Obtaining the Autonomy of Lombardy on the Basis of Being a Linguistic Minority'.[29] In the speech he compared the Lombards to South Tyrol and Val d'Aosta where the linguistic minorities were aided by foreign governments, arguing that since Lombardy had no such allies, the campaign for autonomy for Lombards as a linguistic minority should be abandoned. After this speech, there were very few headlines in the League's propaganda in dialect, and no more official League calls for defence of the dialect. A few supporters continued to graffiti place-names in dialect on road signs, but, until the return to folklore, culture and secession after 1995, did so without Bossi's blessing.

Why the change? The political value of dialect to the League had declined sharply, and it had in fact begun to become a liability, attracting more ridicule than sympathy. Further, given that the linguistic argument was mainly directed at gaining legitimacy for the Lombard case abroad, through claiming 'oppressed minority' status, the abandonment of the dialect reflects loss of hope in that strategy. Clearly, and quite openly, the dialect mobilisation was used because of its results for the mobilisation of the League as a social movement. In this case it was ostensibly for external legitimisation purposes, but surely also (given that this coincided with the foundation of the Northern League) in order to extend the appeal of the League.

In construction of territorial identity, competence in a chosen language is often a condition for membership, those who are incompetent being excluded. In a classically nationalist pattern, a peripheral language may have been ridiculed as backward by metropolitans, it will have been banned from a state-led educational system and defined as a relic. Nationalist language mobilisations are a way of re-describing this stigma as a source of pride. Approbation of skills in such a language is thus a focus of the nationalist discourse, and poets and singers feature loudly in this exercise.[30]

The use of language as a way of constructing a Lombard identity was in fact problematic from the start, basically because it is difficult to identify something that we can call a unique Lombard dialect.[31] The dialect of Milan differed from that of Varese, and Varese from Bergamo. There was certainly no unified grammar, and no apparent desire for one. The problems were summed up in a critical article in *Il Giornale Nuovo* in 1989, when the League was still involved in the politics of their language.[32] Commenting on the publicity for the Lombard League National Congress, the article ridicules the League's use of dialect. In some publicity the meeting was called the '*Congress Nassjonal*', and the article questions the spelling. Indeed there seemed to be no agreement on spelling of dialect. Examples of inconsistencies, and public ridicule of them, abound. Even 'Lombard' was rendered in a variety of ways: Lombardo (standard Italian), Lümbard (with or without umlaut), Lombard, and so on.[33] A unified Lombard dialect simply did not exist. Dialects in Italy tend to vary from city to city or valley to valley, rather than between regions, and are fundamentally dialects rather than languages. Therefore their utility as foundations in the construction of group identity in Lombardy (as boundary markers) was limited, and the movement in fact lost credibility through mobilising in the defence of language. Reference to the dialect has, since Bossi's 1990 speech, been largely symbolic. Bossi is 'il Senatür', his followers 'i Lumbard'.

To summarise, the League had attempted to use the dialect to separate *terroni* from *polentoni,* and at the same time give pride and voice to a section of the population which had long been excluded by the pompous language of the political élite. In the early years, this met with some success. Hearing politicians using local vernaculars aroused the interest of those previously excluded from politics, and dialect networks provided organisational resources for the movement. Because of the dialect's closeness to Italian, however, and its lack of external patronage states (in contrast to the German-speaking community in Tyrol, for example), and the lack of a unified grammar, the linguistic boundary was not effective in legitimising the claims of the movement as an 'oppressed nationality'. As a result of this, and as a result of the changing opportunities open to the League, the dialect was unceremoniously dropped from movement propaganda. This occurred at the point when media coverage, rather than direct address of audiences, became more important to the movement. It thus proved much less sacred than language had done for other self-proclaimed ethno-nationalists. This episode also reveals the continually reconstructed nature of the Lombard identity. The collective identity of the group and the project and goals of the movement are clearly interrelated and balanced. It may have previously appeared to League members that the dialect was an end in itself, but as the context changed it became a means to the end of the vague, undefined goal of autonomy.

It seems that the dialect was a convenience tradition, to be disposed of when it no longer served political mobilisation, and perhaps re-appropriated when it would tie in a few more militants or voters. Is nothing indispensable in the mobilisation? Some incidents, such as the attempt by Bossi to change the name of the movement to Lega Italia – which met with uproar from the grassroots of the movement – give an indication of the limits of strategic use of identity. By the time of the 1993 Pontida rally, the League had adopted a new 'national anthem' to replace the older one. It was in Italian rather than dialect, and less romantic about the landscape of the Lombard or Northern 'nations', focusing instead on the political struggle. The League itself became the main referent, not the territory.[34]

History and the League

History, for the League, was a wardrobe to be plundered for whatever symbols split Italy in the convenient way and achieved the appropriate resonance with the public. The League's was a post-modern history: there were no authorities to refer to, neither references nor footnotes, only haphazard constructions of whatever story fitted the desires and the political opportunities of the day.

Perhaps the best-known myth in the service of the construction of Lombard identity was that of the medieval Lombard League. This provided the name of the Lombard League, and its symbol, a picture of Alberto da Giussano, the hero of the Battle of Legnano. This was fought in 1176 in the name of the original Lombard League when twenty Northern Italian cities united to repel invasions. This historical episode, perfectly genuine by all accounts, was selected and inflated by League propagandists into a claim of a Lombard tradition of resistance to centralising foreign imperialism. This 'tradition' began to be celebrated in the 1980s on the '29 de Masg, Festa Nazional del Popul Lümbard' (dialect for '29 May, National Fete of the Lombard People').[35] These meetings, and the mass meetings at Pontida, built upon such symbolism.[36]

The effect of the League's historical construction was a classically nationalist one of naturalising a political identity by rooting it in the distant past. As one League intellectual described it: 'Bossi rummaged in his cultural history and found the right "myth": the League of twenty cities that allied in the twelfth century to hunt the emperor Federico Barbarossa, the symbol of state centralism' (Vimercati 1990: 8). Ironically, the historical battle and its hero were already well known to Italians. In a classic example of anachronistic historiography, Alberto da Giussano had long had a place in schoolbooks as a hero of the *Italian*, and not the Lombard, nation.

The construction of Lombard history was not limited to party propaganda, however. Medieval symbolism was taken up with enthusiasm in the chants, songs, dress and general symbolic repertoires of party activists.[37] In congresses of the Lombard League, replicas of the statue of the sword-wielding Alberto were omnipresent, and there were invariably some young *Leghisti* posing for photographers wearing chain mail. Moreover, the publication of various new histories of Lombardy must be connected to this politicisation of Lombardness. Perhaps the first such book to appear was the flimsy, home-made looking *Da Ambrogio a Bossi. Lotte per la libertá nella Padania.* A self-financed publication, the book links the popular acclamation of Ambrogio as Bishop of Milan (AD 374), the Battle of Legnano (1176), the free commune of Milan (1447–50), and Bossi's League (1983–), in 120 pages. According to the cover notes these are 'a series of events that have had a single common denominator: the search for freedom and autonomy from central power'. Whereas it is easy to be ironic about such a volume (which was, however, to be seen in display cases in most offices of the Northern League, and sold at League fairs and so on), several more 'serious' histories, such as Gianni Brera's *Storia dei Lombardi* (History of the Lombards) (Brera 1993), were published.[38] Such books are unlikely to have appeared in this period purely by chance. The market for history is highly politically responsive, as any student of nationalism knows.

Another development of Lombard/Northern historical consciousness crucial to the League was the contrast of Austro-Hungarian rule in the North with Bourbonic, or Papal rule in the South. In a projection of current stereotypes into the past, the fact of being ruled for so long from Austria counted in favour of Lombard efficiency and rationality. It is worth noting in passing the anachronism of this view. One of those responsible for administrating Lombardy for the Habsburgs claimed that 'the Lombards have not been able, cannot, and will never be able to get used to the Germanic forms imposed by the administration' (Stanoldo, quoted in Wolf 1973: 253). In general the concern with history, and the claim to status as a 'historical nation', was even more important for the Lombard League's partners, the Venetian League. The Societá Filologica Veneta (a historical and cultural club) was one of the Venetian leader Rocchetta's central concerns in the 1970s and 1980s. Rocchetta put together a book tracing the historical civilisation of the Venetian economy, law, state and people (Rocchetta 1992).

The medieval glories of Lombardy were often the subject of long feature articles in the campaign newsletter *Lombardia Autonomista* that sought to revive interest and pride in 800-year-old triumphs, opposing the imperialism of Barbarossa to the independence of the city republics. This mode of historical representation was convenient to select not because it was part of an existing historical memory, but for reasons connected with the problems of the nation-state of the 1980s and the strategic needs of the political movement. The League was not, after all, alone in identifying the civic culture deficit in the South with its lack of a history of independent communes (Putnam 1993).

As a myth of convenience, the medieval Lombard League served the protest well: it was flexible, since it was possible to present it as a move against state centralisation (Barbarossa's imperial armies) and for free federalism. Thus it fits with the criticism of Roman centralism and state inefficiency and corruption. It provided Lombards with pride in their collective self, as successful warriors and leaders. Further, it included precisely the correct population. The original League was an alliance between twenty Northern cities. Thus, although in the 1980s the Lombard League could be a myth for the Lombards alone (the medieval League was led by Lombardy), the transition to the Northern League (another 'alliance for freedom' according to the League) could use the same mythology and symbolism without contradiction.[39]

Indeed, the responsiveness of League historiography to the changing opportunities and strategies of the League is striking. Apart from the shift of stress on inter-city cooperation in references to the medieval Lombard League (rather than stress on Lombardy) after 1989, there was more free play in the propaganda with historical/geographic references that fitted with the North–South divide. The *Linea Gothica*, *Padana*, even the *Repubblica Cisalpina*, became ways that the League sought to legitimise their separatist claims, and lend their identity a semblance of permanence; with the Italian media at its service the League was able to do this.[40] The praises of Carlo Cattaneo, the as-yet-unsung Lombard federalist hero of the *Risorgimento* were sung, and the 'Celtic substratum' of the Northern peoples was excavated and celebrated. Any pronoun referring to the territory was a potential resource, and the League confronted a broad range of recorded history and selected the convenient episodes.

So why did this historical narrative serve the mobilisation of the League? At the level of activist motivation, a historical reference in a political speech usually has one simple aim: to touch every member of the audience, filling them with righteous anger at past injustices, and making them feel a collective shiver at the thought that they themselves can make history. Anyone at the Pontida meetings, or the congress of the League, has witnessed this atmosphere. Historical reference is of course a tactic used by countless political movements, not only nationalistic ones. The advantage of nationalist history in mobilising action is that it is a direct answer to the central problem of collective action: how to exclude free-riders and make individual contributions to collective action rational (Pizzorno 1986). By rooting identities in the timeless past, history makes it easier for potential movement members to project them into the future. History renders it easier to justify sacrifices in the present by describing it as a contribution to a greater collective good in the future. Without the permanence affected by history, the burden on faith and Utopia is greater.

The invocation of history did more than spur individuals to support the League, however. It also helped organise them. The historical discourse of the Lombard League sought to undermine the idea that the national state was the natural and inevitable form of organisation, and replace it with the idea that a Lombard, or Northern, state was. Further, on a concrete level, many of the organisations that became involved in the League (the Movimento per la Toscana, for example) had been organisations of historical enthusiasts. Like the dialect networks, these were a key organisational resource for the movement.

It is unlikely that the League's reconstruction of Lombard history was successful in gaining the League a great deal of international legitimacy. This is due to the fact that the 'national' claim as a whole was rejected by the majority in Italy and ridiculed by nearly all those in influential positions. The fact that historical constructions of Lombardness did not become generalised and define a new historical actor, however, does not mean that this historical identity work was ineffective. Such discourses can nonetheless undermine existing national identities.

Homo Padanus

All political propaganda is involved in a search for solid, indisputable foundations of meaning which are generally accepted, and can therefore be used as the basis for a call to action. In some periods these have been provided by the authority of 'science' (such as the nineteenth century discourse on race), and in other periods by reference to religious tenets. The League tended to base its calls for action on the social naturalism or primordialist cultural determinism that was a widespread reference in the North of Italy. Like other cases of nationalism (Yack 1996), the League shows the interrelatedness of civic and ethnic views of cultural difference.

Given the mixed success of dialect, history and race in the service of the League, one might be forgiven for arguing that there was nothing like a pre-existing Lombard or Northern 'ethnicity' or identity that was activated by the campaign. This would of course fall into precisely the trap of essentialism that we have criticised, and miss the point. For analytical purposes whether an 'ethnie' 'exists' or not is beside the point: the question is how the claim of its existence should be related to a given political-historical context. It would of course be difficult to deny that an existing sense of difference (one acknowledged on both sides of the boundary) was heightened and politicised in the campaign. This was the general sense that there was a different attitude to life, a different mentality between North and South, and that these mentalities had different implications for the running of the state, which formed a justification for secession.

When Miglio and Rocchetta protested in 1993 against Southerners entering the Alpine regiments of the Italian army, they justified this with the claim that Southerners have a 'different mentality'.[41] The Alps, wrote Miglio, are the habitat of a particular way of living and thinking, which is reproduced in the traditions of the troops. An ex-commander of the feather-hatted regiment disagreed, saying that training the troops in the mountains was enough to make them Alpine. Here, in synthesis, is the League's 'ethnic' position on cultural difference opposed to a 'civic' one. For Miglio, as for many in the movement, cultural differences are natural, embedded in a local habitus, and can only be spoiled by migrations, and individual choices. For Federici, the ex-commander, however, individuals can choose to belong to another group. Even Neapolitans can learn to be mountain men. The difference is in the degree of social naturalism.[42] In the analysis, Miglio represents the argument that cultural differences are given and unchangeable, making separatism inevitable. During his time with the League, Miglio remained close to this line of argument, and eventually left the League rather than compromise when others such as Bossi toyed with the idea of a national League. Rocchetta, who sided with Miglio on the Alpine troops issue, preferred to stay with the League until he was ousted in August 1994.

Bossi was not involved in the debate over the Alpine troops. His position seems to be more 'civic' and less 'ethnic' than were those of Rocchetta and Miglio. In Piedmont in 1990 to address a meeting of League supporters, he was asked how meetings there compared to those in Lombardy. He replied: 'In Lombardy the militants know Carlo Cattaneo by heart. Or they know all of Gioberti. A cultural humus has been created. That doesn't yet exist here.'[43] Part of Bossi's project was thus the construction of a world-view. The world-view he sought to create was not, however, a folkloric revival in the classic nationalist sense, but from the outset the construction of a political consciousness. Thus the League's cultural discourse was Janus-faced: relying on a backward-looking social naturalism while at the same time constructing a future-oriented ideology.

In the 1980s, cultural *Lombardità* was probably seen as an inherited, primordial essence by few, even among League activists. Allegiance to the Lombard flag was a choice, like allegiance to any new political movement. The trick of the ethno-nationalist political formula, however, was to naturalise the allegiance to the movement: to make activists think that the constructed political identity – Lombardness – was in fact timeless and beyond politics. Such a formula generates fierce loyalty. A sense of likeness and of a project, which emerged from under League banners in the 1980s, had been profoundly felt by supporters. The central ideas of this are the same as those hyped by the League: work ethic, honesty and moralistic nostalgia for small-scale communities. As is normal in nationalism, the in-group finds it easier to agree on what they are not than what they are. The South was their enemy, and became the opposition that embodied all political problems and therefore defined the solution to them as autonomy.

It is very hard to imagine the Northern League without the crucial referents of work ethic, honesty, and autonomy and self-reliance, although we can imagine a Northern League without a dialect, or without a local history. These seem indeed to have been excluded from the choices of individuals by the new political self-consciousness of identity generated by the League.

Table 7.1 presents a summary of the key oppositions that made the symbolic boundaries to League identity, and at the same time the central values and goals promoted by the movement.

Conclusions: convenient culture and the uses of nationalism

Thus many of the central themes and boundaries of Lombardness and Northernness were *convenient*, in the senses that they convened people within certain symbolic boundaries, and that they were taken up and dropped as suited the moment. They were also convenient in the sense that the League leadership used whatever symbols were already close to hand – such as well-known historical episodes and cultural stereotypes – to mark the politically useful boundary.

Further, what was held up by the League as the essence of a 'natural' Lombard identity was closely related to the policy problems that the movement claimed to confront. Lombardy and Padania became, in a sense, the exact opposite of the problems of the South, or the Italian state. Since the agreed problems were corruption and inefficiency, the 1980s and 1990s politicisation of Lombardy and Padania's identity was defined in opposition to those. The intense reconstruction of Northern Italians as hard-working, honest, efficient and affluent is linked to the identification of the

Table 7.1 Constructing Padania, constructing Lombardy: repeated oppositions in League discourse

Lombardy/the North	*The South/Rome*
Rich	Poor
Rational	Irrational
Modern	Backward
Mitteleuropa	Africa
Austro-Hungary	Papal States
Germanic	African
Honest	Corrupt
Simple language/dialect	Elaborate Italian politicianese
Polenta	Pasta
The Lombard League of the eleventh century	Arab/papal occupation
First World	Third World
Efficient	Inefficient
Very hard working	Lazy
Independent, autonomist	Assistentialista (dependent on welfare)
Federalist	Centralist
Entrepreneurs	Farmers, bureaucrats
The Milan Judges of the Clean Hands operation	The Mafia, Camorra and N'drangheta
Clean	Dirty

problems of the 'Roman' state as laziness and inefficiency. These identity markers were certainly not the expression of pre-existing 'mythomoteur' in Anthony Smith's terms. If the problems of the Roman state had been others – for example the over-rationalisation of state bureaucracy – the movement for independence (and the heightening sense of collective identity that it involves), might have been entirely different. Lombards may have stressed rural or artistic values, or mystic spirituality, as did romantic peripheral nationalisms.

Did Padania make the League, or vice versa? Does cultural difference make nationalism or the other way around? Do actors make cultural differences, or do their actions simply result from their cultural embeddedness? This is the question behind the problem of self-determination: it is justified where nationalism is *not* a tool. But such questions are very difficult to answer in general terms. Clearly, however, one can begin to understand the dynamic of cultural nationalism by focusing on the relationship of identity discourse to political action in context, the subject to which I now turn.

The wallet factor, the ethnic factor and the freedom factor

The identity discourse was launched as part of a campaign of political mobilisation, and it can only be understood in this context. Alessandro

Patelli, who has been involved in the League campaigns since 1987, and responsible for them as party manager since 1989, said that the League appeal for support worked on three fronts, 'the wallet factor, the ethnic factor and the freedom factor'. He was repeating a formula used by Bossi to describe the overall communications strategy of the League.

The use of this national-separatist strategy by the League had both benefits and limitations as a structuring discourse in the development of movement identity. It enabled the mobilisation of individuals from a variety of sectors and backgrounds, spurring and enticing them into action. At the same time it eventually limited the scope of the action, scuppering attempts by the leadership to develop the League into a nation-wide political movement. Bossi himself often shifted his justifications of identity discourse. He clearly learned of its mobilisation value from the experience of the Venetian League. Asked about the articles in the early League newspapers about Lombard culture and dialect, he replied:

> So all the world that was around us was based on the language, on the dialect. It was the ethnic idea. And the Venetian League was doing so well at that stage. Just like in Union Valdoitaine, you base everything on the language, to try to get the status of the autonomous regions.
>
> (Tambini 1998b)[44]

So how did nationalist discourse help, hinder and generally structure the development of the movement? We are now in a position to overview the points raised earlier in relation to individual motivations, organisation structure, and legitimisation.

1 *Individual motivations.* By appealing to an already latent sense of identity, and by claiming definitions of certain attributes of territorial identity, the League's call to action had a head start on movements that had to start from zero and use arguments of rational intention to inspire support. The appeal worked in various ways. The League clearly presented 'wallet', the economic self-interest Northerners had in supporting fiscal autonomy. Taxes could be lower, they said, and services improved, if the drain of Southern welfare was plugged. At a more emotional level, it rendered the problems of the state attackable, partly because it 'anthropomorphised the enemy'.[45] Previously, corruption and inefficiency had been protected by their invisibility and pervasiveness, and a sense of partial responsibility of Northern citizens. By breaking the identification of the Italian nation with the Italian state, the League

'ethnic' identity work offered Northerners absolution from the guilt implied in the Italian saying that 'Every people gets the political class it deserves'. It released potential militants from their usual fatalistic responses. It seems that the pride released by the approbation of Northern against Italian identity was a crucial factor in mobilising militants.

2 *Organisation.* The strong sense of cultural/territorial identity consolidated the movement, and rendered consistent its spokespeople. The nationalistic mythology also kept the ranks of the League firm and tightly aligned behind Bossi. At crucial points in the history of the League it was demonstrated that it was not merely the centralised control in the hands of the leader Bossi that kept the league from splitting. What kept the varied ideologies within the League from bursting out into factions was its – near paranoid – enemy mythology. A 'they are out to get us' mentality prevailed among League activists. 'They' the enemy in this case were the parties, the Mafia, big business, the media, linked together in behind-closed-doors bargaining: the 'octopus' of occult power. According to Diamanti this paranoia was confirmed in the everyday lives of League activists: 'In their workplaces, in their social relations they received bitter criticism . . . threats, anonymous letters' (Diamanti 1992: 237). This process of social stigmatisation, however, only made them consolidate their commitment to the movement. This siege mentality, rooted in the nationalist Manichaean world-view, permitted organisational moves that would otherwise have been impossible. The barriers to full membership 'to prevent infiltration' and the lack of internal democracy were crucial to the League's unity, and clearly tied to this 'us–them' stance.

The nationalist stance also enabled campaign tactics that might otherwise have been impossible. Broadly, it enabled a wholesale rejection of the existing political system, a set of institutions utterly discredited during the period of League growth. Further, it permitted such tactics as the threats of civil disobedience to have some legitimacy as part of a struggle for freedom. Miglio and Bossi's 1992–3 mutterings about 'arming the North' and setting up a Parliament of the North and the constant threats of a tax strike were examples: it may be true that these threats were never likely to be carried out, but they were effective in forcing change and arguably in attracting votes, since they brought publicity. As an anti-national force the League could make such generalised anti-statist statements much more easily than a political movement with an open commitment to assuming state power.

It was in the construction of movement identity, however, that the nationalist stance was most effective. The use of history, language and culture succeeded in activating a latent sense of cultural difference between Northern and Southern Italy, and lending it an instant permanence. The 'purity' of League identity has remained a crucial symbolic resource of the movement. Initially maintained in relation to the South, the collective identity was constructed along clearly nationalist lines. This had the eventual effect of preventing the expansion of the movement in the South, and caused the League problems when they eventually formed a national government. The social naturalism of the League was necessary to render the otherwise vague cultural boundaries firm and useful to the organisation.

3 *Legitimisation.* In the early years, the League clearly sought external legitimisation through claiming the status of an 'oppressed people'. They failed to get it, however, due to the unfavourable reception these claims had from leaders of opinion, who denied them that status. With Bossi's 1990 speech on the abandonment of the dialect, they abandoned their original claim for Lombard 'self-determination' as it became clear that legitimacy for that claim was not to be had, and a changing set of opportunities emerged in which that way of structuring the movement was no longer convenient (the Northern League). On another level, however, they managed to get some legitimacy by claiming to be one among many movements working for the objective of the Europe of the Regions. Apart from the legitimising effect of the EU institutions, some of which endorse that slogan, the association with other more established regional parties lent the League a more respectable aura.

4 *Nationalism and the media.* The League leadership quickly learned in fact that nationalist posturing gained more notoriety than legitimacy. As a tool of transgression, and therefore of news generation, it proved invaluable, if simply because the boundaries of the public itself are one of the deepest taboos of any national broadcasting and press system: to suggest abandonment of the national public good that forms the background assumption of all media discussion is to offend all institutions of the public sphere. If we assume that a key hurdle for any movement is to 'make news', then the League demonstrated that separatist nationalism, even when it receives little support (as the League did before 1989) will get disproportionately high coverage, which itself feeds the mobilisation. If we see that the key to nationalist mobilisation is presence in public discourse, and the constant undermining of established identities, then nationalism served the League well.

The League: cynical nationalism?

> The most appropriate myth was without doubt the League of the twenty Lombard, Emilian and Piedmontese communes, that allied, in the twelfth century, to fight Emperor Federico Barbarossa.
>
> (Bossi and Vimercati 1992: 41)

Critics have unmasked nationalism: historically pinpointing the moments in which nationalist myths and identities were fabricated, and revealing the cynicism of the nationalist, who was charged with serving individual or class interests behind this smokescreen of folklore and culture (Tambini 1998b). In the case of the League, such an exercise in debunking would be too easy. This is one reason why this account of the League has been more interested in the effects and uses of those myths than the philosophical question of their 'inventedness', or 'truth'.[46] This account has avoided putting the nationalism of the League on trial, or debunking it, opting instead to focus on how that nationalism, however contrived, serves protest. In purely explanatory terms, however, the question still needs to be addressed: was nationalism a tool used knowingly by League leaders, or did Padania use the League?

Clearly, political movements both lead and follow their supporters: no political movement, in a situation of electoral competition, is in such complete control of its followers that it can *use* identity constructions, and clearly no collective interest can be defined independently of subjective perceptions of collective identity, which can be changed at particular historical moments when previous collective identities are no longer convenient. The case of the League illustrates how identity constructions are indeed crucial to mobilising successful protest, and also that these identity constructions use existing and latent resources. It also demonstrates that such a politically-generated identity can become a sorcerer's apprentice, engendering a political dynamic uncontrollable by the leadership if it becomes a dominant means through which individuals define their interests.

According to Professor Gianfranco Miglio:

> 'Federalism' for Bossi and his lackeys was a kind of a crowbar to knock any opposition off its hinges. Many times the leader's 'colonels' would ask me whether a 'federalist revolution' was really in the interest of the movement . . . This instrumentality of the programme was clearest in the obstinate way that Bossi tried to extend the movement in the Southern and Central regions.
>
> (Miglio 1994: 48)

Miglio was not alone in observing the instrumentality of the League's federalist/separatist stance. This has been a conclusion of several academic analysts of the League such as Diamanti (1996a: 79), Rovati and others (Mannheimer 1994). The basic point is that federalism, 'ethno-nationalism', separatism and the cultural stereotyping that go with them were merely tools for organising a protest movement and for the assault on state power by the League. This was all but acknowledged by party manager Patelli himself, in his characterisation of League protest actions as consisting of 'ethnic, wallet and freedom' themes.

But nationalism has also limited the League's scope for action, as the actions of Miglio and others demonstrated. Although the chief architect of Northern autonomy, Bossi wished to play down separatist themes in the period of government; others in the movement rebelled against him, and renewed their calls for the autonomy of the North. It is obvious that for some time much of the leadership of the movement hoped for a nation-wide expansion of the League. They were unsuccessful in gaining that precisely because they were known for their ethno-regional particularism and Northist chauvinism. Further, many left the League when they felt that the separatist aims were being betrayed. The themes of separatism, therefore, are not the disposable, convenience tools that Bossi might have hoped. Miglio, after leaving the League in protest at its abandonment of federalism, put it as follows: 'if Bossi maintains his proposal, in the next Northern League congress, to eliminate the word "North" from the name "Northern League", the movement will certainly fall to pieces' (Miglio 1994: 49). A movement that is tightly centrally organised is more likely to be able to reflect upon and respond to changes in the political context quickly and advantageously. To respond will often mean to attract support from previously untapped social groups, and to quickly provide commentary on new political issues. The League was such a movement. We have already seen that it enjoyed the organisational benefits that result from a clear idea of an enemy and a common identity.

And the Northern League's adventure in national government? It lasted eight months. The League itself brought down the government by refusing to vote with its coalition partners over changes to trust laws. In retrospect, 1994 and the selection of League ministers by Bossi marked one turning point for the League, the moment in which many in the League attempted to lay to rest the nationalist-separatist system of structuring its protest. The pressures of governing, together with Bossi's tendency to put political power ahead of all previous 'principles', had finally led to a situation in which a national separatist stance, and the cultural constructions that went with it, appeared, as a whole, to be no longer convenient. Events during the 1994 period of government, however, show the importance of the central structuring discourse of nationalism for the League: when it was removed, the movement faced serious problems of mobilisation.

8 A smaller tougher movement?

The League since 1995

A new series of posters appeared on the walls of the Northern League offices in Milan in the summer of 1997. Where there had previously hung the notoriously blunt posters and cartoons from the early campaigns, there could be found large reproductions of a letter signed by Bossi. The letter urged all League militants to wear a green shirt or a green handkerchief whenever they were working in the League headquarters. This was necessary, Bossi's note went on, because 'to evangelise for the League we must first believe in ourselves'. Staff generally complied with the wishes of their leader, but many did so in a bashful way, bending the rules like children obliged to wear school uniform. One campaign volunteer had the League handkerchief (green, with the flower design of the Padanian flag) nattily poking from the breast pocket of his blazer, rather than around his neck in the cowboy style preferred by Bossi. Another had fashioned his into a wristband half-hidden by the sleeve of his shirt.

The hardcore militants, however, large numbers of whom attended the Pontida rallies in July, continued to be brazen in their support for the League. They proudly donned their green shirts in front of the cameras, and in front of their friends and neighbours. Such open, public pronouncements of support for the League will be highly significant in the biographies of League supporters that make them, particularly in the small-town contexts where the League has most followers. League members have a strong sense of honour, and are deeply embedded in the recognition of their local community. Few politicians (the historical parallels are obvious) have been able to inspire such open statements of belonging from their followers as those green shirts displayed. But this was not a period of expansion for the League. While long-time militants underlined their commitment in the post-government period, fewer new recruits were joining the League, which in the period 1995–2000 focused its efforts on consolidating existing support. As ever, this involved the League's peculiar brand of nationalism.

The number of League volunteers who were regularly involved in campaigns had by 1996 stabilised at perhaps 15–25,000.[1] The movement had a network of offices in towns throughout the North, a daily movement newspaper, and a radio station, Radio Free Padania, which broadcast on a variety of local frequencies in the North. The movement was still the leading electoral force at a local level in some regions of Northern Italy, but was showing signs of decline in the big cities. For big demonstrations the League could still muster up to 100,000 people in 1996. This was less, in general than the Alleanza Nazionale, even in Milan, and much less than the organised left. League supporters were less infused with the culture of the 'demo' than were other groups, so the poorly attended demonstrations may have masked more widespread support. Indeed, a 'referendum' on secession and an 'election' of 1997 revealed more sympathy with the League, even among those who did not vote for the party.

Bossi's League had suffered its own headaches after dealing its knock-out blow to the 1994 government. For several months the movement was reeling: disorganised, fragmenting, and haemorrhaging support. By 10 February 1995, the parliamentary party consisted of forty-four senators and eighty-three deputies (down from sixty and 114 immediately after the 1994 elections).[2] The decline was due more to defection than to by-elections. The left-wing coalition was looking much more stable in government than had the Polo della Libertá, and the League faced a difficult period of opposition, still competing with Forza Italia. Where to go from there? The answer was simple for Bossi: with no opportunities open that would not compromise the unity of his movement, he returned to the only strategy he knew that would bring it to heel, and galvanise it into further action: Northern nationalism.

The return of the nation: the secession of '*Padania*'

The League quickly intensified its identity discourse in the spring following the fall of the government. The campaign newspaper *Lega Nord* was renamed *La Padania*, and in May 1995, the new 'Parliament of the North' was launched at Mantova, with a minute of silence to commemorate the recent death of the Chechen leader Dudaev.[3] (This latter was to indicate the company with which the League now wished to be associated.) It remained unclear what kind of a role the 'Parliament' would have, since it met only once a month, and resembled a press conference more than a debating chamber. Encouraged by his electoral results, Bossi gradually in the following months intensified the independence-oriented aspect of his speeches and statements, and began to speak of 'soft secession on the Czech model'.[4] At another meeting of the Parliament of the North, on 4 May 1996, Bossi announced that 'Federalism is no use anymore'.[5] This statement, which was similar to his 1989 announcement of the abandonment of the dialect, again revealed the interplay between the goals of the movement and the political opportunities open to it. Federalism, if it is to be discarded when deemed of no use anymore, is revealed as a strategy for gaining support rather than the sacred goal in itself that the League leadership had long claimed it to be. The basic problem was that the term 'federalism' had been taken up by the other parties, such as Forza Italia, and the League needed a new stance to distinguish itself in the electoral market.

The 1996 Festa on the Po, an event with more or less the same mix of folklore, festa and political rally as the Pontida rallies, was announced by the League as the moment at which the North would be rechristened Padania and independence would be declared. The newly-minted symbolism of the weekend was, Bossi explained, based on Celtic ideas of the sacredness of water, and consisted in a symbolic purification: the baptism of Padania. On Friday 13 September, a few hundred League members gathered at the source of the Po river, in Piedmont. There Bossi, dressed casually in a green shirt and multicoloured cardigan, filled a flask with water from the spring. This was taken, via a series of rallies, to a large meeting the following Sunday at Venice, where it was poured into the lagoon. The following declaration of independence was then read:

Declaration of Padanian Independence

The history of the Italian State has become the history of colonial oppression, of economic exploitation and moral violence.

The Italian state has, through its bureaucratic apparatus, systematically occupied the economic and social system of Padania.

The Italian state has systematically annulled every form of autonomy and government from our communes, from our provinces and from our regions.

The Italian state has compromised the security of the future generations of Padania, wasting enormous resources in corruption, clientalism and criminal operations that have brought Padania and Italy to the brink of bankruptcy.

The Italian state has forced the peoples of Padania into a situation in which the products of everyday work are systematically exploited and wasted in the mafia and clientalist assistentialism of the South.

The Italian state has deliberately attempted to suppress the languages and cultural identities of the peoples of Padania through colonising the public school system.

September 15 1996

The identity constructions stressed by the League again shifted at the time of the declaration of independence. The eleventh-century history of the Lombard League communes was now rarely mentioned, and Bossi and other leaders began to speak more of the Celtic background of Padania, as the background to the posited modern differences between North and South. The subject of autonomy was now clearly the entire North of Italy: Padania. In addition to the references to the North, there were references to the regions, provinces and communes as subjects of autonomy. The term 'Padania' was not used in League slogans before this period, though Miglio had used the word to refer to the area of Northern Italy defined by the valley of the Po and its environs: an area that, he argued, formed a natural unit because 'the Valley of the Po is largely homogeneous (the Piedmont, Lombard and Venetian plains are ecologically uniform)' (Miglio 1994 [1989]: 74).

The League continued to test the limits of legality in its secessionist stance. Some local magistrates in Bergamo, Venezia and Mantova started legal proceedings against the League in May 1996, but were wary, not wanting to provide the movement with martyrs.[6] League leaders clearly relished a rather clumsy attempt by the police to raid the League's Milan offices in September 1996. (Maroni was photographed wearing a neck brace for several days afterwards.) Padania's Christening ceremony, the Festa on the Po, was met with a large but careful police presence, and disapproving statements from leading politicians, who began to mention the article of the Italian Constitution that bans 'attacks on the unity of the Italian State'. Turin magistrates added Bossi to the list of people they were investigating as a result of the Festa on the Po, but no arrests were made.[7] The League tried to keep up the momentum of this mass event with another demonstration in Milan two months later, and then the build-up to the referendum on secession, which took place the following May.

That there was little comment on the fact that the referendum on secession took place *after* the declaration of independence reflects the fact that these actions were meant and understood primarily as symbolic actions, and as exercises to keep the movement mobilised: some muscle-flexing by the League. The referendum of 25 May 1997 created quite a stir throughout Italy since it revealed that the organisational capacity of the League was still great. *La Repubblica* reported that the movement provided more than 13,000 polling stations in piazzas across Northern Italy.[8] Though it was generally accepted that the League failed to provide a secret ballot, and they certainly failed to limit people to one vote each, turnout, estimated at between two and four million voters, was impressive. The League reported that over 97 per cent of these responded positively to the question: 'Do you want Padania to become a federal republic, sovereign and independent?' This event should on no account, however, be understood as a genuine referendum. It was in fact a novel and effective way of organising a show of strength, and of taking control of the media agenda. This secessionist posturing took place in the usual media hall of mirrors. Since many of Bossi's supporters were convinced that the 'regime media' work as one against the movement, the League was able to reply to internal critics of secessionist actions that the acts were merely tricks for the media. Those stories reported by sources other than the League's own newspaper were dismissed as distortions and lies.

A key question in our attempt to understand the nationalism of the League is the likely effect that the League's return to nationalist secessionism had on support for the movement. Surveys and subsequent by-elections indicate that highly publicised events like the Festa on the Po and the declaration of independence had the effect neither of alienating the moderate wing of the League, nor of dramatically reducing overall support.

Polls indicate that support for the secessionist idea grew steadily during this period. In 1996 34.7 per cent of a sample of 904 Northerners (excluding Emilia) found 'The independence of the North' unacceptable, 23.2 per cent found it an advantageous and desirable possibility, and 29.2 per cent found it an advantageous but unacceptable possibility (Diamanti 1996a: 77). (See Table 8.1.) Another 1996 poll, conducted for the journal *Limes,* supported the proposition that the independence of the North had support also among those resident in the North who voted for parties other than the League.

Clearly, support for secession is higher among League voters. But what proportion of League voters were prepared at this point to go all the way with Bossi? A survey was made in May 1996 of 500 people, resident in

Table 8.1 Attitudes toward Northern independence, 1996

How would you describe Northern independence?	*PDS (Democratic Party of the Left) %*	*PPI (Italian People's Party) %*	*Forza Italia %*	*Alleanza Nazionale %*	*Northern League %*
An unacceptable proposition	38.7	38.1	29.2	31.9	13.7
A way to disaster	10.3	12.2	8.7	7.6	3.0
Materially advantageous but unacceptable	29.4	30.1	30.1	31.9	25.4
Advantageous and welcome	19.1	16.8	28.8	26.5	54.8
No answer	2.5	2.6	3.2	2.1	3.1
Total	100	100	100	100	100

Source: Diamanti 1996c: 20.

Piedmont, Lombardy, Veneto, Trentino and Friulli, who said they voted for the League. Questioned whether they would follow Bossi to secession, 39.3 per cent said 'yes, certainly', 14.3 per cent said 'yes, probably' and 10.6 per cent said 'yes, perhaps'.[9] Although this makes a total of over 64 per cent in favour of secession, this sample is probably slightly skewed as it consists of a small sample of those voters who *openly* declared support for the League, at a time when the League was promoting the secession argument. But such data do suggest that Bossi can bring many with him: having publicly committed to the League, activists and supporters could not then compromise support for secession without appearing shallow in their support for the League.

Why did the League leadership return to nationalist separatism? To answer that question we have to recall the situation in the party just after the fall of the government coalition. The League leadership had allowed two groups to develop within the party during the period of government. These were known as the Independentists and the Labour (left) factions. We also saw that the end of the period of government was very acrimonious for the party and that a large number of League MPs (perhaps 15 per cent of the total) eventually defected to Forza Italia or splinter federalist groups rather than fight another election under the League banner. At the same time the leadership were aware that grassroots support was trickling away to Forza Italia.

A move to the fanciful discourse of nationalism may in these circumstances appear to have been something of a risky manoeuvre. Would it not worsen the factional splits and alienate part of the movement? Would it not undermine the credibility of the League among potential voters? Even if early polls indicated that it had no such effect, it arguably was not the potential new voters that mattered at this stage, but the need to stop the rot: to maintain party unity and convince existing members to continue to act. Another reason that the League needed a stronger nationalist stance was that editors, journalists and readers were beginning to tire of the same postures that the League had been striking since it became known in the mid-1980s. Federalism was no longer transgressive, since most parties had written diluted federal reforms into their manifestos. In order to make the threats credible, and freshen the League story in the newspapers, the League needed to provide new spectacles such as the Parliament of the North, and the declaration of independence. They did still make the headlines. The 'Senatür' became known as 'Braveheart' to compare him to Hollywood's favourite warrior for Scottish independence, and took to being photographed in the League's military green shirt and scarf, with a Castroesque cigar.

There is no doubt that the move to a nationalist-secessionist stance consolidated Bossi's position within the League leadership. The purges and defections of the previous months had led *'indipendentisti'* such as Rocchetta and Miglio to leave the League. This made Bossi's return to separatism more controversial among his MPs, but it made him the undisputed heir of that faction. The League's big four: Pagliarini (ex-Budget Minister), Maroni (ex-Minister of the Interior), Formentini (Mayor of Milan) and Pivetti (Speaker of Parliament) found it hard to reconcile their serious image as national politicians with the national-separatist pantomime now demanded by Bossi. Maroni, who had been hailed as a potential replacement leader for Bossi by those who left the movement, resigned, and Pivetti was suspended from League activities in August 1996, though she and Maroni were reaccepted into the fold some months later (and both returned as MPs for Varese after they had eaten humble pie and donned green shirts).[10] These less radical politicians presented the secessionist stance in a more moderate way than Bossi: 'We are warning you. If you do not make federal reforms today, you will have secession tomorrow' was how Maroni summed up the position in 1996 (Maroni, in Carraro, Maroni and Diamanti 1996: 50). Such moderates, who seemed unconvincing in a secessionist League, remained in reserve should an opportunity such as involvement in government present itself, and they continued to enjoy the respect of the grassroots of the League.

Bossi did make some revealing statements in an attempt to justify the separatist turn to those who protested against it. When confronting his long-standing spokesman, Luigi Rossi, who left the League in May 1996 in a stand against secessionism, the League leader felt obliged to play down the prospect of genuine secession. Bossi defended the secessionist stance as a strategy, rather than independence as a goal: 'Apart from its strategic value, the discourse on secession is by now inevitable for the North', Bossi said, enigmatically, when confronted with Rossi's resignation.[11] Did he mean that secession, or the discourse on secession, was now inevitable?

Elsewhere in the League, particularly on a local level (where League administrations found such antics a hindrance to the day-to-day problems of government and maintaining their majorities) the reaction to secessionism was cool.[12] Comencino, then secretary of the Venetian League, openly refused to speak of secession, while other moderates attempted to put their own spin on the meaning of the term, exploiting the confusion over its meaning within a united Europe and, like Maroni, continuing to speak of federalism.[13] It seems that many within the League tolerate nationalist secessionism as a pose for the media, but would rethink their position if more was asked of them.

Bossi, of course, claimed at this point that secession was his plan all along, and that even the period of government had merely been preparation for the moment of independence (see the interview in Tambini

1998b). This is an anachronistic reading, however: had other political opportunities presented themselves, the League would not have developed a secessionist stance. Secession however was a word that had only rarely appeared in League propaganda before 1995, and when it did come into the League's vocabulary it was presented by other leaders as a new departure: 'Here at Montecitorio, in the heart of Roman power, our leader has pronounced for the first time the taboo word: secession. Whilst the concept of the North implied a relationship with the South, La Padania defines us alone' (Maroni, in Carraro *et al.* 1996: 47).

In addition to consolidating Bossi's leadership, and compacting the movement, the secessionist stance did in the short term alienate some of the moderates who had come to support the League in the early 1990s. Influential *Espresso* columnist Giorgio Bocca, for instance, began to write disparagingly of the movement. There was an emerging consensus that the League had served its purpose as a tool with which to unblock the Italian political system, and that the new government should be given a chance to reform the state in a more stable atmosphere. This added to the isolation of the movement.

In the elections of 21 April 1996, the League saw its deputies reduced to fifty-nine (of a total of 630) and senators cut to twenty-seven (of a total of 315). The League, in keeping with its stance of distance from the government in Rome, announced that it was not open to offers of involvement in either the centre-left government coalition or the official opposition that now consisted of Alleanza Nazionale and Forza Italia, and was no longer supported by the League. In national terms the League received almost 3.4 million votes, in comparison with the 14.6 million of the Ulivo (centre-left) and 12 million for Forza Italia and Alleanza Nazionale combined. But even if the League had returned to the 'Pole of Liberty' at this point, they would have failed to form a majority in Parliament. Had the League made a deal with the centre-left coalition, they could have rendered unnecessary the difficult participation of the hard-left rump of the old Communist party, Rifondazione Comunista. There was some call for them to do so, but Bossi declined. His experience had taught him that such moves would put strains on movement unity.

The 1996 election underlined the primacy of Lombardy. Of Northern League MPs, twenty-seven came from Lombardy, nineteen from Veneto, four from Piedmont and four from Friuli Venezia-Giulia. Emilia returned two League MPs and Tuscany, Liguria and Trentino one each.[14] The proportions were similar in the Senate. It must be noted, however, that in Veneto, the splinter leagues were more popular, and there is evidence that the Northern League had less of a monopoly on secessionism and localism there than elsewhere. Commentators generally agreed that the overall vote of the League was surprisingly high, though opinion was divided regarding whether it should be viewed as a vote for the new secessionist stance, or as evidence that the League was still picking up the votes of those disappointed either with the opposition performance of the Polo or with the centre-left government.

When many Italians were called to vote in local elections on 27 April 1997 there was another sobering result for the League. They lost Milan, with Mayor Formentini seeing his vote cut from 40.9 per cent in 1993 to 19.1 per cent. In the League's only significant gain, in the medium-sized town of Pordenone, in contrast, their share of the vote rose from 25 per cent to 34.8 per cent over the same period. In general the pattern was one of retreat: the vote becoming ever more concentrated in the sub-alpine regions that Ilvo Diamanti refers to as 'Pedemontana', the strongholds of the pre-1992 Leagues. The share of the vote was halved in Pavia, though it held firm in Mantova, recovering somewhat in relation to the 1996 national elections. In a sample of 102 local authorities of over 15,000 inhabitants nationally, Interior Ministry data revealed that the total League vote had declined by only about 1 per cent over the previous year (to 6.7 per cent of valid votes in all Italy). Bossi's response to the press was that the results confirmed that the big cities are full of Southerners who will not help the North. He made no indication that he would soften the calls for independence.

In Italy, as elsewhere, local elections tend to be fought on national issues, and between nationally-known parties. Given the obvious difference between the actions of the League in local administration, and in the virtual, symbolic world of the national media, however, it is likely that local issues had some salience in the 1997 local elections. In control of the majority of town councils in the subalpine area, League mayors had had the opportunity to impress their electorates on a purely pragmatic assessment of their local performance. The League had no radical policies to be enacted on a local level, and mayors were left more or less to work out a pragmatic programme for themselves. It is possible that they were re-elected despite, rather than because of, Bossi's 'secession strategy'.

The foreign policy of the League

The League was careful, despite the posturing, to stay on the right side of the law. Even where their campaign bordered on illegality, however, law enforcers were hesitant to pursue them. A case could have been made that the secession campaign constituted 'an attack on the unity of the state', but a trial involving such a vague constitutional claim would only have fed opposition and so was not embarked upon. Other League threats made during this period, such as fiscal strikes, burning of television licences and even references to insurrection, remained just that:

threats. The actions of Formentini, the ex-EC official who adopted the role of 'Foreign Minister of Padania' while still mayor of Milan, were no exception. He made no calls for Padania to be recognised abroad.

But all were reminded regularly of the potential for the situation to develop a more serious geopolitical dimension. In a resolution presented to the Chamber of Deputies on 10 January 1996, Bossi outlined the claim of the League and Padania. 'It has been asked of Boutros Ghali' (then General Secretary of the UN) 'if the UN can guarantee, in the absence of a federal reform of the constitution, a referendum to enable the people of Padania to express their free will of self-determination' (Bossi 1996: 135). Bossi later, however, denied that the League had made such moves to have their claim to self-determination recognised internationally, and the UN made no official response (Tambini 1998b). Clearly they were operating within tight legal parameters. Other than the symbolic actions, therefore, little was done. League MPs continued to attend parliamentary sessions in Rome and to lobby for more control of public media, claiming in particular that the League should have control of one of the television networks, to reflect its share of the vote (television networks in Italy are generally shared as electoral spoils).[15]

In Northeastern Italy, in Friuli-Venezia-Giulia, it is likely that the stance of secessionism is taken more seriously than in Lombardy. Trieste and its hinterland joined Italy only in 1918, and the region between there and Istria (the Italian-speaking regions of ex-Jugoslavia) have since been subject to repeated disputes over sovereignty. Antonio Sema has gathered evidence that representatives of the League, which was the leading party in the semi-autonomous region of Friuli in 1996, were involved in informal discussions over Istria in the period 1992–5 (Sema 1996: 79–82), and a local Northern League group was opened in Slovenia. The broad, fragmented and internally contradictory League message is thus likely to be understood differently in the Northeastern regions where territorial politics is a more pressing issue. There secession was taken more seriously as a policy proposal, while the moderates in other regions tolerate secessionism as a mere pose for the cameras.

For the most part the League was able to exist in the grey area between ironic spectacle and genuine politics, quickly retracting statements that stepped over the invisible border between the two. Bossi's deputy Roberto Maroni himself outlined his own vision of the 'foreign policy' of the League in 1996: 'We have decided to create a department of foreign affairs, that has the task of taking us over the Alps. We want to do on a European scale what we have done in Italy: federate the different autonomist movements' (Maroni, in Carraro *et al.* 1996: 53). This was the last heard of this particular plan. Like so many of the League's schemes, the journalists were the first to know, and then little more was done.

Related and splinter groups: was Padania a sorcerer's apprentice?

The broad idea of Northern independence, which has taken up so much space in recent public debate in Italy, may have begun a movement of opinion that benefits actors other than the League. Clearly, although the League got the lion's share of the autonomist vote in the North, it had no monopoly on regionalism/secessionism. Where territorial parties were successful prior to the 1980s, the League made less headway. In 1996 the League managed 9.5 per cent of the valid votes in Tyrol, which lies between League strongholds Lombardy and Veneto, as compared with 25.8 per cent for the German-speaking *Sudtiroler Volkspartei*, and in the French-speaking Val d'Aosta, the League only won 8.1 per cent as against 48.6 per cent for the Francophone party. In the South, there were territorial parties present in most regions, but none of these did better than the Lega d'Azione Meridionale, who received 3.5 per cent of votes in Puglia, or Molise, where Risorgimento del Sud received 2.5 per cent of votes (Ceccarini and Turato 1996: 62). Morawski listed the following Southern autonomist movements as operating in 1996: 'the Southern Movement; the Federal Mediterranean Movement; and the Neoborbonic Movement (newspaper: *Neapolitan Nation*)' (Morawski 1996). These tiny groups were now developing a discourse mirroring Bossi's – of a South exploited by the North – but without great electoral success.

The League were not the only organisation that kept Northern independence in the news in the mid-1990s. Splinter groups that condoned the use of violence in the name of the independence of the North, particularly in Veneto, were particularly active in this period. Best known was the Repubblica Serenissimma movement, whose members proclaimed the independence of the Republic of Venice from the bell tower of St Mark's Cathedral, Venice in May 1997. That they proclaimed independence was not the main focus of press coverage, and the ensuing police inquiry, however. The main problem was the way they arrived at the church. They did so by hijacking a ferry, driving an armoured car onto it and demanding passage to St Mark's. In contrast to the showbiz separatism of the League, however, these men were armed. On arriving they drove past flocks of bemused tourists across St Mark's Square, and then climbed the steps of the bell tower of the Cathedral to read the declaration of independence. Although the Northern League immediately issued a statement denying any link with this isolated movement (and the police inquiry failed to implicate them), the League were inevitably identified with the action: had the Venetians not carried through their threats? The details reveal the performative, spectacular nature of the event. The armoured car had been painstakingly converted from a Fiat 124 and fitted with a false plastic gun turret. It contained, in addition to real guns and ammunition, a few days' food and several changes of clean underwear. These were not needed, however, since the liberation troops were quickly, and peacefully, arrested.

The perpetrators, known as the 'Venice Eight', were at first disowned by Bossi, who claimed the event was a set-up by the secret services. Soon however, sensing a slight shift to more extreme positions in the Venetian wing of the League, and the emergence of more splinter federalist groups in the Northeast, the Leadership began to make statements that appeared to defend the Eight. When they were sentenced, in early July, the League issued a statement criticising the sentences as too harsh. Despite the denials of direct involvement from the League, many held the League responsible for these forms of action, and feared an escalation of terrorist violence. What is more, the constitutional proposals made public by the centre-left coalition in May 1997 were less federalist than many had predicted, and made no attempt to buy off the League.[16] Unlike in Spain, for example, control of police forces and justice would remain centralised, and none of the devolution of fiscal powers demanded by the League would be introduced.

The League to 2000

Throughout its career, which now spanned almost two decades, the League had been strongest at the times when the Italian state looked weak and illegitimate. Towards the end of the 1990s, the Italian state regained some legitimacy, and the League's long retreat continued. The period of 1997–2000 was one of uneasy normalisation in Italian politics. The *Mani Pulite* inquiries into political corruption lost momentum, and the new configuration of Italian politics, in which the League played a vociferous oppositional role, dug in. The criminal charges that Berlusconi, in common with many other politicians, faced, did not appear to tarnish the image of the entrepreneur, who remained high in the polls. The Forza Italia leader was acquitted of most charges, and in any case enjoyed the benefits of a revitalised parliamentary immunity. The time had come for another tactical switch from Bossi, who wasted no time in repairing links with his rival party Forza Italia. The Padanian national revival was put on hold momentarily and the League of government was again a possibility.

Those who had hoped for a realignment of Italian politics into a stable two-party system were disappointed, though the political terrain was clearly now contested between two reasonably coherent poles. On the centre-left the governing coalition included a total of six parties made up mainly of the more centrist elements of the 1980s Communist and Socialist parties. The right-wing opposition was led by the centre-right coalition which consisted of the League, Alleanza Nazionale and Forza Italia, and also the rump of the old Christian Democrats: the CCD-CDU. Until the 1994 coalition was revived in 1999–2000, the League had preferred to sit on the sidelines, and focus on the project of Padania, while watching its vote slowly dwindle. After the by-elections of 28 November, which forced Prime Minister D'Alema to resign and re-form a government, the League began the process of realignment with the Polo, seeing that their share of the vote could again become crucial to the centre-right coalition if they were to form a government.

Umberto Bossi rose to his feet to address the Chamber of Deputies on 3 February 2000 and delivered a speech that summed up the recent revisions to his strategy. It was clear that he would continue to try to ridicule the centre-left government, while trying to work out a way of accommodating his most direct rival, Forza Italia. The attack on the government was weak, even by Bossi's standards: in his inimitable populist style he simply chose to insult them, describing them as the 'Addams Family'. The remainder of the speech was made against a government motion in favour of the *par condicio* laws which would limit Berlusconi's share of the media audience. This represented a dramatic shift of position for the league, and was the fruit of the new alignment of League and Forza Italia (www.leganord.org/documenti/discorsi).

For both coalition partners it was a clear case of 'if you can't beat them, join them'. Forza and Alleanza Nazionale buried their memories of Bossi's fatal right hook in December 1994. The League, whose members habitually call Berlusconi a Mafioso, and see Alleanza Nazionale as a Southern, statist party, held its nose with one hand and shook the coalition partners' hands with the other. The Polo was locked together not because of ideological coherence but because of electoral pragmatism. A repeat of the alliance of 1994 seemed to be the grouping most likely to win an election at this time.

The League's new support for Berlusconi against the *par condicio* media laws may have been exchanged for a commitment to more decentralisation on the part of Forza Italia. The alliance of Forza Italia and the League in Lombardy, for instance, though eventually placing a Forza Italia candidate Roberto Formignoni in the post of president with 62.43 per cent of the votes cast, stood under the slogan 'Per la Lombardia'. The League managed just over 15 per cent of valid votes in Lombardy, which compared with nearly 34 per cent for Forza Italia. This compared with 17.6 and 29.2 per cent respectively in 1995 (www.elezioni.regione.lombardia.it/).

The alliance between Bossi and Berlusconi appeared to involve closer policy coordination than it had done in the past. In the North, where League candidates pooled votes with Forza candidates, and in some cases signed joint policy documents, there was an open commitment to the goal of devolution. A document presented by the centre-right candidates for the presidential candidates in the five northern regions called for devolution of powers for health and education to the regional level. It also called for devolution of police authorities to the local level to institute 'a local police for a more effective action of prevention and repression of petty criminals' (cited in Biorcio 2000: 261). The real power balance in the Polo would not be revealed until it gained power at the national level, which by late 2000 was looking increasingly likely.

The main stumbling block for the genuine devolutionists in the League was the Italian nationalism and centrism of Alleanza Nazionale. Carlo Borsani, the Health Spokesman of Alleanza Nazionale, took a predictably Italo-nationalist position against the League's suggestion that a referendum on devolution should be introduced:

> I am against the idea that from region to region we would have different schools, curriculum, history lessons, culture and tradition. That would be a disaster for our national identity. We would become lots of little weak states in a Europe dominated by states with a strong sense of identity.[17]
>
> (Borsani in *Corriere della Sera*, 29 July 2000)

The direct opposition between these two coalition partners over the national question would seem to suggest that any government formed by these parties will be unable to undertake a radical programme of reform which involves either centralisation or devolution.

The regional elections of 16 April 2000

The League and Forza Italia used the slogan 'the return of hope' in their joint campaign for the regional elections of 16 April 2000. The results, which signalled a decline in absolute terms for the League, but a chance that the party could play a crucial leverage role in the coming national elections, were greeted in the League's newspaper as a victory for the 'League of government'. In the League stronghold in Veneto there were some signs of a retreat. In Treviso the League gained almost 20 per cent of the vote, in Vicenza 15.4 per cent, Verona 12.2 per cent, Belluno 11.6 per cent, Padova 8.6 per cent, Venezia 7 per cent and Rovigo 4.8 per cent (*La Padania*, 18 April 2000). In the other stronghold of the League, Lombardy, the results are shown in Table 8.2.

The challenge for the League was, again, to retain its identity when the pressures to go into some kind of a merger with Forza Italia were growing daily. No doubt, Bossi was rummaging in his nationalist toolkit

Table 8.2 League share of the vote in the regional elections of April 2000, Lombardy

Area	*% valid votes*	*Number of votes*
Bergamo	27.2	136,637
Brescia	20.5	114,022
Como	19.8	55,440
Cremona	13.2	23,135
Lecco	21.3	30,104
Lodi	11.7	11,397
Mantova	12.7	23,954
Milano	9.5	178,000
Pavia	11.6	27,933
Sondrio	23.4	18,347
Varese	20.5	83,641

Source: Region of Lombardy Election Service (www.elezioni.regione.lombardia.it/).

and thinking of new ways to grab the headlines in the build-up to a national election in April 2001. The League did not seem to have too many tools left to use. Journalists had bored of the publicity-grabbing antics, and the League was beginning to feel the adverse effects of the resulting lack of 'oxygen of publicity'. Having declared independence, launched Lombard and Padanian currencies, passports, a parliament, and enacted dozens of other nationalist stunts, what more could they do to grab the headlines? There were no more daily pages dedicated to the League in the national newspapers, and the League's own media such as the newspaper *La Padania*, Radio Padania Libera and tiny local television station TV Padania were hardly a match for Berlusconi's media interests.

Behind Bossi's hyperbole, the change since 1996 was clear: the League no longer enjoyed the widespread support that they had enjoyed in the early 1990s. As Roberto Biorcio put it, commenting on the state of the League early in 2000, 'despite the strong base of the party in the Pedemontana area – where they had more than 40 per cent of the vote – the League failed to deepen their political hegemony' (Biorcio 2000: 258). A movement with support limited to such a small geographical part of a broader political community would always have to rely on partners to gain power.

Still convenient? The nationalism of the League

Was the League still nationalist by the turn of the millennium, or had the movement finally exhausted its repertoire of national symbolic actions? They had at least one card left to play. On 18 June 2000, while the European soccer championships were being played in Belgium and Holland, the League organised a football match: Padania versus

England. The media stunt, which involved paying English professionals from Aston Villa to put together an unofficial England side, resulted in press articles in most Italian dailies, with photos of the League leader complete with scarf and cigar. The sound-bite from Bossi: 'The UK has organised things better than we have. Over there, Wales and Scotland have their own national teams.' The implication was obvious: why not the Italian regions? Any Englishman who knows the significance of 1966 will have an answer to that question, but the point is made, and a few thousand League fans have had a chance to wear their scarves, and perhaps some of them felt the mass collective emotions that only stadium football can provide. The result was disappointing for the League. Losing 4–2 against England is a respectable result for a team representing a nation that many would argue does not exist, but only 2,000 people attended the match, according to *La Repubblica*, and empty stands featured in the press photos and television reports. The first international soccer game of Padania only made page 27 (not the back page) of *La Repubblica*, the sensationalist national paper in which the League had enjoyed a regular spread on pages 2 and 3 throughout the mid-1990s.

Bossi's ethnic, wallet and freedom propaganda formula clearly still structured the discourse at the turn of the millennium, as reproduced in the daily newspaper *La Padania*. The flexibility of the movement is striking. One feature that has become clear is the constant reference to Padania. Lombardy, Veneto and the other regional entities are still present in League propaganda and speeches, but the notion of Padania, which the League adopted only in 1996, is now stabilised in the Italian public consciousness. The crucial discursive move of having a geographical pronoun recognised by the entire Italian population has been successful. However negative or positive a light the term is held in by citizens, Padania is recognised and thus forms a resource for the League.

Mazzini and D'Azeglio would have felt increasingly frustrated watching the performance of the League during the 1990s. The movement was, with some success, reversing the process of cultural nation-building that had proceeded apace during the twentieth century in the Italian peninsula. Few would deny the effect of the League's nationalist discourse in the 1990s: citizens of the Italian state, both North and South, were more likely to question political discourses that had uncritically maintained the notion that Italy is the master frame of identity and common interest. This is supported by poll data which shows that the number of people in the North of Italy who support increased autonomy of the North from the rest of Italy actually increased whilst the vote of the League declined (Sondaggi Doxa/Abacus, cited in Biorcio 1999: 65). The League could justifiably claim to have had a hand in this process of fragmentation by mobilising nationalist constructions through the media (Sciortino 1999: 321).

Clearly, nationalism remains the key discourse motivating, organising and legitimising the movement. The term federalism had now been dropped from the official League discourse, and had been replaced with independence or 'devoluzione'/devolution, a reference to the decentralising reforms put in place by the Blair government in the UK.

The new politics of xenophobia

By mid-2000 a harsh anti-immigration theme had moved back into the discourse of the League. To a certain extent this was opportunism. Many Italian newspapers tend to anti-immigration positions. The League, as the party with the roughest language and a long tradition in anti-immigration statements, was in a good place to turn this sentiment into votes.

The anti-immigration stance resonated with many voters, but created some new problems for the League. Despite a widespread sympathy in Italy with anti-immigration politics, entrepreneurs in Lombardy – a key constituency of the League – were beginning to warm to immigration. As *l'Espresso* reported in July 2000, Northern industrialists need immigrants desperately. As Italy entered a new period of intense economic growth, Labour shortages were becoming evident, and they were forecast to worsen in the context of a greying population. While anti-immigration statements might in the short-term win votes, in the long-term they undermine the interests of the core constituency of the League. Forza Italia, who also represented Northern industry, did not indulge this form of rhetoric.

German Chancellor Gerhard Schroeder had already made his objections to the discourse on immigrants clear in February 1999, when he stated that Italy could face exclusion within Europe should a coalition involving Fini and Bossi come to power. (This followed a difficult wrangle between the European Commission and Austria concerning the inclusion of Georg Haider's Freedom Party in the Austrian Government from 1999.) It is true that the anti-immigration statements made by the League at this time were on a par with those of the Austrian Freedom Party, and with the prospect of a Polo government looking more likely in 2000, there was a growing prospect of Schroeder's warning being put to the test.

The League remained secretive about the level of support they enjoyed from their militants in this period, but if attendance at League events is a guide, it is likely that it has declined more sharply than has the vote. The League remained a strictly hierarchical organisation whose members were not consulted on policy. Supporters were a dwindling crowd, swayed by the renegotiation of interest and identity promoted by the League.

In terms of international law and the doctrine of self-determination, the legitimacy of the Padanian claim was no stronger than was the claim of the Lombard League a decade previously. However, the dramatic changes in the structure of governance and economy in Europe during the 1990s tended to support such claims in general terms, and the media campaign of the League had had some success in loosening previously stable Italian ideas of sovereignty and national community. European monetary integration, and the processes of devolution and federalisation in other countries, were continually referred to by the League themselves. However the international image of the party was heavily tarnished by the immigration stance of the League, perpetuating as it did the knee-jerk negative stereotypes of immigrants that prevent their successful integration.

The three nationalisms of the League

In the first two decades of its existence, the League used nationalism to develop a very effective new script for protest action. It proved effective precisely because it challenged state nationalism, the key legitimising discourse of the state. But nationalism, like all effective tools, is dangerous. It has inherent tendencies to promote enemy logic and intolerance, and the movement leadership was never entirely in control of the identity discourse it generated.

The nationalism of the League stood in general for smaller independent units against large, centralised bureaucracies, and variously championed federation on the Italian and the European level, Italian regions such as Lombardy, and new inventions such as Padania. The only stable aspect was what it was against: the Italian state at Rome. Nationalism in the hands of the League also developed at times into a negative anti-immigration nationalism. Identifying immigrants from outside the EU as the enemy served various purposes, but it was particularly useful at motivating the excluded non-voters, and distracting attention at moments in which the League was failing. In all these variant forms, the tool of nationalism, whether consciously or unconsciously wielded, proved an excellent means to motivate, organise and legitimise protest against the Italian state. We have seen how the media management machine of the League harnessed the inherent transgressiveness of nationalist discourse that challenges existing national public spheres. And we have seen how a nationalist enemy logic spurred collective action and totalised the movement. As nineteenth-century nationalisms mobilised vernacular cultural revivals in the media of song, poetry and art among the emerging bourgeois vernacular reading publics, so the League used the dominant electronic media of the late twentieth century to gain resonance for their contestation of Italian nationhood.

We have seen that the League cannot be reduced to a sum of its parts. It must be understood as a loose configuration, moving through time, made up of a shifting variety of individual commitments, and varied motivations of voters, militants, and leadership. These motivations are united not by a pre-existing cultural structure of primordial belonging, but by an unstable identity construction and organisational structure, depending on shifting definitions of goals and enemies. Each of these elements can be understood separately for analytical purposes, but in practice they are intertwined in the achievement of collective action. Identities exist only in context, and are at once products and preconditions of collective action. This non-essentialist understanding of the League, and indeed of Northern, Lombard and Padanian identity, cannot offer means to predict the future path of the League. It can, however, help us identify the nationalist trajectories that the League has used, and is likely to use again.

During the history of the movement, three Leagues have competed for prominence: the Padanian League, the League of Government and the Regional League. After describing these various incarnations of the movement, I outline some of the other more worrying consequences of the League's virtual secession.

The Padanian League

The League's main posture between 1995 and 1999 was the struggle for Padanian liberty. During this period, the movement worked on two fronts, staging a virtual secession for the cameras, while trying to hold on to some influence both in Rome and at the local level. There are several reasons that this position is difficult to maintain. One is the 'ratchet effect' by which the League media spectacle is involved in an inflationary spiral due to news value depreciation. Actions that yesterday got headlines are not news today. Threats, when they are not carried out, tend to sound ever less credible. In so far as the League's aim is to retain media coverage, the party is forced to engage in ever-more-extravagant spectacle in order to do so. Given the apparent consensus in the press that the League should be denied blanket publicity, and the strains this puts on the grassroots militants, the League are unlikely to be able to pursue Padanian nationalism much further. A second difficulty for Padanianism is that the large number of supporters who support secession as a stance, but not a project, are likely to leave the League if it promotes secession. For such reasons, but also because new opportunities were emerging, particularly following elections, the difficulties in Padanian nationalism were already evident in 2000.

The League of government

In 1993–4 and again during 1999–2000, the nationalist/secessionist discourse was suddenly reined in as the party prepared for government. In both cases, it was replaced with a degree of anti-immigration rhetoric, and with a cautious and pragmatic approach to coalition government. The League leadership was not above a taste for executive power, and chances of taking part in government were keenly welcomed in the party. Bossi was able to tolerate the government stance as long as it did not threaten his personal power or party unity. The evidence, however, is that the party cannot survive for long in the Italian government, because governing from Rome challenges its very *raison d'être*. During the government of 1994 the League haemorrhaged support and the Parliamentary party fractured with a lack of common purpose. How the 20,000 or so committed activists might respond to a further period of office in Rome is not clear. Having invested a great deal of their personal pride and identity, not to speak of their time, money and energy, in the project of Northern or regional independence, it will be difficult for them to support a governing party, particularly if the long-term decline of the League continues.

The regional League

The existing regions of Northern Italy (Piedmont, Veneto, Lombardia) were the key subjects of League nationalist discourse until the formation of the Northern League in 1989. Since then they have featured in League propaganda, but been progressively replaced with the notion of the North, or Padania. The regions remain as latent possibilities for a renewed politics of the regions, but while the Padanian party continues to function, a retreat to the regions is unlikely. The various 'national' Leagues that make up the League do still exist as power centres within the Northern League, however, and would be likely to re-emerge should the party split or face a serious decline.

The consequences of nationalism

A small, dangerous League

The League, while using threatening language, stayed within the law in its first two decades. But there are dangers in demobilisation, and it is worth noting the possibility that if the League enters a phase of terminal decline, some activists will move to extraparliamentary tactics. A minority of those involved in the movement of 1968 went on to support terrorists in the Red Brigades and other no-compromise factions when the initial wave of the movement subsided. It is possible that a small minority of committed activists might turn Bossi's threats of armed insurrection, uttered sarcastically on a sunny Sardinian beach in 1994, into a prophecy.

Research into why people continue to support movements of this type reveals that many individuals do so not because they think that it will bring them economic benefits in the future. They work for the movement because they enjoy it, because their friends do, because they identify strongly with the movement, and because they have made large investments of personal identity in the movement. Similar explanations inform us of the rationality of seemingly irrational actions, such as facing down the tanks in Tiananmen Square, which make sense only when they are viewed in terms of the personal biographies of participants in movements (Calhoun 1991). I have mentioned how League activists described their new-found pride and self-respect when they were first recognised as a politically strong force within Italy. I showed how the mobilisation of the League took on new ritual forms, displacing to a certain extent the rituals of the declining church and communist traditions in some parts of Italy. I showed that the League leadership has cunningly cemented its relationship with its militants by having them 'come out' in public through the use of green shirts, badges and stickers. A glance at the League's stronghold communities as the League hovers on the brink of decline shows that there is a distinct possibility that the warrior of Giussano is moving into hiding, but has no intention of going to sleep. Many thousands are still militant enough to wear green shirts in their town piazzas, manning the electoral gazebos of the League. If the retreat of the League into the movement's small-town strongholds in the subalpine valleys continues, and particularly if Bossi himself in such a scenario is unable to accept compromise or retirement, there is a potential for an isolated, dangerous rump movement to emerge, which is prepared to pursue illegal methods. It is likely that the members would be relatively few in number, and many would only take that direction if Bossi himself led them there.

Padania without Bossi?

Nationalism was used as a mobilisation tool by the League, and might be discarded. But it is clear that, like the sorcerer's apprentice, it has in the meantime developed a life of its own. Padania exists, as a project and as a recognisable pronoun, in at least some of the ways that Italy existed in the mid-nineteenth century when it was dismissed by Metternich as a 'mere geographical expression'. The facts that support for Northern independence is widespread also outside the ranks of the League, and that a number of splinter groups have taken up the mantle of regional autonomy in Italy, indicate that the League is not in complete control of its protest 'tool'. It has been unable to completely control the identity dynamic that its use of the media had engendered. The simple but powerful ideas it has presented, which undermined the nationalising state of Italy, and proposed to replace it with an alternative structure, have also been taken up by groups it can not control. In the event of a collapse of the League, or a return of the League of government, it is likely that the project of Northern autonomy would be carried forward by these and other actors, probably with an influential splinter group peeling off from the League. For there are still headlines to be written about Northern separatism, for the League or for anyone else wishing to strike that pose.

No secure predictions can be made on the basis of the generalisations that have been made in this book. The League is a movement that has been declared dead many times, and has found in nationalism a way to reunite, remobilize, and gain more support than had been thought possible. This book has tried to illustrate in particular the importance of the identity work of the League in that process of movement construction and mobilisation. It has sought to provide an explanation of why seemingly irrational, folkloric identity constructions were a rational strategy for the Leadership, how they rendered certain actions on the part of the support of the League more justifiable and rational, and how they served to organise and legitimise the movement.

One thing is clear. It is not the strategic intentions of the leaders that will be decisive in the fate of Padania, Lombardy and the League. It is the interaction between leadership strategy, identity constructions, the structure of the League, and the political opportunities open to it, that will decide the answer to the current national question in the Italian peninsula. The League, like post-Soviet and post-colonial nationalism, benefited above all from the fact that its rise coincided with a regime crisis. The movement exploited the fissures in the previous identities of Italian society: not only the fragile, young national identity, but also the two main belief systems of Catholicism and communism. The peculiar nationalist formula of League 'news management' proved a hugely effective means to grab the headlines and thus mobilise identity constructions that contest the prevailing nation-state sense of collective interest. The history of the League thus illustrates how actors that challenge the very idea of the nation can benefit when a nation-state polity suffers a general crisis of legitimacy. And in the transition to the second Italian republic it was not any one party, but the entire party system and state that was indicted. If Italy continues to be normalised, the League's moment may have passed.

Internationally, identity politics dominates. Even where absolute cultural differences decline, and nation-states falter, nationalism remains an effective means for mobilising political movements. We should not expect the current transformation of the nation-state to coincide with the end of nationalism in politics. The opposite is likely to be true: in an integrating Europe within a globalising world, where sovereignty and citizenship increasingly part company with national publics and democratic systems, contestations of territory, sovereignty, citizenship, subsidiarity and rights are set to continue. Because those institutions depend on nationalist constructions for their motivations, organisation and legitimacy, nationalist counter-constructions, mobilised by parties such as the League through spectacle-driven media, are likely to be key weapons in the new politics.

Notes

1 Virtual nationalism?

1 See interview with Gianfranco Miglio in *Il Giornale*, 30 May 1994.
2 For more on this subject see Tambini 1994.
3 Article Three of the League's programme from 1983–91 had called for direct democracy and referenda. No details were ever specified, and no substantial reforms implemented.
4 The League's anti-immigration position, in that it is not based on biologically reductionist theories of racial superiority, resembles the new right parties such as Le Pen's Front National in France, rather than the old-style racism of the British National Party in Britain.
5 Biorcio's research was carried out in 1989–90, before the launch of Forza Italia.
6 According to Bossi, 'federalism is the expression of the national unity of a country' and to Rocchetta it 'means a system of government in which the different parts of Italy can each develop the best form of self-government and reciprocal co-operation' (Tambini 1994).
7 See De Luna (1994: 43), Schmidtke (1996) for examples.
8 In Bossi's own words: 'era il periodo etno-nazionalista, era il periodo in cui noi presentavamo la regione come nazione e quindi il territorio era fonte di cultura, in quei tempi la era fonte di identitá storica. . . . La seconda fase, io la chiamo neo-regionalismo.' ('Intervento del Segretario Federale', Umberto Bossi in 'Conference Proceedings: Nuovo Federalismo Europeo' Novara 25–6 June 1993: 204).
9 Melucci defends a similar position:

> contemporary collective action, in its empirical unity combines different orientations and meanings. Unless such components are distinguished and identified, it is impossible to compare different forms of actions. One ends up by considering the movements as 'characters' moving on the historical scene, and affirming a sort of essence.
>
> (Melucci 1985: 336)

10 Melucci (1985: 331) advised analysts of social movements to conceive of them as 'a multipolar action system, developing out of the tensions between ends, means, and environment'.
11 *Lombardia Autonomista*, anno 8, no. 7, Luglio 1989. The front-page article, with the headline 'Grande vittoria elettorale del nationalismo lombardo contro l'oppressione coloniale dei partiti romani' was written by Francesco Speroni, who became Minister for Institutional Reform in 1994.
12 See also Giorgio Bocca 'Padania: il paese che non c'e', *La Repubblica*, 26 May 1997.

Rusconi (1994: 19) takes the nationalist claims of the League more seriously as a national alternative.

13 Miroslav Hroch made extensive research into what explains the progress of movements from purely cultural concerns to politics. He argued that nationalist agitation alone did not explain these changes. However he did not interrogate the interrelation of cultural and political nationalism, or the degree to which they are dependent on one another, or the role of international legitimation.

14 Habermas (1992) contains a discussion of the role of nationalism in social movements and in citizenship regimes. See also Craig Calhoun (1995: 231–5).

15 The debate over whether 'the nation' pre-exists nationalism, however, is more than a debate about historical explanation. It is a debate about legitimacy: the legitimacy of individual nationalist claims, and the legitimacy of nationalism as a way of justifying state power.

16 Thus while Kedourie ([1960] 1993) argued that nationalism 'was a doctrine invented at the beginning of the nineteenth century', Gellner (1964, 1982) convincingly argued that it was the changing structural context – particularly modernisation – that determined the take-up of the nationalist principle.

17 Controversy in nationalism theory concerns the role of culture in action. Is nationalism best explained as a response to culture-as-structure, i.e. as setter of preferences, as would appear to be the case for Anthony Smith (Smith 1991a), or as a tool used to gain access to other goods (Hobsbawm 1990; Barth 1967)? (See Tambini 1998a.)

18 Breuilly (1982) was the first theorist to treat nationalism in this broad sense as a 'form of politics'. This model draws on his innovation, but brings it closer to the relevant theoretical work in the theory of social movements and political protest.

19 As Touraine (1978: 109) put it, 'The social movement is present as a combination of a principle of identity, a principle of opposition, and a principle of totality. In order to struggle we first need to know in the name of whom, against whom, and on which terrain we struggle.'

20 The theories of Melucci, Touraine and Pizzorno have been associated with the identity school of social movements analysis.

21 Much of the innovative new work on nationalism seeks to incorporate these motivations into explanations (Calhoun 1991: 54; Scheff 1994a). For a discussion, see Tambini (1998a).

22 Charles Tilly and Sidney Tarrow refer to this as a 'repertoire of actions' (Tarrow 1994).

23 For an application to ethnic protest see Nielsen (1980).

24 The anthem runs, 'From Bernina to the Tonale a voice/ has woken the Lombards down to the Po/ a voice clear and angry/ the clear water that flows through the valleys/ and the flames that burn in the hearts/ are history, our poetry/ that for all have only one name: LOMBARDY.' (Vimercati 1990: 87, my translation.)

25 See 'Primitive Classification' by M. Mauss and E. Durkheim, reprinted in Lash (1991).

26 Note that this is very closely related to the 'revaluation of values' argument described earlier. Whereas Barth himself did not address the seeking of emotional goals by boundary drawing, I attempt to incorporate this motivation.

27 Those few rational-choice or Marxist approaches that imply that nationalist constructions of identity are a mere smokescreen for bourgeois interests therefore exaggerate the degree of control that élites can have on the processes of construction and recognition of identity.

28 Gellner (1964) called these the 'scraps and patches' of culture that national

identities were made of. Smith (1991a) disagreed, arguing that pre-existing cultural differences do indeed predict nationalist constructions.

29 There is some controversy over the nature and virtues of such explanation (Cohen 1981). I will skip over these here, and show in relation to the model, and using empirical cases, why such reasoning is justified.

This critique of functionalism is based on the discussion of the functionalist basis of historical materialism of Elster (1979) and Cohen (1981).

30 Anderson saw the print media as a necessary condition of the emergence of 'imagined communities' on the scale of nations: Deutsch described national identities as resulting from what he called rapport, or 'complimentary of communication' itself dependent on new forms of communication.

Mosse (1975) made an analysis of the aesthetics of national representation in Germany, showing the importance of symbolising unity in these meetings and in architecture.

31 Given the undermining of national public broadcasting and the increasing internationalisation of media production distribution and consumption processes, and given the proliferation of new forms of media, we can expect the conditions of nationalist identity mobilisation to be altered in the contemporary context, but this goes beyond the period of the rise of the League.

2 The movement in context

1 Especially Sicilia, Catania, Puglia and Lazio.

2 Surnames and some subtle aspects of physical appearance might make them recognisable.

3 The area of Lombardy is 24,000 sq. km (Italy is 301,000 sq. km). The region has 9 million inhabitants (Italy 57 million). With 16 per cent of the population it provides 21 per cent of the GNP of Italy (Della Peruta 1994).

4 All unreferenced quotes in this section come from interviews with militants carried out at the Congress of the Northern League in December 1993.

5 Instituto Centrale di Statistica (1987), vol. 34. Tomo 1 table 2.4.

6 In February 1992 the first arrests of top politicians were made on charges of accepting bribes, in a scandal that would eventually involve over 200 of Italy's parliamentarians.

7 The phrase was coined by Edward Luttwak.

8 Pizzorno (1993a) has stressed the distinction between *politica palese* and *politica occulta* (open politics and hidden politics) in Italy.

9 For electoral figures and discussion, see Natale (1991).

10 The *pentapartito* was made up of Democrazia Christiana, Partito Socialista Italiano, Partito Repubblica Italiano, Partito Social Democratico Italiano, and Partito Liberale Italiano.

11 The first regional elections were in 1970. The new regional jurisdictions (based on pre-*Risorgimento* political boundaries) were invested with limited powers to legislate on housing, health, social welfare and agriculture (Ginsborg 1990: 327).

12 The five who gained autonomy were Valle d' Aosta, Sardegna, Trentino-Alto Adige, Sicilia, and Friuli-Venezia Giulia.

13 The spread of votes was not completely uniform. The Christian Democrats traditionally held the balance of power in the South and North. The Socialists and Communists were dominant in the 'red belt' in the centre between Rome and Bologna.

14 See Salvemini (1955) for an overview of the Southern Question from a socialist point of view.

15 The Goths, when they invaded Italy in the sixth century, after the fall of the Roman Empire, were stopped in the Padana plains, south of where Milan is today, by the Longobardi. Hence the 'Gothic Line'.
16 Figures from Bocella, N. *Mezzogiorno Piu Lontano dal Nord*, p. 429, in Ginsborg (ed.) (1994).
17 *La Repubblica*, 10 August 1995. Whatever the accuracy of this figure, its presence on page one of the popular daily indicates a heightened awareness of division, and it is above all with this subjective aspect that we are concerned.
18 The sudden rush of corruption trials started by the Milan magistrates in 1992 became known as *Tangentopoli*: Backhander City.
19 The League was electorally active only since the 1970s, however.

3 The rise of the League

1 Dialect rendition was relatively easy: in most cases place names can be translated into dialect by deleting the last syllable.
2 Several militants interviewed by the author mentioned particular cartoons as influencing their decision to join the League.
3 *Lombardia Autonomista*, anno 2, no. 12, May 1983.
4 Leoni became a Member of Parliament for the League in 1989.
5 See Natale, in Mannheimer *et al.* (1991).
6 Some of these have been published in an edited collection (Fusella 1993).
7 *Il Giornale*, 31 October 1989.
8 This was in fact noted at the time by commentator Guido Passalacqua: 'La Marcia dei Lumbard', *La Repubblicca*, 7 December 1989.
9 *Lombardia Autonomista*, anno 2, no. 14, September 1983.
10 *Eco Delle Valli*, 9 May 1989.
11 *Lombardia Autonomista*, December 1988.
12 This was identified as early as 1989 by Guido Passalacqua. ('La Marcia dei Lumbard', *La Repubblica*, 7 December, 1989.)

4 The dilation

1 Some interregional ambitions were there from the start:

> In the Italian state, the Lombard people and the *other peoples of the North* represent a clear minority in respect to the Southern Peoples. This form of ethnic coexistence condemns the peoples of the North to suffer the choices of the political class that is mainly made up of Southerners.
> (*Lombardia Autonomista*, anno 2 no. 14, September 1983: 3. Stress added)

2 December 1993 interview with Hon. Riccardo Fragassi, Lega Nord-Toscana MP since 1992, and Tommaso Fragassi, leader: Lega Nord-Toscana. Interview with U. Bossi, 10 June 1997. For brief histories of the seven regionalist movements that went on to form the Northern League, see Cappelli and Maranzano (1991: 59–95).
3 Interview with Hon. Riccardo Fragassi, and Tommaso Fragassi, 2 December 1993.
4 Interviews with militants, December 1993. See also Fusella (1993: 48).
5 *La Nazione*, 10 February 1991: 15.
6 '*Extracommunitaria* immigration' literally means immigration from outside the EU. In practice it is a euphemism for immigration from the Third World, especially Africa.
7 *La Repubblica*, 7 December 1989; *Sole 24 Ore*, 8 December 1993.

8 Gianfranco Miglio (b. 1918) was a constitutional theorist at the prestigious Catholic University of Milan. Early in the post-war period he was active in the Christian Democratic Party, though since the 1960s he had been a consistent and vociferous critic of the Italian government. Though most known in Italy for his support for the League, and anti-Southern, Germanophile polemics, he has had an accomplished academic career. As a leading figure in the self-styled Milan Group of constitutionalists he published *Towards a New Constitution* (*Verso una nuova Costituzione*, Milan: Giuffrè) in 1983. The only established academic openly supportive of the League, Miglio had a difficult relationship with the movement, first seeing his proposals adopted, and then seeing them dropped. He ceased to work with the League in 1994 when denied his coveted post of Minister for Constitutional Reform.
9 *Panorama*, 9 May 1993.
10 See *Lega Italia Federale*, section distributed with *Lega Nord*, November 1993.
11 'La Lega Meridionale Sbarca a Milano', *Corriere della Sera*, 3 December 1989.
12 *La Repubblica*, 8 December 1989.
13 *La Repubblica*, 8 June 1993.
14 *Corriere della sera*, 16 June 1993.
15 'La Lega di Bossi Corteggia il Psd'Az.', *La Nuova Sardegna*, 24 April 1993.
16 According to Pasquino (1993: 7–8):

> The Lega has so far been unable to make inroads in the Southern electorate. It is not that the party system is better entrenched or more resilient in the South; it is simply that in Southern politics the element of personality was more important and still remains capable of tying many voters to some popular parliamentarians and candidates. Furthermore, the appeal of the Lega is couched in anti-Southern terms, or at least it is rightly or wrongly perceived in this way.

17 The Italian Socialist Party has been called the 'League of the South', because of the concentration of its support in the South. But it is by no means regionally oriented, being still close to conventional nation-state nationalism.

5 The League in government, 1994

1 This had come to serve the League as a 'national' anthem. No wonder that they protested when on 18 May Prime Minister Berlusconi announced that he was considering changing the Italian national anthem: to Verdi's *Va' Pensiero.*
2 See Frei (1993) for a colourful description of these events.
3 *Indipendente*, 11 May 1994.
4 '*Bossi: "Se Silvio non rispetta i patti, alzeremo la voce"', Il Giornale*, 1 November 1994.
5 *La Repubblica*, 31 August 1994.
6 *La Repubblica*, 31 July 1994. At a congress of the Venetian League, of which Rocchetta was general secretary, Bossi made a series of outspoken interventions ridiculing him, and used his personal influence to rally all support behind a candidate who pledged support for Bossi. For a comparison of the positions of Rocchetta and Bossi, see Tambini (1994).
7 'Bossi "richiama" Miglio', *La Repubblica*, 23 October 1994.

6 Leader, activists and organisation

1 The Northern League was not founded until 1990. In this section I refer to the supporters of the Lombard League and the Venetian League, which could be considered its main predecessors.

2 The journal itself by 1985 claimed that 27,000 newspapers were distributed (*Lombardia Autonomista*, anno 2, no. 2).
3 The nearest he gets to providing evidence is to generalise indirectly about average levels of education in the localities in which the League gained a high vote (Moioli 1990: 156–8).
4 A research project by the Catholic University of Milan, commissioned by the regional Christian Democrats.
5 These data, however, are based on self-identification and we could expect that many of those interviewed to assign themselves to a higher category.
6 The data from these studies must be used with caution for two reasons. First, the 1989 study was commissioned by the Christian Democrats, who later used the results in a propagandic way in the press. Second, according to the League, supporters were told not to cooperate with such studies and to give bogus answers (Vimercati 1990: 96–7). That they nonetheless contradict the claims of the early Italian political research on the League should therefore be even stronger evidence that those claims are not justified. The 1980s League voter was more likely to be male than female, otherwise the profile was more or less average.
7 Ilvo Diamanti, in Mannheimer *et al.* (1991).
8 See Corbetta (1993), Mannheimer (1993), Natale (1991) and especially Diamanti (1993: 104–8).
9 The total number of experiences was forty-six because some reported experience with more than one party.
10 See Schmidtke (1996), Mazzette and Rovati (1993) and De Luna (1994) for other examples of stage models.
11 In Bossi's own words: 'It was the first phase, the ethno-nationalist period, in which we presented the region as a nation: the territory as a source of culture, and historical identity. I call the second phase, "neo-regionalism."' (Speech of Umberto Bossi to conference: 'Nuovo Federalismo Europeo', Novara, 25–6 June 1993. Conference Report: 204.)
12 In his congress speech in 1991, Bossi made reference to the 'economic plan, unanimously chosen by the congress of Segrate, and sworn in at Pontida' (Speech to Congress, Umberto Bossi, 1991: 6).
13 Bossi, Speech to Congress, 1991.
14 The seven nations represent the main Northern regions. There are more if we include Trentino, Friuli and other small regions of the extreme North.
15 *La Repubblica*, 1 August 1994.
16 'E la Lega "boccia" Rochetta', *La Repubblica*, 29 July 1994.
17 Source: Northern League office of organisation.

7 The uses of nationalism

1 See 'Razzisti. Volantino Contro i Terroni. La Lega Lombarda: Non è Nostro', *Corriere della Sera*, 3 May 1989.
2 The picture is still more complex after 1990 with the rise of the Northern League. The more established 'national' secretariats (regional offices) already had their own organs (such as *Mondo Veneto* of the Venetian League) and their own slogans and preoccupations, many relating to local issues. All regions then had some editorial freedom in producing their own local pull-out section in the *Lega Nord* newspaper.
3 Speech Entitled '*La diffusione di malattie tra gli extracommunitari*' delivered by Piergianni Prosperini. Congress of the Lombard League 1990. From the archives of the Northern League.

4 The frame metaphor I borrow from Goffman (1986), and from the more recent work of Gamson (1992), and other communications analysts. It simply means that facts in communication are generally placed within a framework (frame) that guides the decoder in constructing meaning.
5 This opposition of one region being more modern, European and wealthy, and another poor, backward and non-European, was crucial in the Czech–Slovak split, according to Tom Nairn (1993), and also in recent Catalan nationalism.
6 It is widely accepted that the proportion of Southern Italians in jobs in state bureaucracy is much higher than that of Northerners. Lega supporters may argue that they were put there by corrupt Southern politicians, but others prefer the theory that this reflects the lack of other opportunities in the South.
7 This thinking is quite clear in the writing of Gianfranco Miglio (1992; 1993). The American political scientist Putnam started a public debate in early 1993 when he published in Italian a work that explained the 'civic feeling' in Northern Italy as the result of the experience of the free towns in the medieval period, thus supporting the League's basic argument (Putnam 1993). (See commentary in *Corriere della Sera*, 12 February 1993.)
8 *Lombardia Autonomista*, anno 5, no. 7, July 1989: 1.
9 A quantitative study has been made of the incidence of these themes in the media during the period of the rise of the League (Ruzza and Schmidtke 1992).
10 Gambetta in Ginsborg (1994: 350).
11 An example of a documentary series specialising in this kind of reporting was Michele Santoro's series 'Samarcanda'.
12 A *carroccio* was a standard-bearing wagon towed into battle by the armies of medieval city states. It carried the colours of the city, and its loss in battle was regarded as a great defeat. During the 1980s the term became synonymous with the Lombard League, and later the Northern League, because of the movement's use of medieval symbols.
13 Allievi points out that the freedom proposed by the League is always negative freedom: freedom from, rather than freedom of, or freedom to (Allievi 1992: 14).
14 'Laburisti, ma anticomunisti' interview with Daniele Vimercati, *Il Giornale*, 18 June 1994.
15 This was the point that emerged from the work of Barth, discussed earlier.
16 Mario Borghezio, 'Ethno-Cultural Affinities Between the Peoples of the North (Padania)', a speech approved by the first congress of the Northern League in 1990, and reprinted in *Lombardia Autonomista*.
17 In 1991 a large, well-publicised exhibition entitled 'The Celts' took place in Venice.
18 Speech delivered to the congress of the Northern League, 1991, by Piergianni Prosperini.
19 *La Stampa*, 3 March 1993.
20 This appears to be the background project of *Le Parole Della Lega* (Allievi 1992). The author attempts to deduce the position of the League from his own particular reading of the propaganda. The result is that he probably credits it with too much sophistication.
21 See Weber (1979) for a long-term historical study of the development of French national custom and tradition.

I use the term 'habitus' after Bourdieu to describe forms of cultural practices in everyday life, and to avoid terms like 'cultures' or 'cultural identity', which reify nationalist ideas.
22 'Polenta. Un Piatto Povero per un Grande Popolo', headline in *Lombardia*

Autonomista, 26 July 1989. And 'Nord-Sud riuniti da una polentata', *Il Giornale*, 16 July 1989. The alternative is pasta, made from highly refined flour and shaped into dozens of varieties, each with different names. Heavy, no frills polenta, still rarely eaten outside Northern Italy, is simple and filling by contrast. It is food for hard workers. The Lombard embrace of polenta might be compared to the Scottish predilection for porridge. (A Southern Italian taunt of Northerners was that they are *polentoni* – polenta heads.)

23 'Bossi has already expressed his preference for Protestantism, which is close to him also geographically' (Baget Bozzo, quoted in *La Stampa*, 24 September 1992).

24 Interview in *La Stampa*, 22 July 1993.

25 As Giesen has shown for the work ethic in post-war German identity formation, it enabled approbation in non-militaristic terms: 'The construction of national identity escaped to a new domain: The economy, the indisputable economic miracle of post-war Germany based on the old virtues of industriousness, reliability and discipline' (Giesen 1993).

26 In Giesen's (1993) terms they are cultural boundaries, and as such inclusive of others, rather than exclusive.

27 A verse from the anthem of the Lombard League (sung at rallies, for example Pontida 20 May 1990): 'Oramai su la nostra bandera/ Gh'e on lombard con la grinta on poo scura/ Pien di rabbia e senza pagura' (*La Repubblica*, 22 May 1990).

28 For a collection of dialect poems given pride of place in the movement newspaper, see *Lombardia Autonomista*, December 1988, no. 42 (translations into Italian included). All of the poems are loaded with melancholy nostalgia and nature worship.

29 Speech delivered to the first Lombard League congress, 1989.

30 See Greenfeld (1992) for an account. Such an exercise in the redescription of provinciality is central in the mobilisations in the Irish, Welsh and Catalan cases, for example.

31 According to Roberto Biorcio,

> The existence of an autonomous Lombard culture based on a specific language and traditions would appear difficult to verify. The use of local dialects is more diffuse in peripheral areas of other provinces. And neither can you find a unified Lombard language. In many areas the dialects resemble the dialects of bordering provinces rather than dialects of other parts of Lombardy.
>
> (Biorcio 1990: 68)

32 'Una Lega Poco Lombarda', *Il Giornale Nuovo*, 27 November 1989. '"Congress" va bene, anche se manca l'accento sull'e', ma "Nassjonal", secondo il vocabolario Cherubini, la massima autorità . . . in milanese si scrive "nazional".' Many articles doubting the authenticity of the claims surrounding the Lombard dialect appeared in the late 1980s.

33
> I would like to know what the League means in referring to 'the Lombard language'. Is that *milanese, bergamasco, comasco, legnanese, pavese* or *bresciano*? Maybe some descendant of Alberto da Giussano intends to step into Dante's clothes, and rewrite de Vulgari to show us which dialect is pre-eminent in the 'Lombard nation'.
>
> (*Il Giornale Nuovo*, 27 November 1989)

34 La Lega e il popolo/ la tigre giustiziera/ divora questo secolo/ ma apre una frontiera . . . abbatti l'arroganza/ guida il Carroccio verso la speranza. (The League is a people/ the tiger of justice/ devours this century/ but opens a

frontier . . . knocks down arrogance/ drives the *Carroccio* towards hope.) (Fusella 1993: 141.)

35 See *Lombarda Autonomista*, 1986, no. 6.

36 Pontida was the site of the signing of the treaty founding the original Lombard League, in 1167.

37 For example, 'Alberto da Giussano: Umberto da Cassano' (Bossi) chanted at the first congress of the Lombard League in 1989. (See *La Notte*, 11 December 1989.) In later years the medieval symbolism moved, literally, to the background. The backdrop for the congress of the Northern League/Lombard League in 1993 was a cardboard replica of a medieval town, complete with turrets and towers.

38 Brera was a nationally famous sports journalist. Many books also sought to counter this slight Balkanization of Italian historiography. One of the most blatant attempts at this was Spadolini (1994).

39 The cities of the medieval Lombard League were: Bergamo, Brescia, Cremona, Mantova, Milano, Lodi, Piacenza, Parma, Venezia, Verona, Vicenza, Padova, Treviso, Ferrara, Modena, Bologna, Novara, Vercelli, Tortona, Varese, Como, Asti, Alessandria, Pavia and Reggio Emilia.

40 The Repubblica Cisalpina was formed by the territories that now make up Emilia-Romagna and Lombardy between 1797 and 1802.

41 'La polemica sui meridionali nelle truppe alpine', Gianfranco Miglio/Luigi Federici in *Noi* (magazine), 11 March 1993.

42 The phrase is from Pier Paolo Poggio in De Luna (1994).

43 Carlo Cattaneo and Vincenzo Gioberti are considered the founding fathers of Italian Federalism. For a discussion see Vimercati (1991).

44 Sicily, Sardinia and several other regions in Italy have semi-autonomous status, with strong regional parliaments and tax concessions. Extension of this status to Lombardy was the early goal of the League.

45 Manconi, quoted in Bocca (1990: 26).

46 David Miller has made a similar point about the importance of understanding the positive functions of nationalism, but focuses on its implications for citizenship, rather than its implications for protest and mobilisation (Miller 1995).

8 A smaller tougher movement?

1 This is an estimate based on the membership figures for 1993, and the numbers that the League has been able to mobilise in organising protest actions. The League has kept more recent figures secret. The degree of commitment of these militants will vary.

2 'Bossi: non mi ritiro neanche per sogno', *Corriere della Sera*, 10 February 1996.

3 *Corriere della Sera*, 5 May 1996.

4 'Voglio due Italie come hanno fatto i cecoslovacchi', *La Repubblica*, 5 May 1996.

5 Umberto Bossi, speech to the Parliament of Padania, 4 May 1996 (Luvera 1996: 37).

6 'Lega, e scontro sulla "mano dura"', *La Repubblica*, 1 June 1997.

7 'Veltroni rompe il silenzio', *Il Manifesto*, 12 September 1996.

8 *La Repubblica*, 25 May 1997. This figure is the same as that printed in *La Padania* of 25–6 May 1997.

9 Survey conducted by SWG for *Famiglia Christiana* magazine. Reported in *La Repubblica*, 7 May 1996.

10 *La Repubblica*, 9 August 1996.

11 'Rossi: no alla secessione, Carroccio addio', *Corriere della Sera*, 17 May 1997.

12 See: 'Enti Locali. Niente governo con la Lega? Il Pds temporaggia', *Il Manifesto*, 14 September 1996.

13 Comencino's comments were reported in 'In Veneto della protesta. "Qui lo Stato non c' è"', *La Repubblica*, 4 May 1996. For other moderates, see 'Ma nel Norde-Est il Carroccio e dei moderati', *Corriere della Sera*, 13 May 1997.

14 *La Repubblica*, 23 April 1996.

15 See *La Repubblica*, 29 June 1996.

16 *La Stampa*, 15 May 1997.

17 'Borsani (AN) alla Lega: L'Alleanza in regione e ancora in rodaggio', *Corriere della Sera*, 29 July 2000.

Bibliography

Alberoni, F. (1981) *Movimento e istituzione.* Bologna: Il Mulino.
Allievi, S. (1992) *Le Parole della Lega.* Milan: Garzanti.
Anderson, B. (1983) *Imagined Communities.* London: Verso.
Archer, M. (1988) *Culture and Agency.* Cambridge: Cambridge University Press.
Armstrong, J. (1982) *Nations Before Nationalism.* Chapel Hill: University of North Carolina Press.
Axelrod, R. (1984). *The Evolution of Cooperation.* New York: Basic.
Babha, H. (1990) *Nation and Narration.* London: Routledge.
Banfield, E. (1958) *The Moral Basis of a Backward Society.* Chicago: Free Press.
Banton, M. (1983) *Racial and Ethnic Competition.* Cambridge: Cambridge University Press.
Barth, F. (1967) *Ethnic Groups and Boundaries.* Boston: Little, Brown.
—— (ed.) (1977) *Scale and Social Organisation.* Boston: Little, Brown.
Bauman, Z. (1987) *Legislators and Interpreters.* Cambridge: Polity.
—— (1990a) *Modernity and Ambivalence.* Cambridge: Polity.
—— (1990b) 'Modernity and Ambivalence', *Theory, Culture and Society* 7(3).
—— (1995) *Life in Fragments. Essays in Postmodern Morality.* Oxford: Blackwell.
Belotti, V. (1990) *La Lega Lombarda. Saggio critico.* Bergamo: Editrice San Marco.
—— (1992) 'La rappresentanza politica locale delle leghe', *Polis* 6(2): 281–90.
Biorcio, R. (1990) 'La Lega come attore politico: Dal Federalismo al Populismo Regionalistica', in Mannheimer, R. (ed.), *La Lega Lombarda.* Milan: Feltrinelli.
—— (1992) 'The Rebirth of Populism in Italy and France', *Telos* (90): 43–56.
—— (1999) 'La Lega Nord e la Tranzizione Italiana', *Rivista Italiana di Scienza Politica* 29(1).
—— (2000) 'Bossi-Berlusconi, la nuova alleanza', *Il Mulino* 389(3).
Bocca, G. (1990) *La disunità d'Italia.* Milan: Garzzanti.
Bolla, G. C. and Imperatore, L. F. (1992) *Da Ambrogio a Bossi: Lotte per la Libertà nella Padania.* Milano: Edizioni B.I..
Bollati, G. (1983) *L'Italiano. Il carattere nationale come storia e come invenzione.* Turin: Einaudi.
Bonora, P. (1990). *Regionalità. Il concetto di regione nell' Italia del secondo dopoguerra.* (1943–1970). Milan: Franco Angelli.
Bossi, U. (1995) *Tutta La Verità. Perché ho partecipato al governo Berlusconi. Perché l'ho fatto cadere. Dove voglio arrivare.* Milan: Sperling and Kupfer.
—— (1996) *Il Mio Progetto.* Milan: Sperling and Kupfer.

Bossi, U. and Vimercati, D. (1992) *Vento dal Nord. La Mia Lega La Mia Vita.* Milan: Sperling and Kupfer.

—— (1993) *La rivoluzione. La Lega: Storia e Idee.* Milan: Sperling and Kupfer.

Bourdieu, P. (1979) *La Distinction. Critique sociale du jugement.* Paris: Les Editions de Minuit.

—— (1980) 'L'identité et la representation. Elements pour une reflexion critique sur l'idée de région', *Actes de la Recherche en Sciences Sociales* 35: 63–72.

Bourdieu, P. and Coleman, J. (1991) *Social Theory for a Changing Society.* Boulder: Westview.

Brera, G. (1993) *Storia dei Lombardi.* Milan: Baldini and Castoldi.

Breuilly, J. (1982) *Nationalism and the State.* Manchester: Manchester University Press.

—— (1985) 'Reflections on Nationalism', *Philosophy and Social Science* 15(1): 65–73.

—— (1993) *Nationalism and the State* (2nd edn). Manchester: Manchester University Press.

Brubaker, R. (1992) *Citizenship and Nationhood in France and Germany.* Cambridge, Mass.: Harvard University Press.

—— (1997) *Nationalism Reframed. Nationhood and the National Question in the New Europe.* Cambridge: Cambridge University Press.

Buchanan, J. (1991) *Secession: The Morality of Political Divorce from Fort Sumner to Lithuania and Quebec.* Boulder: Westview.

Bull, A. and Corner, P. (1993) *From Peasant to Entrepreneur: The Survival of the Family Economy in Italy.* Oxford: Berg.

Bull, M. and Rhodes, M. (1997) 'Between Crisis and Transition: Italian Politics in the 1990s', in *Western European Politics* vol. 20, 1–13.

Caciagli, M. and Spreafico, A. (eds) (1991) *Vent'anni di Elezioni in Italia 1968–1987.* Liviana: Padova.

Calhoun, C. (1989) 'Social Issues in the Study of Culture', *Comparative Social Research* 11: 1–27.

—— (1991) 'The Problem of Identity in Collective Action', in Huber, J. (ed.), *Macro-Micro Linkages in Sociology*, pp. 51–75. Beverly Hills, Calif.: Sage.

—— (1993) 'Postmodernism as Pseudohistory', *Theory, Culture and Society* 10: 222–42.

—— (ed.) (1994) *Social Theory and the Politics of Identity.* Cambridge, Mass.: Blackwell.

—— (1995) *Critical Social Theory.* Oxford: Blackwell.

Cantieri, R. and Ottaviani, A. (1992) *I cento giorni della Lega* (Preface by Franco Rocchetta). Verona: Edizioni Euronobel.

Capelli, S. (1990) *La gente e La Lega: Un' ipotesi divenuta realta'.* Milan: Greco and Greco.

Capelli, S. and Maranzano, D. (1991) *La Gente e La Lega.* Milan: Greco and Greco.

Carr, E. H. (1961). *What is History?* London: Penguin.

Carraro, M., Maroni, R. and Diamanti, I. (1996) 'O Federalismo Subito, o Independenza', *Limes: Rivista Italiana di Geopolitica* 1: 47–53.

Cartocci, R. (1991) 'Localismo e Protesta Politica', *Rivista Italiana di Scienza Politica* (Dec.) 21(3): 551–80.

Cassese, A. (1994) *Self-Determination of Peoples: A Legal Perspective.* Cambridge: Cambridge University Press.

Castellani, A. (1996) *Umberto Bossi Una Biografia Politica.* Unpublished thesis: Universita degli Studi di Firenze.

Ceccarini, L. and Turato, F. (1996) 'Atlante Geopolitico delle Leghe', *Limes: Rivista Italiana di Geopolitica* 3: 59–71.
Cesario, V., Rovati, G. and Lombardi, M. (1989) *Localismo politico: il caso Lega Lombarda.* Comitato Regionale Lombardo. Varese: Democrazia Cristiana/La Tipografia Varesina.
Clarke, J. C. D. (1990) 'National Identity and History', *History Workshop* (29): 43–71.
Clogh, S. B. (1992) *The Economic History of Modern Italy.* New York: Columbia.
Cohen, A. (1981) 'Functional Explanation, Consequence Explanation and Marxism', *Inquiry* 25: 25–56.
—— (1985) *The Symbolic Construction of Community.* London: Tavistock.
—— (1986) *Symbolising Boundaries: Identity and Diversity in British Cultures.* Manchester: Manchester University Press.
Cohen, J. (1985) 'Strategy or Identity? New Theoretical Paradigms and Contemporary Social Movements', *Social Research* 52(4): 663–716.
Colley, L. (1992) *Britons: Forging the Nation. 1707–1837.* New Haven: Yale University Press.
Collins, R. (1990) *Culture, Communication and National Identity. The Case of Canada.* Toronto: University of Toronto Press.
Confalonieri, M. (1990) Si avanza uno strano guerriero. Ulisse. Bollettino del Circolo Culturale *'Ulisse'.* (3): 3–7.
Connor, W. (1978) 'A Nation is a Nation, is a State, is an Ethnic Group is a . . .', *Ethnic and Racial Studies* (Oct.) 1(4): 377–99.
—— (1990) 'When is a Nation?' *Ethnic and Racial Studies* 13(1): 92–103.
—— (1993) 'Beyond Reason: The Nature of the Ethnonational Bond', *Ethnic and Racial Studies* (July) 16(3): 373–89.
Conversi, D. (1990) 'Language or Race? The Choice of Core Values in the Development of Catalan and Basque Nationalisms', *Ethnic and Racial Studies* (Jan.) 13(1): 50–70.
Corbetta, P. (1994) 'La Lega e lo sfaldamento del sistema', *Polis* (Aug.) 7(2): 229–52.
Costantini, L. (1993) *Dentro La Lega.* Rome: Koiné Edizioni.
Cross, J. (1990) 'The Lega Lombarda: A Spring Protest or the Seeds of Federalism?' *Italian Politics and Society* (32): 20–31.
Crouch, C., Eder, K. and Tambini, D. (eds) (2001) *Citizenship, Markets and the State.* Oxford: Oxford University Press.
Della Peruta, F. (1994) 'Lombardia: primato economico, e proposte politiche', in Ginsborg, P. (ed.), *Stato dell'Italia,* pp. 126–30. Milan: Mondadori.
De Luna, G. (1994) *Figli di un benessere minore. La Lega 1979–1993.* Scandicci (Florence): La Nuova Italia Editrice.
De Mauro, T. (1994) 'Lingue e dialetti', in Ginsborg, P. (ed.), *Stato dell'Italia,* pp. 61–6. Milan: Mondadori.
Deutsch, K. (1953) *Nationalism and Social Communication.* Cambridge, Mass.: MIT Press.
Diamanti, I. (1991) 'Una tipologia dei simpatizzanti della Lega', in Mannheimer, R., Biorcio, R., Diamanti, I. and Natale, P. (eds), *La Lega Lombarda.* Milan: Feltrinelli.
—— (1992) 'La mia patria e' il Veneto. I Valori e la proposta politica delle leghe', *Polis* (Aug.) 6(2): 225–55.
—— (1993) *La Lega: Geografia, storia e sociologia di un nuovo soggetto politico.* Rome: Donzelli.

—— (1996a) *Il male del nord. Lega, localismo, secessione.* Rome: Donzelli.
—— (1996b) 'Dietro il Fantasma della Lega', *Il Mulino* 367: 879–88.
—— (1996c) 'Il Nord Senza L'Italia?' *Limes: Rivista Italiana di Geopolitica* 1: 2–36.
Diamanti, I. and Feltrin, P. (1983) 'Societa e territorio nelle elezioni del 26 Giugno. Il caso di Treviso e di Vicenza', *Strumenti* (2): 29–87.
Diani, M. (1996) 'Linking Mobilization Frames and Political Opportunities. Insights From Italian Regional Populism', *American Sociological Review* 61.
Di Virgilio, A. (1994) 'Dai partiti ai poli: la politica delle alleanze', in Bartolini, S. and D'Alimonte, R. (a cura di) *Maggioritario ma non troppo. Le Elezioni Politiche del 1994*, pp. 177–232.
Douglas, M. (1982) *Essays in the Sociology of Perception.* London: Routledge and Kegan Paul.
—— (1984) *Purity and Danger.* London: Ark.
Durkheim, E. and Mauss, M. (1963) *Primitive Classification.* London: Cohen and West.
Eder, K. (1985) 'The "New Social Movements": Moral Crusades, Political Pressure Groups, or Social Movements?' *Social Research* 52(4).
Elster, J. (1979) *Ulysses and the Sirens.* Cambridge: Cambridge University Press.
—— (1989a) *The Cement of Society: A Study of Social Order.* Cambridge: Cambridge University Press.
—— (1989b) *Nuts and Bolts for the Social Sciences.* Cambridge: Cambridge University Press.
—— (1989c) *Solomonic Judgements.* Cambridge: Cambridge University Press.
—— (1990) *Psychologie Politique.* Paris: Les Editions de Minuit.
Etzioni, A. (1995) *The Spirit of Community. Rights, Responsibilities and the Communitarian Agenda.* London: Fontana.
Fadda, A. (1993) 'Classe ed etnia. Dal Partito d'Azione al Partito Sardo', in Mazzette, A and Rovati, G. (eds), *La protesta dei forti. Leghe del nord e Partito Sardo d'Azione.* Milan: Angeli.
Fishman, J. A. (1972) *Language and Nationalism. Two Integrative Essays.* Rowley, Mass.: Newbury House.
—— (1986) *The Rise and Fall of the Ethnic Revival: Perspectives on Language and Ethnicity.* The Hague: Mouton.
Foster-Carter, A. (1993) 'A Shrimp Among Whales: Notes on Nationalism and the National Question in Korea', *Oxford International Review* 4(1).
Frei, M. (1993) *Getting the Boot. Italy's Unfinished Revolution.* New York: Westbury.
Fusella, A. (1993) *Arrivano I Barbari.* Milan: Rizzoli.
Gamson, W. (1988) 'Political Discourse and Collective Action', *International Social Movement Research* 1.
— (1992) *Talking Politics.* Cambridge, Cambridge University Press.
Gellner, E. (1964) *Thought and Change.* London: Weidenfeld and Nicolson.
—— (1973) 'Scale and Nation', *Philosophy of the Social Sciences* 3: 1–17.
—— (1982) 'Nationalism and the Two Forms of Cohesion in Complex Societies', British Academy: Radcliffe-Brown Lecure in Social Anthropology.
—— (1983) *Nations and Nationalism.* Oxford: Blackwell.
—— (1987) *Culture, Identity and Politics.* Cambridge: Cambridge University Press.
—— (1991) 'Nationalism and Politics in Eastern Europe', *New Left Review* (Sept.).
—— (1994) *Encounters With Nationalism.* Oxford: Blackwell.
Giddens, A. (1990) *The Consequences of Modernity.* Cambridge: Polity.

—— (1991) *Modernity and Self-Identity. Self and Society in the Late Modern Age.* Stanford, Calif.: Stanford University Press.

—— (1985) *The Nation-State and Violence* (2 vols). Cambridge: Polity.

Giesen, B. (1993) *Die Intellektuellen und die Nation. Eine deutsche Achsenzeit.* Frankfurt am Main: Suhrkamp.

Giesen, B. and Eisenstadt, S. (1995) 'The Construction of Collective Identity', *Archives Europeenes de Sociologie* 36: 72–105.

Ginsborg, P. (1990) *A History of Contemporary Italy.* London: Penguin.

—— (ed.) (1994) *Stato dell'Italia.* Milan: Mondadori.

Goffman, E. (1986) *Frane Analysis: An Essay on the Organisation of Experience.* Northeastern University Press.

Gramsci, A. (1971) *Selections From the Prison Notebooks.* London: Lawrence and Wishart.

Greco, M. and Bollis, A. (1993) *Carroccio a Nordest. Storia, programma, uomini della Lega Nord del Friuli-Venezia Giulia.* Milan: MGS Press.

Greenfeld, L. (1992) *Nationalism: Five Roads to Modernity.* Cambridge, Mass.: Harvard University Press.

Habermas, J. (1992) 'Citizenship and National Identity: Some Reflections on the Future of Europe', *Praxis International* 12(1).

Hechter, M. (1995) 'Explaining Nationalist Violence', *Nations and Nationalism* 1(1): 53–68.

Hechter, M. and Levi, M. (1979) 'The Comparative Analysis of Ethno-Regional Movements', *Ethnic and Racial Studies* 2(3): 260–74.

Hirschman, A. O. (1981) *Essays in Trespassing. Economics to Politics and Beyond.* Cambridge: Cambridge University Press.

Hobsbawm, E. (1990) *Nations and Nationalism since 1780: Programme, Myth, Reality.* Cambridge: Cambridge University Press.

Hobsbawm, E. and Ranger, T. (eds) (1982) *The Invention of Tradition.* Cambridge: Cambridge University Press.

Horowitz, D. (1985) *Ethnic Groups in Conflict.* Los Angeles and London: University of California Press.

Hroch, M. (1985) *Social Preconditions of National Revival in Europe.* Cambridge: Cambridge University Press;.

—— (1990) 'How Much Does Nation Formation Depend on Nationalism?' *East European Politics and Societies* (4).

—— (1991) 'From the National Movement to the Fully-Formed Nation. The Nation-Building Process in Europe', *New Left Review.*

—— (1994) 'The Social Interpretation of Linguistic Demands in European National Movements', EUI Working Papers (European Forum) 94(1).

Huber, J. (ed.) (1991) *Micro-Macro Linkages in Sociology,* pp. 51–75. Beverly Hills, Calif.: Sage.

Iacopini, R. and Bianchi, S. (1994) *La Lega ce l'ha crudo.* Milan: Mursia.

Ionescu, G. and Gellner, E. (eds) (1970) *Populism: Its Meaning and National Characteristics.* London: Weidenfeld and Nicolson.

Istituto Poster (1993) *Cittadini, Valori e Politica. Sondaggio in due aree della Lombardia e del Veneto* (1992–3). Vicenza.

Jensen, J. and Phillips, S. (2001) 'Redesigning the Canadian Citizenship Regime. Remaking the Institutions of Representation', in Crouch, C., Eder, K. and Tambini, D. (eds), *Citizenship, Markets and States.* Oxford: Oxford University Press.

Kedourie, E. (1993) *Nationalism* (4th edn). Oxford: Blackwell.

Koopmans, R. and Statham, P. (1999) 'Challenging the Liberal Nation-State? Postnationalism, Multiculturalism, and the Collective Claims Making of Migrants and Ethnic Minorities in Britain and Germany', *American Journal of Sociology* 105(3).

Lamont, M. (1992) *Money, Morals and Manners. The Culture of the French and American Upper Middle Class.* Chicago: University of Chicago Press.

Lamont, M. and Fournier, M. (eds) (1992) *Cultivating Differences. Symbolic Boundaries and the Making of Inequality.* Chicago and London: University of Chicago Press.

Lash, S. (ed.) (1991) *Post-Modernist and Post Structuralist Sociology.* Aldershot: Elgar.

Lash, S. and Friedman, J. (eds) (1992) *Modernity and Identity.* Oxford: Blackwell.

Lazar, M. (1992) 'L'Italie Existe-T-Elle? Entretien avec Franco Rocchetta', *Politique Internationale* (Winter 1992–3): 129–47.

Legnante, G. and Corbetta, P. (2000) 'Cambiamento politico e stabilità elettorale', *Il Mulino* 389 (3).

Lepre, A. (1986) *Storia del Mezzogiorno.* Naples: Liguori.

Levi, M. and Hechter, M. (1985) 'A Rational Choice Approach to The Rise and Decline of Ethnoregional Political Parties', in Tiryiakan, E. and Rogowski, R. (eds), *New Nationalisms of the Developed West.* London: Allen and Unwin.

Levi-Strauss, C. (1952) *Race et Histoire.* Paris: Unesco.

Lombardi, M. (1990) 'La Lega Lombarda: Manifestazione politica del localismo', *Studi di Sociologia* 28(4): 48.

Lukes, S. (1985) *Marxism and Morality.* Oxford: Clarendon Press.

Luvera, B. (1996) 'Internazionale Regionalista. Tra Maschera e Volto', *Limes: Rivista Italiana di Geopolitica* 3.

McAdam, McCarthy and Zald (1988) 'Social Movements', in Smelser, N. (ed.), *Handbook of Sociology*, pp. 695–739. London: Sage.

Malcolm, N. (1994) *Bosnia: A Short History.* London: Macmillan.

Mannheimer, R. (1993) 'L'elettorato della Lega Nord', *Polis* (Aug.) 7(2): 253–74.

—— (1994) 'Per la Lega Nord e' strategico il federalismo', *Federalismo e Societa* 1(2).

Mannheimer, R., Biorcio, R., Diamanti, I. and Natale, P. (1991) *La Lega Lombarda.* Milan: Feltrinelli.

Marino, G. (1979) *Storia del Separatismo Siciliano.* Editori Riuniti, 1986, Rome: Donzelli.

Mazzette, A. and Rovati, G. (eds) (1993) *La Protesta dei Forti: Leghe del Nord e Partito Sardo d'Azione Collana di Sociologia.* Milan: Angeli.

Mazzoleni, G. (1992) 'Quando La Pubblicità Elettorale Non Serve', *Polis* (Aug.) 6: 291–304.

Melucci, A. (1982) *L'invenzione del presente: Movimenti, identità, bisogni individuali.* Bologna: Il Mulino.

—— (1985) 'The Symbolic Challenge of Contemporary Movements', *Social Research* 52(4).

—— (1988) 'Getting Involved: Identity and Mobilization in Social Movements', *International Social Movement Research* 1.

—— (1989) *Nomads of the Present: Social Movements and Individual Needs in Contemporary Society.* Philadelphia: Temple University Press.

Melucci, A. and Diani, M. (1983) *Nazioni senza stato: i movimenti etnico-nazionali in occidente.* Turin: Loescher.

Miglio, G. (1990) *Una costituzione per i prossimi trent'anni. Intervista sulla terza repubblica.* Bari: La Terza.

—— (1992) 'Toward a Federal Italy', *Telos* (90).

—— (1993) 'The Cultural Roots of the Federalist Revolution', *Telos* (93): 33–9.

—— (1994) *Io, Bossi e la Lega.* Milan: Mondadori.

Miller, D. (1995) *On Nationality.* Oxford: Clarendon Press.

Moioli, V. (1990) *I nuovi razzismi. Miserie e fortune della Lega Lombarda,* Rome: Edizioni Associate.

Morawski, P. (1996) 'La secesione visto dal sud', *Limes. Rivista Italiana di Geopolitica* 4.

Morley, D. (1992) *Television, Audiences and Cultural Studies.* London: Routledge.

Mosse, G. (1975) *The Nationalisation of the Masses: Political Symbolism and Mass Movements in Germany from the Napoleonic Wars through the Third Reich.* New York: Fertig.

Nairn, T. (1977) *The Breakup of Britain. Crisis and Neo-Nationalism.* London: New Left Books.

—— (1993) 'Where Egotism Defines the National Boundaries', *CEU Gazette* 4.

Natale, P. (1991) 'Lega. Lombarda e insedimento territoriale: Un analisi ecologica', in Mannheimer, R., Biorcio, R., Diamanti, I. and Natale, P. *La Lega Lombarda.* Milan: Feltrinelli.

Nielsen, F. (1980) 'The Flemish movement in Belgium after World War II: A Dynamic Analysis', *American Sociological Review* 45: 76–94.

Olson, M. (1965). *The Logic of Collective Action.* Cambridge, Mass.: Harvard University Press.

Palmieri, M. (1984) 'Milano e Lombardia. Un laboratorio per l'informazione radiotelevisiva', *Problemi dell' informazione* 22(1): 33–45.

Parekh, B. (1995) 'Ethnocentrism of the Nationalist Discourse', *Nations and Nationalism* 1(1): 25–52.

Parisi, A. (1992) 'Leghe Leghisti Legami', *Polis* (Aug.) 6(2): 221–3.

Pasquino, G. (1985) *Il Sistema Politico Italiano.* Bari: La Terza.

—— (1991) 'Meno Partito Più Lega', *Polis* (Dec.) 5(3): 555–64.

—— (1993) 'Introduction: A Case of Regime Crisis', in Pasquino, G. and McCarthy, P., *The 1992 Elections in Italy.* Bologna: Johns Hopkins.

Piccone, P. (1992) 'The Crisis of Liberalism and the Emergence of Federal Populism', *Telos* (90).

Pizzorno, A. (1983) 'Identità e Interesse', in Sciolla, L. (ed.), *Identità.* Turin: Rosenburg.

—— (1986) 'Some Other Kind of Otherness: A Critique of Rational Choice Theories', in Foxley, A. *et al.* (eds), *Development, Democracy and the Art of Trespassing.* Notre Dame, Ill.: University of Notre Dame Press.

—— (1993a) *Le Radici della Politica Assoluta e Altri Saggi.* Milan: Feltrinelli.

—— (1993b) 'Categorie Per Una Crisi', *Il Mulino* (96).

Poche, B. (1995) 'The New Northern League: End of a Grand Design?' *Telos* 101.

Putnam, R. D. (1993) *Making Democracy Work. Civic Traditions in Modern Italy.* Princeton: Princeton University Press.

Recchi, E. (1997) *Giovani Politici.* Padua: CEDAM.

Renan, E. (1961) 'Qu'est-ce qu'une nation?' in *Ouevres Completes.* Paris: Gallimard.

Ricolfi, L. (1992) 'Politica senza fede: l'estremismo di centro dei piccoli leghisti', *Il Mulino* (2): 53–69.

Robertson, R. (1990) 'Mapping the Global Condition', in Featherstone, M. (ed.), *Global Culture.* London: Sage.

Rocchetta, F. (1992) 'L'Italie Existe-T-Elle? Entretien avec Franco Rocchetta', *Politique Internationale* (Winter 1992–3): 129–47.

Romano, L. (1992) 'La Fine del sistema democristiano perfetto. Dalla Liga Veneta alla Lega Nor', *Nuvole* 3–4.

Rovati, G. (2000) 'Liguria: il centrosinistra passa la mano', *Il Mulino* 389(3).

Rusconi, G. (1992) 'Il Volto Della Lega. Etnodemocrazia e cittadinanza nazionale', *Il Mulino* (3).

—— (1993) *Se Cessiamo di Essere Una Nazione*. Milan: Il Mulino.

—— (1994) 'Razionalità politica, virtù civica, e identità nazionale', *Rivista Italiana di scienza politica* 24(1).

Ruzza, C. and Schmidtke, O. (1992) 'The Making of a Regionalist Movement: Mobilization Dynamics in the Lombard League', *Telos* (90).

Said, E. (1979) *Orientalism*. New York: Random House.

Salvemini, G. (1955) *Scritti Sulla Questione Meridionale* (1896–1955). Turin: Einaudi.

Salvi, S. (1973) *Le nazioni proibite. Guida a dieci colonie interne dell'Europa occidentale*. Florence: Vallecchi.

—— (1975) *Le Lingue Tagliate. Storia delle minoranze linguistiche in Italia*. Milan: Rizzoli.

Samuel, R. (1988) *Patriotism: The Making and Unmaking of the British National Identity*. London: Routledge.

Sassen, S. (1996) *Losing Control? Sovereignty in the Age of Globalization*. New York: Columbia University Press.

Savelli, G. (1992) *Che Cosa Vuole La Lega*. Milan: Longanesi.

Scannel, P. and Cardiff, D. (1982) 'Serving the Nation: Public Service Broadcasting Before the War', in Waites, B., Bennett, T. and Martin, G. (eds), *Popular Culture: Past and Present*, pp. 161–80. London: Croom Helm.

Scheff, T. (1990) *Microsociology. Discourse, Emotion and Social Structure*. Chicago: Chicago University Press.

—— (1994a) *Bloody Revenge: Emotions, Nationalism and War*. Boulder: Westview.

—— (1994b) 'Emotions and Identity: A Theory of Ethnic Nationalism', in Calhoun, C. (ed.), *Social Theory and the Politics of Identity*. Cambridge, Mass.: Blackwell.

Schlesinger, P. (1987) 'On National Identity: Some Conceptions and Misconceptions Criticized', *Social Science Information* 26(2).

—— (1991) *Media, State and Nation. Political Violence and Collective Identities*. London: Sage.

Schmidtke, O. (1996) *The Politics of Identity, Ethnicity Territories and the Political Opportunity Structure in Modern Italian Society*. Sinheim Pro Universitate Verlag.

Sciortino, G. (1999) 'Just Before the Fall. The Northern League and the Cultural Construction of a Secessionist Claim', *International Sociology* 14(3): 321–36.

Segatti, P. (1992) 'L'offerta politica e i candidati della Lega alle elezioni amministrative del 1990', *Polis*. (Aug.) 6(2): 257–80.

Sema, A. (1996) 'Leghismo di Confine e Secessionismo nel Friuli-Venezia Giulia', *Limes: Rivista Italiana di Geopolitica*. 3: 71–88.

Smith, A. D. (1971) *Theories of Nationalism*. London: Duckworth.

—— (1979) *Nationalism in the Twentieth Century*. Oxford: Oxford University Press.

—— (1981) *The Ethnic Revival*. Cambridge: Cambridge University Press.

—— (1984) 'Ethnic Myths and Ethnic Revivals', *Archives Européennes de Sociologie* 25: 283–305.

—— (1990) 'Towards a Global Culture', *Theory, Culture and Society* 7: 171–91.

—— (1991a) 'The Nation: Invented, Imagined, Reonstructed?' *Millennium* 13(2): 200–17.

—— (1991b) *National Identity*. London: Penguin.
—— (1995) 'Gastronomy or Geology? The Role of Nationalism in the Reconstruction of Nations', *Nations and Nationalism* 1 (1): 3–23.
Smolicz, J. (1988) 'Tradition, Core Values and Development in Plural Societies', *Ethnic and Racial Studies* 11 (4).
Sollors, W. (1986) *Beyond Ethnicity: Consent and Descent in American Culture*. New York and Oxford: Oxford University Press.
Sorella, A. (1982) 'La Televisione e la lingua Italiana', *Trimestre, Periodico di Cultura* 14(2,3,4): 291–300.
Soysal, Y. (1994) *The Limits of Citizenship. Post National Membership in Europe*. Chicago: University of Chicago Press.
Spadolini, G. (1994) *Nazione e Nazionalità in Italia*. Rome-Bari: Laterza.
Streuss, L. (1977) *L'identité*. Paris: Bernard Grasset.
Swidler, A. (1986) 'Culture in Action, Symbols and Strategies', *American Sociological Review* (51).
Tambini, D. (1994) 'Strategy or Identity? The Northern League at a Crossroads', *Telos* (98–99): 229–48.
—— (1998a) 'Nationalism: A Literature Survey', *European Journal of Social Theory* (Nov.) 1(2): 137–54.
—— (1998b) 'Virtual Nationalism. Padania Declares Independence', *Telos* (101–2): 314–29.
Tarrow, S. (1994) *Power in Movement. Social Movements, Collective Action and Politics*. Cambridge: Cambridge University Press.
Taylor, C. (1990) *Sources of the Self: The Making of Modern Identity*. Cambridge: Cambridge University Press.
—— (1992) *Multiculturalism and 'The Politics of Recognition'*. Princeton: Princeton University Press.
Therborn, G. (1991) 'Cultural Belonging, Structural Location and Human Action. Explanation in Sociology and in Social Science', *Acta Sociologica* (34): 177–91.
Thompson, E. P. (1980) *The Making of the English Working Class*. London: Penguin.
Tilly, C. (1996) 'The State of Nationalism', *Critical Review* 10(2): 299–306.
Tiryakian, E. and Rogowski, R. (eds) (1985) *New Nationalisms of the Developed West*. London: Allen and Unwin.
Todesco, F. (1992) *Marketing Elettorale e Communicazione Politica. Il Caso Lega Nord*. Dissertation, Università Bocconi, Milan.
Touraine, A. (1978) *La Voix et la Regard*. Paris: Editions du Seuil.
—— (1981) *Le Pays Contre L'état*. Paris: Editions du Seuil.
—— (1985) 'An Introduction to the Study of Social Movements', *Social Research* 52(4): 749–87.
—— (1988) *Return of the Actor. Social Theory in Postindustrial Society*. Minneapolis: University of Minnesota Press.
Urbani, G. (1992) *Dentro la Politica: Come funzionano il governo e le istituzioni*. Milan: Il Sole 24 Ore.
Vermullen, H. and Govers, C. (1994) *The Anthropology of Ethnicity. Beyond 'Ethnic Groups and Boundaries'*. Amsterdam: Het Spinhuis.
Vimercati, D. (1990) *I Lombardi alla Nuova Crociata*. Milan: Mursia.
—— (ed.) (1991) *Carlo Cattaneo. Stati Uniti d'Italia. Il Federalismo, Le Leghe*. Milan: Sugarco.
Wallman, S. (1978) 'The Boundaries of "Race": Processes of Ethnicity in England',

Man (June) 13(2): 200–15.
—— (1982) 'The Application of Boundaries Theory to the Study of Boundaries Processes', in Mason, D. and Rex, J. (eds), *Theories of Ethnic and Race Relations.* Cambridge: Cambridge University Press.
—— (1983) 'Identity Options', in C. Fried (ed.), *Minorities: Community and Identity.* Berlin, Heidelberg, New York: Springer-Verlag.
Ward, W. (1993) *Getting It Right in Italy.* London: Bloomsbury.
Weber, E. (1979) *Peasants into Frenchmen. The Modernisation of Rural France.* (1870–1914). London: Chatto and Windus.
Wolf, E. (1973) *Storia d'Italia. Dal primo settecento al'unità.* Turin: Einaudi.
Woods, D. (1992a) 'The Centre No Longer Holds: The Rise of Regional Leagues in Italian Politics', *West European Politics* 15(2): 56–76.
—— (1992b) 'Les Ligues Regionales en Italie', *Revue Française de Science Politique* (Feb.) 42(1): 33–58.
Yack, B. (1996) 'The Myth of the Civic Nation', *Critical Review* 2(2): 193–212.
Zariski, R. (1972) *Italy. The Politics of Uneven Development.* Illinois: Dryden.

Index